*If sorrow is our own nature, then we
should have no cause for sorrow at all.
We should all be happy being sad.*

— SWAMI DAYANANDA SARASWATI

यच्छ्रेयः स्यान्निश्चितं ब्रूहि
तन्मे शिष्यस्तेऽहं शाधि मां

HOBBLEBUSH BOOKS · Brookline, New Hampshire

An Ordinary Life
Transformed

Lessons for
Everyone from
the *Bhagavad Gita*

तन्मे
त्वां प्रपन्नम् _{Sloka 2.7}

Rev. Stephanie Rutt

ISBN-13: 978-0-9760896-6-7
ISBN-10: 0-9760896-6-1

Library of Congress Control Number: 2006932461

Book design by David Jonathan Ross

Composed in Janson Text and Veronika at
Hobblebush Books, Brookline, New Hampshire

Printed in the United States of America

Bhagavad Gita translation by George Thompson
Cover painting by Jan Mercuri Grossman

Published by:
Hobblebush Books

17-A OLD MILFORD ROAD
BROOKLINE, NEW HAMPSHIRE 03033

www.hobblebush.com

Contents

Jnana Yoga: *The Path of Wisdom*

To Joe

Joe

I was over forty before I found out about Joe. I was rummaging through my grandmother's cedar chest as I had done so often in the past during my summer visits. All the old pictures were there—mostly those taken "down home" where my grandmother had grown up. Among the yellowed and torn pictures were the familiar faces of those I had long known, mixed in with others I did not recognize. One such picture was of what looked to be a teenage boy. He was standing alone out in the yard.

Although I had run across this picture before, this time the face staring back at me held my attention and roused my curiosity. I walked into the kitchen where my grandmother was busy cleaning, moving pots and pans from the stove to the sink. "Nanny," I said, "who's this?" She looked at the picture briefly and said rather matter-of-factly, "That's Joe," as she continued to move the pots and pans. When no further explanation came, I said, "Well, who's Joe?" My grandmother never stopped her work nor looked at me as she offered her brief explanation. "Joe was my younger brother. But, he was never right." It was clear she was not about to be drawn into any type of conversation about it.

I was stunned. It seemed incomprehensible to me that there had been a family member I had not known about. I was the one who had created photo albums of the family, wandered through graveyards with my grandmother to gather information about births and deaths and had started researching our family tree. At one point, I remembered an old family Bible in which my great-grandmother had placed a sheet of paper listing the names and birth dates of her children. The bottom of the sheet of paper had been torn off but there remained what looked like the top part of the capital letter 'O' at the bottom where the last name would have been added. I had never paid any attention to the mark before. Now I knew it was the top part of the letter 'J' written in cursive as the other names had been.

I remember my great-grandmother as a tiny, fast moving woman of few words. My great-grandfather was tall and had a rather hard expression about him. They were farmers who spent their days literally making their daily bread and doing what was necessary for simple survival, as rural folk did in the early part of the nineteen hundreds. Joe was the sixth and last child to be born. But there was no doubt he would change life for all of them forever.

I have come to have the deepest compassion for my family and the secret we have carried. I can only imagine how difficult and challenging it must have been for all of them, particularly the other children whose job it was to look after Joe, as there was little he could do for himself. I learned that as he approached adulthood the daily care became overwhelming and the difficult decision was made to put him into an institution. When the day came to take him, I was told, my otherwise stern great-grandfather "wailed" as he shaved. No one had ever seen him cry before. And, what was being buried deep in the heart of the one who tore Joe's name off the list to go in the Bible?

Each of us has secrets and parts we feel should not be brought into the light. We fear that if others could really see us they would not accept or love us, when, in fact, it is we who do not accept and love ourselves. And all families have "something"—secrets, perceived flaws, lies, wrongdoings, injustices—things most family members believe are best kept hidden from the world. But, what is *true* will not let us go.

This is why the Bhagavad Gita opens with the protagonist Arjuna standing on a battlefield about to go to war with, principally, his own family—his cousins. In his family's case, an overt injustice has occurred and it is Arjuna's duty to restore righteousness. But, seeing his family before him, he falters and offers all his good reasons, rationalizations, for not being able to confront the injustice he knows is there.

And, at times, so it is with us.

Until one day our desire to live open and free becomes greater than the need to hide. Our secrets seek the light of day. Our perceived flaws seek transformation in the crucible of self-acceptance. And our lies, wrongdoings and injustices seek to be made right.

And Krishna, or God within, smiles.

Welcome home, Joe.

Your Personal Pilgrimage

How This Commentary Differs from Others

For the past nine years, I have been privileged to facilitate study groups of the Bhagavad Gita with participants from all religions and walks of life. I have witnessed again and again that it doesn't matter if you are passionate about a particular religion, don't have a religion, or have simply become disenfranchised. Study of the Bhagavad Gita makes a Methodist a better Methodist, a Jew a better Jew, a Catholic a better Catholic, a Buddhist a better Buddhist. For those not connected with a faith tradition or perhaps feeling disenfranchised, I have often seen the study rekindle a remembering, a yearning, to reconnect with the One about whom all religions speak.

I am a hands-on, how-does-it-show-up-in-daily-life teacher. I am most interested in how we navigate the storms of life when the rudder breaks and darkness falls. This is where we meet Arjuna at the beginning of the Bhagavad Gita and where we meet ourselves each time fear descends. And like us, Arjuna is an ordinary human. So, as we listen in on Krishna's (God's) council to Arjuna, we know with certainty that He is speaking directly to us as well.

There are very useful translations and commentaries of the Bhagavad Gita which provide in-depth analysis of this great epic poem. This book

is different. It does not pretend to be a scholarly or an exhaustive commentary on the multiple levels of meaning of the Bhagavad Gita. There
are many authors more qualified than I to offer such commentary. I have
a different goal. The intention here is to provide a description of the
Bhagavad Gita as an allegory of the spiritual journey and to distill the
essence of each chapter in such a way as to make the concepts readily
available for application to everyday living.

This book invites you, the reader, to embark on your own personal
pilgrimage. Do not shrink from its challenge. The Potter's wheel awaits
you. The touch of grace will shape you and the fire will transform you.
This book is filled with real-world stories and examples of how ordinary
people have found the courage to stand up and do what needs to be done.
How ordinary people have discovered that when they speak, live and act
from their deepest impulse, Truth is served. How ordinary people have
*fallen in love with that which is the same in all of us and how that experience
changes everything.*

Simply, I am an ordinary woman who loves God. One of the things I
tell myself every day is *I am enough and I am nothing.* To me, this is the
entire essence of Krishna's message to Arjuna. When Arjuna succumbs
to despondency on the battlefield, Krishna admonishes him to get up
and get over it! He reminds him that he is a skilled warrior and there's a
war to be fought *and* victory is guaranteed if he will only take refuge in
Him. Like Arjuna, we too are *enough*, as we have a unique part to play in
the Divine plan. And, like Arjuna, we are *nothing* when—in those glorious
moments—we take refuge in our God, crying out in sweet surrender, "Thy
will be done!"

And, in an instant, we are free.

Welcome Home.

Why Study the Bhagavad Gita?

From Sorrow to Joy

Bhagavad Gita means *Song of God*. Its purpose is to bring about an end to sorrow through the realization that *we are That which we seek*. All of us seek peace, happiness and joy, but *within* ourselves is not usually the first place we look. Instead, we look outside ourselves, searching from place to place, experience to experience, teacher to teacher for *That which we already are*. It never occurs to us that what we're looking for is literally as close as our breath—that we *already have all we need to be content in any circumstance*.

In our desperate search, we overlook the place of true joy—our inner sanctuary, where joy resides, not in response to a particular set of circumstances, but simply as a humble response to continued self-acceptance. Here, *all* is received. Here, the quiet truth whispering softly from the center of our being can be heard. Here, joy is immune to the changing tides of outward circumstance. By turning inward to embrace all, we find what we have so desperately been seeking. It's called freedom.

But, we are not aware. So, we search.

And, then, something happens. Maybe it's an event that unceremoniously catapults us out of our comfortable existence. An unexpected diagnosis, accident, loss of a job, divorce, death of a loved one. Or maybe it's just waking up from a long period of sleepy boredom that shouts, *something's got to change!* Like Arjuna, we find ourselves in unfamiliar territory, feeling overwhelmed, inadequate, unable or just simply unwilling to meet the challenges ahead. Our rudder is broken and night is falling fast. Desperately, we may continue searching for someone or something *outside* ourselves to save us. But, this time, nothing satisfies.

It's a critical juncture. We can continue the old ways of coping or we can choose a less familiar route called *surrender.* At first, this surrender route does not appear to be such an attractive option. We fear the loss of control. But this time, as skeptical as we are of the surrender route, we are even more reluctant to repeat the same old patterns. And, so it is with Arjuna. His rationalizations for not rising up to do his duty aren't working. His familiar ways of thinking aren't providing escape from his self-imposed bondage. Overwhelmed and desperate, he chooses *surrender* and cries out to his Lord for guidance.

And, where he thought he would lose himself, he finds himSelf.

But, the old ways are not so easily shed. Again and again, Arjuna, and we too, must choose. Over time, we start to trust this new route called surrender, for a joy comes that passes all our old understanding. Slowly, we start to trust the Potter within. We begin to suspect that each experience is just a stroke of the Potter's hand molding us for a higher purpose. We begin to see that surrender makes us free.

And, more and more, we start to fall in love. Not with what used to make us happy or even with what we think will make us happy—but with the Potter Himself, *for nothing will satisfy now short of the Potter Himself.* Loneliness and our sense of separateness fade. We start to see with new eyes as the Potter reveals His face—the face of God—everywhere.

There is God bagging our groceries, cashing our check, finding the right size shirt, bringing our food. We start to notice that it doesn't matter what mood folks are in, what they have or haven't done, what they believe or don't believe. All we see is God. And when we hear an ambulance or fire engines or learn about "collateral damage" on the news, our heart aches for the one whose name we don't even know. Because now no one is outside the bounds of our love. *No one.*

Now, we love our neighbor as our self.

And, like water to parched lips, this is the only joy that matters. It is all that can truly sustain us through the changing seasons of our life. It is our compass when the storm hits, the rudder breaks and darkness falls. It is what is left when we fear all is lost. It is what brings us to our prayer mat. It is what looks at the enemy and sees our self. It is what can raise the sword of courage to combat hatred without hating. It is what can love the saint and sinner the same.

This joy sees what's the same in all of us.

And having seen, knows.

And knowing, is never the same.

A Story of Yogic Wisdom

The Bhagavad Gita is the essence of Eastern spirituality, drawing from the Hindu tradition in general and yoga philosophy in particular. Yoga means the *yoking* of individual finite consciousness to infinite consciousness. It is through this yoking that we come to realize *we are That which we seek.*

If we really want to understand ourselves, good questions to ask are, "What is God?" or "How would I describe God?" I have noticed that how a person answers these fundamental questions can predispose a whole range of beliefs and behaviors. For example, if I believe that God is some kind of being or energy outside of my self, I will most likely ask or plead when I pray to God. Feeling separate, I may believe that God is sometimes with me and sometimes not, or that some people have God and others don't. When life is going well I may feel connected to God, but, when life hands a painful blow, I may feel abandoned.

But, if I believe that God is the creative force that brings forth all creation, something shifts. Now, I pray *with* God, not *to* God. Now, the challenge becomes to *affirm*, not plead. Since God is our creator residing within, I realize I could *never be alone*—regardless of what I may think or feel or what I have or haven't done. And, as I look out at my brothers and sisters, I know that there, too, is God—regardless of what he or she may think, feel, have or haven't done.

As I turn away from the belief in a separate God and toward the realization of my unity with all that is, infinite joy begins to replace limiting fear. Wonder replaces speculation. And the more I surrender the old, familiar sense of separateness, the more I come to land in the soft hand of God—wanting nothing more than to be shaped and formed by that joy that passes all understanding.

And, suddenly, realizing God is *That which is the same in all of us*, the basic precepts of spiritual teachers across faith traditions begin to make sense. Jesus: "Love your neighbor as yourself." Mohammad: "None of you are true believers until you love for your brother what you love for yourself." Buddha: "If you truly loved yourself you could never hurt another."

So, the question becomes, "If God is within all and totally accessible, why is there so much suffering in the world?" Yogic wisdom offers that the answer lies in understanding that there are two manifestations or expressions of God: the infinite and the finite. We suffer because we only identify with the finite expression of God and, therefore, do not feel connected to our infinite Source.

The infinite, or Brahman, also referred to as Christ Consciousness, is the eternal, unchanging, omnipresent force—not describable by words—Source of all that is—*That which is the same in all*. The finite, or *prakriti*, is the transient, changing aspect of God, inherent in all creation, expressing all the variations or differences. Like flowers of the field, we are each unique, yet all brought forth by the same Source.

But, because we only identify with the variations and differences of prakriti, we think that our unique body, thoughts and feelings are who we are. So, for example, if, through our conditioning, we come to believe we are inadequate—as most of us do in one way or another—then, that's what we think: *we* are inadequate. Because such beliefs are brought about by outside circumstances and influences, we set out to fix the unfortunate condition through outside sources. When we do well and get good feedback, we think we are "good." When we fail or are rejected, we think we are "bad." We become slaves to finding our validation, happiness and success outside ourselves. It is never enough.

However, when Arjuna falters on the battlefield of life, he discovers that the only thing that will save him is to look *within*, to hear the counsel of his own inner Divinity—Brahman within—personified by Krishna. In this way, he learns to distinguish between the personal conditioning of his human journey and the deeper truth of who he is—between his will and Divine will.

And like Arjuna, we too, realizing *we are Brahman, That which we seek*, can transform our conditioning, trading in moments of fleeting happiness based on external circumstances for the joy illuminated solely from within. We, too, can become our Self.

And, the potential to realize our Self is the great gift of the human journey. As humans, we have evolved to have the joy and responsibility of being given a body-mind so we may *experience the realization of our Divinity*. To help us along, we're given two laws: free will and karma. Here, in what is often called the *field of prakriti*, we use our free will to grow whatever we want and the law of karma gives us the results of our actions. By reaping what we sow, we learn.

And, over many incarnations, we learn that God is not something to be earned but, rather, *realized*.

And, that the very searcher is God.

This belief in an omnipresent, non-dualistic God is the essence of what is called Vedanta philosophy. The realization that we are a unique expression of the One helps us to understand why we are here, how we manifest our experience and, ultimately, how to know God. In the following chart, "Overview of Vedanta Principles," we see how this realization informs personal awareness, dispels sorrow, and allows for the most freeing outcome to prevail.

> *Ye shall know the Truth and*
> *the Truth shall make you free.*
>
> —THE BIBLE

	Realization	Personal awareness	How sorrow is dispelled	Outcome
Brahman *Eternal, unchanging*	God is the infinite, unchanging source of all.	I and God are one.	Takes away feelings of separateness and isolation.	"I see myself in all and all in myself."
Prakriti *Transient, changing*	God is expressed through the finite changing manifestations of all creation – all that is born, lives, and dies.	That which is born will die. I am eternal.	Takes away fear of death.	"I know that 'I' was never born and never die."
Why we have come	God animates the body-mind so we may experience the realization of our divinity.	I am here to experience my divinity and to manifest my part in the Divine plan.	Takes away envy, jealousy, and the need to compare with others.	"My only job is to offer my gifts in service to all."
How we manifest	All creation is manifested in response to free will and according to the law of karma.	I reap what I sow.	Takes away feelings of being a victim.	"This is the schoolhouse for souls. I learn as I go."
How to know God	Heaven on earth happens when I align my will to thy will.	I am enough and I am nothing.	Takes away attachment to outcome.	"Thy will is my will."

Historical Context

The Events Leading to War

The Bhagavad Gita was written by the illumined sage, Vyasa, sometime between the fifth and third centuries BC. It occurs in the sixth book of an expansive Hindu epic poem, the *Mahabharata*, which is seven times the size of the *Iliad* and the *Odyssey*. It is interesting to note that the *Mahabharata* has eighteen books, the Bhagavad Gita has eighteen chapters and the battle of Kurukshetra, the backdrop for the Bhagavad Gita, lasted eighteen days.

Maha means *great* and *bharata* is the name of the family about whom this ancient epic is written. It tells the story of two sets of cousins within this great Bharata family, the Pandavas and the Kauravas, who are about to go to war to determine who will rule a territory in ancient India. The protagonist, Arjuna, is a Pandava. As he looks across the battlefield and sees the faces of his cousins, he loses his will to lead his army into battle. Full of despondency, he begs Lord Krishna to counsel him so that he may see clearly and rise to do his duty. The Bhagavad Gita is the dialogue that occurs between Arjuna and Lord Krishna—*the same dialogue that occurs between us and our God when we feel unable to meet the challenges of life and surrender to the Potter's wheel.*

In order to set the stage for this timeless dialogue, let's take a closer look at the historic events that have led these two armies to face one another in battle.

The Story Behind the Bhagavad Gita

There once lived King Bharata who ruled a kingdom in ancient India. King Bharata had two sons. One son became known as King Pandu. King Pandu was unable to have children but was given five sons through Divine grace. The middle son was Arjuna. The five sons became known as the Pandavas. King Bharata's other son was King Dhritarashtra. King Dhritarashtra was blind and had one hundred sons. They became known as the Kauravas.

King Pandu died young and his five sons were sent to live with their one hundred cousins. They grew up together but there was much turmoil. The five Pandavas were known for their goodness, intelligence and bravery, and terrible jealously rose among the Kauravas. Eventually, they decided to live apart and rule separate parts of the kingdom. Over the years, the Pandavas ruled their part of the kingdom very well and became more and more powerful. This made the Kauravas increasingly more envious and jealous. Eventually, the Kauravas plotted to destroy the Pandavas.

The oldest son of the Kauravas, the reigning King Duryodhana, invited the oldest son of the Pandavas, Yudishthria, to a game of dice and defeated him through trickery and cheating. Yudishthria, although losing, continued to play until all was lost—even the part of the kingdom ruled by the Pandavas. It was a shameful moment for the Pandavas, but, being of righteous mind, they agreed to the conditions of their defeat.

It was decided that the Pandavas would go to live in the forest for twelve years and remain incognito for a thirteenth year. Should they be discovered during that final year, they would have to return to the forest for another twelve years. If the Pandavas could fulfill these conditions, at the end of the thirteenth year their share of the kingdom would be returned. Meanwhile, the Kauravas would rule the land.

Because of their faith and devotion, the Pandavas were able to fulfill all of the conditions of the agreement and at the end of the thirteenth year asked for their share of the kingdom to be returned. But, the Kauravas refused, saying that the Pandavas would have to fight for what they wanted.

Now, as a battle was certain, both sides wanted the help of Lord Krishna. King Duryodhana, representing the Kauravas, and Arjuna, representing the Pandavas, went to see Lord Krishna. Lord Krishna, knowing they were coming, pretended to be sleeping. When King Duryodhana arrived, he seated himself behind Krishna's head. When Arjuna arrived, he stood at Lord Krishna's feet. Both waited for Lord Krishna to awake.

When Lord Krishna "awoke," he decided to be neutral and impartial, offering each a part of Himself. One could have his whole army. The other could have only him—unarmed and he would not fight. As Arjuna was the younger of the two cousins, he was allowed to choose first. King Duryodhana was nervous because he was hoping that Arjuna would not choose the army.

But Arjuna said, "Without you, Sir, what can I do with your army? It's enough just to have you." And, Arjuna fell at the feet of his Lord.

King Duryodhana was relieved. He said, "That's fine with me. What am I going to do with you? I want your entire army, your power." Lord Krishna said that each was getting what he wanted and that this was good.

When King Duryodhana left, Lord Krishna asked Arjuna what he could do for him since he would not be fighting.

Arjuna said, "If I enter the field of battle with you as my charioteer, the world will see virtue established. Please drive my chariot."

Finally, the armies of the Pandavas and the Kauravas were arrayed opposite each other on the battlefield of Kurukshetra. At this point, although Arjuna knows the enemy well, he asks Lord Krishna to drive his chariot into the middle of the field so that he can have a better look at the opposing army. This is where the Bhagavad Gita begins.

Symbolism of the Outer and Inner Battle

To appreciate the Bhagavad Gita as an allegory of the spiritual journey, we must have an understanding of the rich symbolism in this Song of God. In this way, we begin to see that the outer battle is nothing more than a reflection of the inner battle occurring within each of us since the beginning of time.

Krishna and Arjuna

Krishna is God personified within us—the eternal knowing beyond our transient, changing, more superficial, mind chatter—the deeper truth we access in moments when the mind is still—the joy that is illuminated solely from within. Arjuna, the middle of the five Pandu sons, represents equanimity born of self-control, determination and the fire of spiritual practice required to live a divine life. He also represents our human journey, the ego and results of our mental conditioning. In addition, while skilled in his craft, he is not a revered priest or esteemed intellectual. He is an ordinary human. Like us. This exemplifies that we are each equally capable of full realization and liberation.

Pandavas and Kauravas

The Pandavas and Kauravas represent the good and bad tendencies in all of us. "Bad" is seen here as a result of being "blind" or ignorant. This is why King Dhritarashtra is blind. That most of us operate more from our blind places than from our enlightened ones (!) is represented by the 100 sons. The Kauravas represent the forces of ignorance. "Good" is represented by the pure King Pandu. The Pandavas represent the forces of righteousness.

The Game of Dice

In any form of gambling, there is always the risk of losing. Though Yudishthria begins to lose, he continues until all is lost. This represents those times when even the most pure of heart among us falters and succumbs to weakness. Once we start down a road of self-destruction, it is very difficult to turn back. That King Duryodhana invites Yudishthria to play, knowing that he intends to win by cheating, represents those parts of us that sometimes feel so envious, inadequate or fearful that we'll resort to anything to get what we want.

Pandavas Accept the Conditions of Defeat

Even though the Pandavas suspect that the Kauravas have won through trickery, they accept the conditions of their defeat. This symbolizes the willingness of the righteous to assume responsibility for their actions. They agreed to participate and are therefore willing to assume responsibility for the outcome.

Twelve Years in the Forest and a Thirteenth Year Incognito

According to yoga philosophy, we advance in our spiritual evolution in twelve-year cycles. The thirteenth year represents time spent in meditation during which we make ourselves ready for the battles in life by developing discernment. Discernment allows us to see clearly beyond the emotions of the moment so we may act in ways that serve Truth and the greater good.

Visiting the Sleeping Lord Krishna

The sleeping Lord Krishna symbolizes the neutrality of God through the gift of free will. We are equally free to rely upon the ways of the world, Krishna's army, or to seek guidance from God within, Krishna alone. King Duryodhana waits at the head, symbolizing reliance on thinking or intellectual processes. Arjuna waits at the feet, symbolizing his willingness to surrender the outcome to God within.

The Choice

Both King Duryodhana and Arjuna are looking for what they believe will help win the war. King Duryodhana chooses to rely on the external sources of power. He chooses to place his faith and trust in something outside of himself. The large army will give him the victory he wants. The risk in relying upon things on the outside to give us what we want is that outward conditions are always changing. So, one "victory" doesn't satisfy very long. Soon, we need the next victory, or thing, to make us happy. Arjuna chooses to rely on the internal source of all power. By asking Krishna to be his charioteer, Arjuna is relying upon God within that is unchanging and eternal. In addition, he chooses to trust that, by surrendering to God within, a righteous outcome will prevail.

The Chariot

The chariot symbolizes the body through which we experience the human condition. The human condition is symbolized as a battlefield because each of us must overcome the enemies within in order to live a divinely inspired life. But, simple desire is not enough. We must engage in the challenging task of reining in attachment to the sense pleasures of the world symbolized by the horses. When we have slackened the reins on the senses, discernment fails, control slips and life is soon driving us. We find ourselves barely hanging on, steering from one direction to another, desperately looking for the next thing we hope will satisfy—and more is always better. More food, a bigger house, nicer outfit, wider acclaim, next promotion, a better relationship, more peak experiences, and so on. We become reactive to the conditions of life.

Arjuna chooses not to fall prey to the world of the senses that would logically tell him to choose Krishna's vast army for victory. Instead, he chooses discernment, and puts Krishna in charge to rein in the senses. In this way, he achieves victory over himself and the battle is won. Now he can fulfill his destiny in service to the greater good.

OUTER BATTLE:	INNER BATTLE:
Krishna — *Charioteer*	Divine personified: Supreme wisdom
Arjuna — *Devotee*	Ordinary man: Human experience
Chariot — *Contains both Krishna and Arjuna*	Body
Reins	Brain
Horses	Senses
Pandavas	Forces of righteousness in the family of humankind
Kauravas	Forces of ignorance in the family of humankind
Battlefield	Human condition

Standing back from the story to gain a full view of this spiritual allegory, we see only our self. We are both Krishna and Arjuna. We are the chariot, the reins and the horses and have equal potential for fighting as a Pandava or a Kaurava on the battlefield of our life.

Through the gift of free will, the choice is ours.

The winds of grace blow all the time.
All we need do is set our sails.

—RAMAKRISHNA

✿ *A Story of Yogic Wisdom*

✿ *Historical Context: The Events Leading to War*

✿ *Symbolism of the Outer and Inner Battle*

✿ *TVAM TAT ASI, "Thou That Art"*

TVAM TAT ASI

"Thou That Art"

Keeping in mind that the purpose of the Bhagavad Gita is to bring about an end to sorrow through the realization that we are *That which we seek*, we can better understand the overall structure of this Song of God. The Bhagavad Gita contains 700 Slokas, or verses, over the eighteen chapters that are divided into three sections. Together the three sections represent the profound truth—Tvam Tat Asi—"Thou That Art."

Scholars of Hindu scripture will recognize this as a re-ordering of the well known Tat tvam asi, That thou art. As this famous saying captures the essence of the Bhagavad Gita, I have respectfully used it as a teaching device to organize the lessons of this Song of God into three sections.

The first six chapters focus on the path of Karma, or action, and provide guidance on what we must do to realize that we are, in fact, individual expressions of the one God, the "Thou" or Tvam. As individual expressions, we are called Atman. The second six chapters focus on the path of Bhakti, or devotion, and describe the nature of God to be realized, the "That" or Tat. This omnipresent force is called Brahman. The last six chapters focus on the path of Jnana, or wisdom, and discuss the relationship between Atman and Brahman, the "Art" or Asi, and how this relationship is experienced.

The Bhagavad Gita is often spoken of in relation to yoga. This is because the goal of the Bhagavad Gita and the goal of yoga are one and the same—to yoke the individual finite consciousness to infinite consciousness. This is why the paths paralleling the three sections of the Bhagavad Gita are called Karma Yoga, Bhakti Yoga and Jnana Yoga.

When we hand the reins over to Krishna (action), we live as Atman. When we truly live as Atman, we are filled with a love so profound (devotion) that all we see is God, Brahman. This realization, that we are truly expressions of the one God, brings all there is to know (wisdom).

The chart at the beginning of each of the three sections of this book, "From Sorrow to Joy," provides an overview of how each of the chapters fulfills this promise.

AN ORDINARY LIFE
TRANSFORMED

Karma Yoga
The Path of Action

What we must *do*
to realize we
are Atman

नयितं कुरु कर्म त्वं
कर्म ज्यायो ह्यकर्मण
शरीरयात्रापि च ते न
प्रसधि्ये दकर्मणः Sloka 3.8

Overview of Chapters 1-6

Chapter 1: The Face of Sorrow
Rise Up to Defend Righteousness or Truth
Here we clearly see our human journey—all of our "good reasons" for not showing up to do what we truly know needs to be done. Here we see that we are Arjuna.

Chapter 2: Realizing Who We Are
Surrender to the Voice of the True Self
This chapter offers an overview of the Bhagavad Gita. Krishna offers a theoretical explanation of the true Self, reminds Arjuna of the importance of doing his duty and gives practical suggestions for realizing Atman within.

Chapter 3: Actions of Sacrifice
Offer Every Action as a Sacrifice in Service to the Greater Good
Krishna expounds on the virtues of selfless service—making our actions offerings of sacrifice. We are reminded that it is better to do our own work, or dharma, imperfectly, than to do another's perfectly. Krishna also provides a warning against the two enemies of spiritual growth: desire and anger.

Chapter 4: Seeing with New Eyes
Identify with the Observer Within

Krishna differentiates between action and inaction, introducing the notion of the Observer, or witness consciousness. By identifying with the Observer, God within, we naturally surrender our actions, release all attachment to outcomes, and joyfully engage in selfless service.

Chapter 5: Renounce and Be Free
Renounce All That Is Fleeting to Realize the Eternal

Krishna explains that by disciplining the mind through *Jnana Yoga*, meditation, and purifying the mind through *Karma Yoga*, selfless service, illumination from within can occur. Such illumination leads to *moksha*, or liberation.

Chapter 6: The Inner Sanctuary
Discipline and Refine the Mind through Meditation

By focusing and disciplining the mind, the practice of meditation slowly allows us to identify with the Observer, or *Atman*, within.

In the face of sorrow, surrendering to God within reveals our true nature. With this realization, our actions become offerings of sacrifice. We see with new eyes and naturally begin to renounce all that is fleeting and transient. More often we find ourselves resting in our inner sanctuary.

Slowly, we begin to know ourselves as Atman—individual expressions of the eternal bliss of God.

What We Must Do To Realize We Are Atman:
Rise Up to Defend Righteousness or Truth

*Truly, it is in the darkness that one finds
the light, so when we are in sorrow, then
this light is nearest of all to us.*

—MEISTER ECKHART

CHAPTER I

The Face of Sorrow

We begin where we are. Here we meet Arjuna and recognize our self. We
see our human journey and encounter all our "good reasons" for not showing up to do what we know needs to be done. We see that *we are Arjuna*.

And, the stage is set. Historically, the illumined sage, Vyasa, author of
the *Mahabharata*, bestowed upon the visionary, Sanjaya, the spiritual vision
to see from a distance the entire Bhagavad Gita so that he could report
the events of this legendary conflict to the blind King Dhritarashtra.
Remember that King Dhritarashtra is father to the one hundred Kauravas
sons who represent the forces of ignorance.

The dialogue opens with King Dhritarashtra asking Sanjaya to describe
what happened on the battlefield of Kurukshetra, the field of action, the
day his sons faced the sons of King Pandu ready to wage war. Sanjaya
begins by reporting to King Dhritarashtra the conversation that occurred
between his oldest son, the reigning King Duryodhana, and his archery
teacher, Drona. As we listen in, we are first introduced to a few of the key
Pandava and Kaurava warriors.*

---

* A list of Sanskrit names and terms that are introduced in the author's commentary,
with a pronunciation guide, will be found at the end of each chapter. A complete
alphabetical list may also be found in Appendix A on page 225.

Slokas 1–11

Dhritarashtra spoke:

1.1   On the field of Dharma, on the battlefield of Kurukshetra, they are assembled and eager to fight, my men on one side and the sons of Pandu on the other. What did they do, Sanjaya?

Sanjaya spoke:

1.2   Your son King Duryodhana saw the army of the Pandavas drawn up for battle, and then he approached his teacher [Drona] and spoke these words:

1.3   "Teacher, look at this magnificent army of Pandu's sons and their men all drawn up and led by your wise student [Drishtadyumna], the son of Drupada!

1.4   There they are, warriors, great archers, all of them equal in battle to Bhima and Arjuna, Yuyudhana and Virata, and Drupada as well, the great chariot-warrior!

1.5   And Dhrishtaketu and Cekitana and the king of Kashi, a heroic man! And also Purujit and Kuntibhoja, and that bull among men, the king of the Shibis!

1.6   Also there is that broad-striding Yudhamanyu, and Uttamaujas, also a heroic man, and Subhadra's son, and Draupadi's sons – all of them great chariot-warriors!

1.7   And now notice, O best of Brahmins, these others, the most distinguished among us, the leaders of my army: I tell you their names so that you will remember them!

1.8   You lord [Drona] yourself, and Bhishma and Karna, and Kripa, the winner of many battles! And Ashvatthama and Vikarna, and Somadatta's son as well!

1.9   And many other warriors willing to give up their lives for my sake, with their many swords and arrows, all of them war-seasoned!

1.10   The strength of this army of ours is unmatched, led as it is by Bhishma, whereas this army of theirs, led as it is by Bhima, is easily matched!

1.11   And so in all of your strategic movements, stationed wherever you are ordered to be, may all of you, all of you, protect Bhishma!"

Bhishma, leader of the Kaurava army, is the head of the Kaurava family and a very saintly person. This exemplifies that there is no person or situation which is all ignorant or dark. That he chooses to fight with the Kaurava army shows that it is our predestined duty to stand with our family in times of conflict. Bhima, leader of the Pandava army, is Arjuna's older brother, the second son of King Pandu, king of the Pandavas.

And, the readiness for war is expressed by the roar of conch-shells, drums, cymbals, tabors and trumpets!

Slokas 12–19

1.12 It brought on great delight in Duryodhana, when the aged grandfather of the Kurus [Bhishma] roared out a lion's roar and blew his conch-shell, full of fire.

1.13 Then conch-shells and drums, and cymbals, and tabors and trumpets, all at once resounded. The sound was thunderous!

1.14 And standing there on their great chariot yoked to white stallions, Krishna and Arjuna, the son of Pandu, also blew their celestial conch-shells.

1.15 Krishna blew the Pancajanya horn, Arjuna blew the Devadatta horn, and fierce wolf-bellied Bhima blew the great Paundra horn.

1.16 Yudhishthira the King, the son of Kunti, in turn blew the Anantavijaya horn, the horn of eternal victory, while Nakula and Sahadeva blew the sweet-toned Sughosha and the jewel-toned Manipushpaka shells.

1.17 The King of Kashi, a master-archer, and Shikandhin the great chariot-rider, and Dhrishthadyumna, and Virata and Satyaki the unconquered,

1.18 and Drupada and the sons of Draupadi and the mighty-armed son of Subhadra – all at once, my king, they all blew their conch-shells, over and over again and in all directions!

1.19 That sound pierced the hearts of Dhritarashtra's men and the thunder of it made heaven and earth shake!

It is important to note that the war is actually begun by the Kauravas, the forces of ignorance or darkness, when their leader, Bhishma, sounds his conch-shell. In Sloka 1.16, we meet Arjuna's other three brothers: Yudhishthira, Nakula and Sahadeva. Recall, that Yudhishthira, the oldest son of King Pandu, was the one who gambled all away in the game of dice with King Duryodhana, the oldest son of King Dhritarashtra, initiating these historic events. Arjuna, the middle son of the five Pandu brothers, represents equanimity. See a visual of the lineage in the chart (opposite).

But, at the critical moment, posed for greatness, fully prepared with Krishna as his charioteer, our mighty hero, Arjuna, hesitates.

Slokas 20–23

1.20 Then Arjuna, his war-banner displaying the sign of the monkey, looked upon Dhritarashtra's men, just as the clashing of the weapons was to begin. And then he raised his bow.

1.21 And, my king, he spoke these words to Krishna: "O unshakable one, stop my chariot here in the middle, between these two armies,

1.22 where I can see these men fixed in their positions and eager to fight, these men who are ready to fight against me in the strain of war.

1.23 I see them gathered here, these men who are set to fight, hungry to please in battle Dhritarashtra's reckless son.

Arjuna is stalling—putting off what he knows must be done.

Slokas 24–30

1.24 O Dhritarashtra, descendant of the family Bharata, Krishna heard the words that Arjuna spoke and he stopped that excellent chariot between the two armies.

1.25 Standing face to face with Bhishma and Drona and all of the great kings, Krishna spoke: "Arjuna, here they are, the assembled Kurus. Look at them!"

1.26 Arjuna looked upon them there where they stood, fathers and grandfathers, teachers, uncles and brothers, sons and grandsons, and companions,

1.27 fathers-in-law and dear friends, in both of the armies. Seeing them all standing there, his kinsmen,

1.28 Arjuna was overwhelmed by deep compassion and in despair he said, "Krishna, yes, I see my kinsmen gathered here and ready to fight.

1.29 My arms and legs have grown heavy. My mouth is dry. My body is trembling and the hair on my head stands on end.

1.30 My Gandiva bow drops from my hand, and my skin—it burns. I cannot stand still, and my mind just wanders.

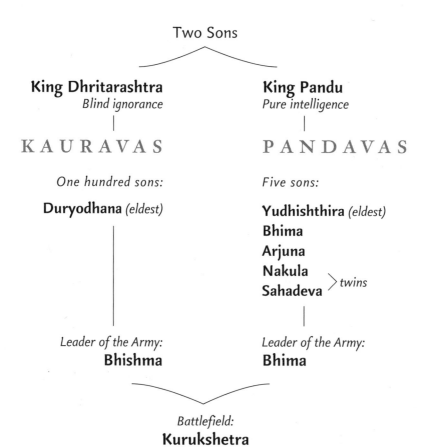

Two Sons

King Dhritarashtra
Blind ignorance

King Pandu
Pure intelligence

K A U R A V A S

P A N D A V A S

One hundred sons:

Duryodhana *(eldest)*

Five sons:

Yudhishthira *(eldest)*
Bhima
Arjuna
Nakula
Sahadeva ⟩ *twins*

Leader of the Army:
Bhishma

Leader of the Army:
Bhima

Battlefield:
Kurukshetra
The field of action

Anyone who has suffered the anxiety of sheer mental and emotional paralysis will recognize the symptoms Arjuna exhibits. Our mind becomes cloudy and our body weak. Our mouth becomes dry. Fear holds us hostage. We're unable to exercise our will. An ancient Zen proverb says, "Sit, walk, or run, but don't wobble." Arjuna is wobbling. We, too, wobble in anxiety, fear and depression until we confront the untruths and injustices within our own lives, our relationships and community. And, like Arjuna, every day we are forced to confront our own fears in relation to those closest to us.

It is not easy to confront the truth and it is impossible not to—for eventually what is true will beg for recognition: the job that is not bringing satisfaction—the relationship which needs a healthy dose of honest communication—the addiction we or a loved one is struggling with—the healing of an old wound we spend our energy hiding. Daily, we lay down our weapons and say, "I cannot." Daily, we collapse in sorrow because the pain and fear are just too great. And, yet, what is *true* will not let us go.

Ultimately, we find the courage to rise up, *when facing the truth becomes more important than being right or maintaining our position*. For example, getting help for our child we suspect has an eating disorder becomes more compelling than continuing to make excuses for the signs we see. It is for this reason that fighting for the truth, or *dharma*, although it may at first feel overwhelming, is *always freeing*. It is freeing because we have found the courage to rise above our personal fears or agendas to do what we know needs to be done. To not do so creates bondage, or *adharma*. This is the sorrow of Arjuna and ours as well, each time we put off saying or doing what we *know* needs to be said or done.

Overcoming our fear to rise up and defend the dharma is the central theme of the Bhagavad Gita. Recall from the events leading up to the war, the Kauravas have not held up to their part of the agreement. An injustice has occurred. They have left the Pandavas no choice but to fight for what is rightfully theirs. Arjuna must stand up and confront the deceit and injustice within his family and those around him in order to be victorious on the battlefield of life.

And, so must we.

Sometimes we get derailed with the notion of *fighting*. We think of great spiritual teachers such as Gandhi or Martin Luther King, Jr., whose lives were supreme examples of how to confront injustice with non-violence. I would suggest here that it is not the action itself but the *motivation* behind the action that determines the outcome for us.

For example, if you saw a helpless person being attacked on a street corner, would you just walk by? If someone broke into your home and was going to kill a loved one, would you do nothing?

Can we conceive of the possibility that we can show up to stop a hurtful action without hating the perpetrator? That, indeed, it is our duty to do so? This is the great challenge spiritual teachers such as Gandhi and Martin Luther King, Jr., demonstrated. They showed us a different way. They showed that it is possible to stand up to injustice without becoming unjust—to stand up to hatred without hating. *This is the challenge of fighting as a Pandava on the battlefield of life.*

However, Arjuna, a great Pandava warrior, cannot rise up to defend the dharma because he is lost in emotional turmoil. So, he seeks solace in his rationalizations.

Slokas 31-45

1.31   O Krishna, I see bad unfavorable signs here, and I can see nothing good in killing my own people in battle!

1.32   I have no desire for victory, Krishna, nor a kingdom, nor the joys of life. What is a kingdom to us, Krishna, and what are pleasures, or life itself?

1.33   It is for their sake that we desired a kingdom, pleasures and the joys of life, these men assembled here in battle, men who are prepared to give up their lives and their fortunes.

1.34   Our teachers, our fathers and sons, and our grandfathers as well. Uncles, fathers-in-law, grandsons, brothers-in-law, all of them our kinsmen!

1.35   I do not want to kill them, even if they kill me, Krishna, not for the sake of kingship over all of the three worlds, much less for the earth itself!

1.36   What joy would there be for us, Krishna, if we kill Dhritarashtra and his men? Evil will follow us if we kill them, even as they draw their bows against us.

1.37   It is not right for us to kill Dhritarashtra's men. They are our own kin! How can we gain happiness, Krishna, if we kill our own kin?

1.38   Even if they don't see it, blinded as they are by the greed that has destroyed their reason, it is wrong to destroy one's family and to betray one's friends.

1.39   How could we not have the wisdom to turn away from this evil thing, since we can see that the destruction of the whole family is a great crime?

1.40   If the family is destroyed, then the timeless traditional laws of our family will die too. If our traditional law [dharma] dies, then chaos [adharma] will overwhelm the entire family.

1.41   If the family is overwhelmed by chaos [adharma], then the women of the family will be corrupted, and when the women are corrupted, Krishna, all social order will collapse.

1.42   This collapse drags the family and those who destroy it down into hell, and their ancestors fall with them, since the offerings of rice and water will no longer be observed.

1.43   The crimes of those who destroy the family cause the social order to collapse. They undermine the unchanging laws and caste-duty and family duty.

1.44   Krishna, we have been taught that a place in hell is saved for men who undermine family duty [dharma]. This is our tradition.

1.45   Oh no, no! We are intent on committing a great evil here, driven as we are by greed for a kingdom and pleasures, to kill our own kinsmen!

We, too, have our good reasons for not showing up to confront the truths we need to confront. Yet, as Arjuna, we must confront the rationalizations, good reasons, well-honed excuses, those *enemies within*, in order to see clearly and respond appropriately.

True seeing is true love.

Yet, confronting and overcoming the enemies within is not for the weak minded. Fighting for truth is not a sentimental act based on emotion but an act of courage based on clarity. And this is the courage needed to battle our inner demons. This is why serving the greater good—or truth—*is not related to emotional feeling*. Sometimes, what serves best may, at first, feel the worst. Still, truth is the only doorway to freedom.

Slokas 46–47

1.46   If Dhritarashtra's men with all their weapons were to kill me here as I am, unarmed and unresisting, that would bring me greater peace."

1.47   Saying these things in the midst of a war, Arjuna sank down into his chariot seat. He dropped his bow and arrows. His mind was tormented by grief.

Unable to do his duty, Arjuna sinks into martyrdom. In *The Living Gita, The Complete Bhagavad Gita and Commentary*, Swami Satchidananda says Arjuna has become "like a judge who loses his neutrality when he sees a relative in the dock." This illustrates how even a mature person can become temporarily lost in sentimental attachments. Confused, he is unable to rise up and offer his skills in service to the greater good.

And, like us, he will suffer until he does.

But, fortunately, his despair leads him to seek help from his Lord and the ensuing dialogue becomes this Song of God.

In chapter 2, Krishna begins his counsel, telling Arjuna what must be done to overcome sorrow and rise up to become a fierce warrior for truth and justice on the battlefield of life.

Key Points

1. We are forced to confront our own inner dragons or issues in relation to those closest to us—our family and peers.
2. We all have our rationalizations, good reasons, for not confronting the difficult issues in our lives.
3. To fight for truth is not a sentimental act based on emotion but an act of courage based on clarity.

Characters and Terms
In the Order They Appear in the Text and Slokas

SETTING THE STAGE

Arjuna (*Are*-joo-nah) warrior in Pandava army who receives Krishna's instruction

Vyasa (*Vyah*-sah) illumined sage; author of the *Mahabharata*

Mahabharata (Mah-ha-*bar*-ah-tah) epic poem of which the Bhagavad Gita is a part

Sanjaya (Sun-*jah*-yah) visionary; narrator of the Bhagavad Gita

Bhagavad Gita (*Bah*-gah-vahd *Gee*-tah) the Song of God

King Dhritarashtra (King *Drit*-ah-*rah*-shtrah) blind king of the Kauravas

Kauravas (*Cow*-rah-vahs) forces of ignorance

Kurukshetra (Koo-roo-*kshay*-trah) field of action; battlefield where the Bhagavad Gita occurs; the body

King Pandu (*Pahn*-doo) king of the Pandavas

King Duryodhana (King Door-*yo*-dah-nah) oldest son of King
  Dhritarashtra

Drona (*Drow*-nah) archery teacher of warriors on both sides; fights
  with the Kauravas

Pandavas (*Pahn*-dah-vahs) forces of righteousness

WARRIORS DESCRIBED:

Dhrishtadyumna (*Drish*-tah-*dyoom*-nah) son of Drupada; Pandava
  warrior

Drupada (*Drew*-pah-dah) Pandava warrior

Bhima (*Bee*-mah) Arjuna's older brother; leader of the Pandava army;
  second son of King Pandu, king of the Pandavas

Arjuna (*Are*-joo-nah) Pandava warrior who receives Krishna's
  instruction

Yuyudhana (Yoo-*yoo*-dah-nah) Pandava warrior

Virata (Vir-*ah*-tah) Pandava warrior

Dhrishtaketu (Dir-ish-tah-*kay*-too) Pandava warrior

Cekitana (Chay-*kit*-tah-nah) Pandava warrior

King of Kashi (King of *Kah*-shee) Pandava warrior

Purujit (*Poo*-roo-jit) Pandava warrior

Kuntibhoja (Koon-tee-*bow*-jah) Pandava warrior

Shibis (*She*-bees) Pandava warrior

Yudhamanyu (Yoo-dah-*mahn*-yoo) Pandava warrior

Uttamaujas (Oo-tah-*mau*-jahs) Pandava warrior

Subhadra (Soo-*buhd*-drah) wife of Arjuna; their son's name is
  Abhimanyu (Ah-bee-*mahn*-yoo) Pandava warrior

Drupadi (*Drew*-pah-dee) daughter of Drupada; her sons are not
  named warriors, but represent qualities that arouse a longing for
  God and the turning away from the material world

Brahmins (*Brah*-mins) those who are one with Brahman

Drona (*Drow*-nah) archery teacher of warriors on both sides; fights
  with the Kauravas

Bhishma (*Bee*-sh-mah) leader of the Kaurava army

Karna (*Kar*-nah) Kaurava warrior

Kripa (*Kree*-pah) Kaurava warrior

Ashvatthama (Ash-*vah*-tah-mah) Kaurava warrior

Vikarna (*Vi*-kar-nah) Kaurava warrior

Somadatta (*Sew*-mah-*dah*-tah) son of Somadatta is Somadatti (Sew-mah-dah-tee) Kaurava warrior

BLOWING OF CONCH–SHELLS:

Bhishma (*Bee*-sh-mah) leader of the Kaurava army; blows conch to begin war

Kurus (*Koo*-roos) short for Kauravas

Krishna (*Krish*-nah) God within; charioteer and guide of Arjuna

Pancajanya (*Pahn*-cha-*jan*-yah) conch blown by Krishna

Devadatta (*Day*-vah-*dah*-tah) God-Given conch blown by Arjuna

Paundra (*Pound*-rah) Bhima's conch

King Yudhishthira (King You-*dish*-ti-rah) Arjuna's oldest brother; eldest son of King Pandu, king of the Pandavas

Kunti (*Koon*-tee) first wife of King Pandu; mother of King Yudhishthira, Bhima and Arjuna

Anantavijaya (Ah-*nahn*-tah-vi-jay-ah) endless victory conch blown by King Yudhisthira

Nakula (*Nah*-koo-lah) Arjuna's younger brother; twin of Sahadeva. Nakula and Sahadeva's mother is **Madri** (*Mah*-dree), second wife of King Pandu

Sughosha (Soo-*go*-sha) sweet-toned conch blown by Nakula

Sahadeva (Sah-ha-*day*-vah) Arjuna's younger brother; twin of Nakula

Manipushpaka (Mah-nee-*poosh*-pah-kah) jewel-toned conch blown by Sahadeva

King of Kashi (King of *Kah*-shee) Pandava warrior

Shikandhin (She-*kun*-din) Pandava warrior

Dhrishthadyumna (Drish-*tahd*-dyoom-nah) son of Drupada; Pandava warrior

Virata (Vir-*ah*-tah) Pandava warrior

Satyaki (*Saht*-yah-kee) Pandava warrior

Drupada (*Drew*-pah-dah) Pandava warrior

Drupadi (*Drew*-pah-dee) daughter of Drupada; her sons are not named warriors, but represent qualities that arouse a longing for God and the turning away from the material world

Subhadra (Soo-*bahd*-rah) wife of Arjuna; their son's name is
Abhimanyu (Ab-hee-*mahn*-yoo) Pandava warrior

ARJUNA FALTERS

Bharata (*Bar*-ah-tah) lineage of both the Pandavas and Kauravas (See chart on page 11.)
Gandiva (Gahn-*dee*-vah) Arjuna's bow
Dharma (*Dar*-mah) traditional or spiritual law; truth
Adharma (*A*-dar-mah) chaos; untruth

Personal Reflection

1. What issues in your life are you avoiding?
2. What are your very good reasons—rationalizations—for not showing up?
3. Describe the difference between acting from emotion and acting from clarity. Can you recall a time from your own experience?

What We Must Do To Realize We Are Atman:
Surrender to the Voice of the True Self

> *Junah's problem is simple.*
> *He thinks he is Junah.*
>
> **—THE LEGEND OF**
> **BAGGER VANCE**

CHAPTER 2

Realizing Who We Are

This chapter offers an overview of the entire Bhagavad Gita. Krishna offers a theoretical explanation of the true Self, reminds Arjuna of the importance of doing his duty and gives practical suggestions for realizing Atman within. As Atman, an individual expression of the One, Arjuna, and we, may experience the outer world of the senses while holding awareness of true Self within. We may be *in* the world but not *of* the world.

Many key concepts are introduced here that will be revisited in later chapters.

Slokas 1-3

Sanjaya spoke:

2.1   Arjuna sat there overwhelmed by compassion, his eyes blurred and filled with tears. And then Krishna spoke these words to him:

The Blessed One spoke:

2.2   Where does this weakness in you come from, Arjuna, at this time of crisis? It is not fitting to a nobleman. It does not gain you heaven. It does not bring you any honor.

2.3   Don't give in to this impotence! It doesn't belong in you. Give up this

petty weakness, this faintness of heart. You are a world conqueror,
Arjuna. Stand up!

Krishna sees that Arjuna is overcome with despair and wastes no time
delivering a scathing rebuke. Remembering that Krishna is God personified in us, *it is really our own inner knowing that is offering this rebuke. This
means that there is a part of us that knows exactly what we should be doing in any
situation to bring about the greatest good.* The problem is, lost in emotional
turmoil, we stop listening to our inner knowing. Instead, we only hear the
familiar tapes of our thoughts and feelings. Arjuna asked Krishna to be his
charioteer but is allowing fear to drive instead.

Krishna does not coddle Arjuna at this critical juncture. He challenges
him to wake up and remember who he is, a Pandava, and it is his duty to
defend the dharma or righteousness in the kingdom. Sometimes, a good,
swift kick in the backside is what it takes to wake us up!

In the early 90s, I witnessed a beautiful example of what can happen
when one person has the courage to show up as a Pandava on the battlefield of life. It happened, surprisingly, on a TV talk show. On this particular
day, the audience was filled with black people and, on stage, were people
representing various white supremacy groups. The atmosphere was very
volatile, with a lot of shouting back and forth. It seemed everyone was
feeding on the frenzy.

Then, a guest, a white man, was introduced. He had written a book
about how a black man had taught him to love and how the experience
had changed him. As a result, he had been able to give up his membership
in a hate group.

I don't remember a word the man said. What I have never forgotten
was the silence that fell over the audience as he spoke. All the shouting and
frenzy stopped. The mood shifted. Then, after a break for commercials,
the show returned, the man was gone and the frenzy resumed.

Recall from our earlier discussion in "A Story of Yogic Wisdom," the
nature of God *is that which is the same in all of us—the one Essence from which
all variations arise.* This awareness of the one Essence behind all variations
allows a Pandava on the battlefield of life to see beyond the duality of
black and white, to confront hatred without hating, and, in doing so, to
elevate all onto the common ground of love. But, many of us are uncom-

fortable when confronted with our sameness, as it causes us to give up the comfort of our positions and the security of our viewpoints.

However, any time we are able to rise above the duality of having to be right or having to win, we come upon a neutral ground where we may simply seek to serve the greater good. Notice that it is often the emotion of anger that keeps us positioned in our corners ready to come out fighting. The black people in the audience and the white people on the stage were simply mirrors of one another in their mutual hate and anger.

When we hand over the reins of our chariot to Krishna, God within, it is no longer about "us" and "them." Now, it's just "us." We are free to rise up and take action in the name of goodness and truth. We are able to act instead of react, and the forces of ignorance dim in direct response to our resolve. It is not that the world becomes different. *We* become different.

This is exactly what Dr. Martin Luther King, Jr., did in his "I Have a Dream" speech. He challenged us to rise above hatred to arrive on the common ground of what we all want for our children. This is why this short speech is so remembered and so loved. It is worth noting here that Dr. Martin Luther King, Jr., was a great admirer of Gandhi, who often referred to the Bhagavad Gita as a manual for daily living.

Acting as a Pandava on the battlefield of life, Krishna is our charioteer. We "walk through the valley of the shadow of death" and we "fear no evil" for the Light of Lights guides our way. Krishna is stern with Arjuna because his very soul is at stake.

And so is ours.

But, Arjuna is not persuaded.

Slokas 4–9

2.4   But how can I engage Bhishma and Drona in battle, Krishna? How can I fight them with my arrows, these two men who deserve my devotion instead?

2.5   No, instead of killing my gurus, these men of great authority, it would be better for me to eat the food of a beggar here in this world. If I were to kill my gurus here, even though they seek their own ends against me, it would be like eating food smeared with blood.

2.6   And we do not know which is the heavier burden: whether we should win the fight, or whether they should win. Dhritarashtra's men stand there, drawn up before us. If we were to kill them, we ourselves would no longer wish to live!

2.7   My compassion is an error that harms my very being. I ask you because my understanding of duty [dharma] is confused. What would be better? Tell me unambiguously. I am your student. You are my refuge. Teach me!

2.8   Even if I could attain unrivalled wealth on this earth and a prosperous kingdom and lordship over the gods, I still would not be able to see what might dispel this sorrow which so distracts me from my senses.

Sanjaya spoke:

2.9   So Arjuna, the conqueror, spoke. "I will not fight!" he said to Krishna, and having spoken thus, he became silent.

Arjuna repeats the same logic he expressed in Chapter 1 as to why he does not want to fight. We, too, find ourselves repeating the same recordings of our notions and beliefs. It's comforting and familiar. It also serves us. Stuck in this rut, we don't have to face the fear of moving forward.

Sloka 2.7 represents the critical turning point without which the rest of the Bhagavad Gita could have taken place. *My compassion is an error that harms my very being.* Arjuna knows he is lost. His rudder is broken and night is falling fast. And, at this critical juncture, he chooses *surrender.* He takes refuge in his Lord and now he is ready to listen. It is often our suffering that brings us to our knees. We lay down our weapons and with head bowed we confess we are lost. How free it feels to come to this place—how strangely unencumbered.

Unencumbered by all our notions about how things *should* be, we become a kind of blank slate upon which our deepest knowing may write. It is the place of prayer, when we have come to the end of all we know. And, it is the beginning of all true knowing. We pray that God will remember us in our hour of need, although we may have rarely visited our inner sanctuary. After all, we had thought that we could make it alone. But, nonetheless, there awaits the grace of God that has never left us. How could it? It *is* us.

Arjuna, though, has forgotten who he is—*Atman—an individual expression of the One eternal Brahman—never born nor die—That which is the same in all.* He has forgotten that this eternal expression of Brahman or God is not affected by the changing conditions of the nature, the world of the senses, prakriti. So, Krishna reminds him.

Slokas 10–18

2.10 O my lord of the Bharatas, Krishna responded, it seemed with a smile, as Arjuna sat there between the two armies. These were his words.

The Blessed One spoke:

2.11 You grieve for those who are beyond grieving, and you talk like one with wisdom, but the truly learned grieve neither for those who have lost their lives nor for those who still have them.

2.12 But in fact there never was a time in the past when I did not exist, nor you, nor any of these other lords. And there never will be a time in the future when we do not exist.

2.13 Just as in this body the embodied person experiences childhood, and youth, and old age, in the same way one enters other bodies. The wise are not disturbed by this.

2.14 O Arjuna, encounters with the material world induce sensations of coldness and heat and pleasure and pain. They come and they go. They are impermanent. You are a Bharata! Endure it!

2.15 For these sensations do not make a man waver who is a bull among men, a man for whom pain and pleasure are the same, a truly wise man. Such a man is fit for immortality!

2.16 What does not exist cannot gain existence, and what does exist cannot lose existence, but the border between these two – existence and non-existence – can be perceived by those who can see things as they really are.

2.17 But know that this is imperishable, this which pervades the whole world. No one can bring about the destruction of what is imperishable.

2.18 These our bodies are said to have an ending, but they belong to an embodied one who is unending, who does not perish and is beyond measure. For this reason, O Bharata, you should fight!

A beautiful Sufi aphorism says, "When the heart weeps for what it has lost, the spirit laughs for what it has found." This is why Sloka 2.10 says that *Krishna responded, it seemed with a smile.* No, it is not the fun part of the journey to confront our rationalizations, good reasons, fears, weakness and sorrow. But Krishna knows that Arjuna just needs a reminder—to remember—and his condition can be transformed.

Recall in "A Story of Yogic Wisdom," our discussion of the two aspects or expressions of God: the eternal, unchanging, never-born-nor-dies Brahman; and, the transient, changing aspect, prakriti, that brings forth the ongoing cycle of birth, death and rebirth in all creation. Arjuna is suffering because he is only identifying with the changing aspect, prakriti, and therefore, only sees the personalities of his family and friends before him.

Krishna knows that Arjuna has lost his will to fight because he has mistakenly made the fight *personal*, and, as a result, has become overwhelmed with sentimentality.

And how easy it is to become sentimental when it comes to truly seeing ourselves or a family member. How easy it is to overlook the signs of our teenager's drug habit because she or he "is really such a good kid" or, more importantly, because we don't want to feel like a bad parent. We cannot rise up to face the truth of what is happening because our vision has become clouded with personal concerns. What courage it takes to say, "This is happening and we all need help." To paraphrase a line from the Simon and Garfunkel song "The Boxer," we only hear what we want to hear and disregard the rest. Lost in sentimentality, we, like Arjuna, serve no one.

There is also a different intention behind fighting *for* righteousness, truth, help for our family and fighting *against* someone or something. Mother Teresa once remarked that she would not participate in an anti-war rally but would gladly attend a create-peace rally. Fighting *against* leaves us in duality, often with strong personal attachments to outcome. Fighting *for* truth or dharma elevates us to a higher ground where we can serve all for the greater good.

So, Krishna reminds him that *what is the same in all*, the true Self, is eternal and cannot kill nor be killed. He is challenging Arjuna to rise up and *confront the injustice*—not the personalities—before him, and, in doing so, *defend the dharma*.

Slokas 19-30

2.19 Whoever thinks that this one is a murderer, or who thinks that that one has been murdered, in both cases they are wrong. The one does not kill, nor is the other killed.

2.20 One is not born, nor does one die—in any way! Once one exists, one can never not exist! Unborn, eternal, permanent, primordial – one is not killed when the body is killed!

2.21   How can one who knows that he is imperishable and eternal and unborn and unchanging, how can this person kill, or cause anyone else to kill?

2.22   Just as a man discards worn-out clothes and gets others that are new, so one who is embodied discards worn-out bodies and enters others that are new.

2.23   Weapons do not cut him, fire does not burn him, water does not wet him, the winds do not dry him out.

2.24   He cannot be cut or burned, he cannot be made wet or dried out: he is unchanging, everywhere, immovable, and eternal.

2.25   He is called the unmanifest, the inconceivable, the immutable. Therefore, once you have understood that this is so, you should not mourn for him.

2.26   But even if you think that he is constantly born and constantly dies, even then, Arjuna, you should not mourn for him.

2.27   For death is certain for anyone who has been born, just as birth is certain for anyone who has died. Since this condition cannot be avoided, you should not mourn.

2.28   The origins of all things are inaccessible to us. Here in the midst of life things are accessible. But the ends of all things are also inaccessible. So what is there to lament?

2.29   It is a rare and wonderful thing when someone sees him, rare and wonderful when another speaks of him, and rare and wonderful also when another hears of him. But to have heard about him is not to have known him.

2.30   The embodied [self] which dwells in the body of each one of us is completely beyond harm. Therefore, you should not mourn for any being whatsoever.

But, just in case Arjuna is not persuaded by the more esoteric truths of the real and the unreal, Krishna makes the argument more personal, challenging Arjuna to do the duty of his nature.

Slokas 31–36

2.31   Also, reflect upon your own caste-duties [svadharma]. You should not get agitated. For a warrior there is nothing more noble than a war of duty.

2.32   The opportunity arises by pure chance and the doors of heaven open. Arjuna, those warriors are happy who gain the opportunity to fight such a war!

2.33   But if you will not participate in this war of duty, you will have abandoned your caste-duty and your honor, and you will have won only evil for yourself.

2.34   The whole world will talk only of your permanent dishonor, and for someone of your stature dishonor is far worse than death.

2.35   These great chariot-warriors will think that you have fled from the battle out of fear, and you will become a small and despised man among men who once thought so highly of you!

2.36   Your enemies will say many scandalous things and they will ridicule your competence. What could be more disgraceful than this?

In the book, *The Legend of Bagger Vance*, by Steven Pressfield, a young man called Junah is involved in a golf match with two well-known competitors. The game is an exhibition match being played in Savannah, Georgia during the Depression. Although Junah has Bagger Vance, God personified, as his caddy, he is losing miserably because he cannot get out of his own way. He is trying too hard. Although, he has the potential to win, he cannot see it and continues to create his own nightmarish experience.

Finally, one of the elders of Savannah, Judge Anderson, can take the embarrassment no longer and goes over to find out what "fool nonsense" the caddy might be putting into their champion's ear. He approaches the caddy and asks for an explanation.

> "Junah's problem is simple," Bagger Vance said. "He thinks he is Junah."
>
> "What in damnation does that mean?" The judge's face flushed crimson. "He *is* Junah, you damn twit!"
>
> "I will teach him that he is not Junah," the caddy answered with his accustomed calm. "Then he will swing Junah's swing."

Bagger Vance states beautifully, "I believe that each of us possesses, inside ourselves, one true authentic swing that is ours alone." His job as caddy is simply to reconnect Junah with his authentic swing because, in doing so, *winning* becomes the *only* possibility. Like Junah, in order for us to reconnect with our authentic swing and *sink the putt*, we must be willing to move out of our own way—to stop being a problem to ourselves. We must surrender to the advice of Krishna, our caddy.

When we recognize the golf game as a metaphor for the game of life, we see that our one true authentic swing comes to represent those times when we are acting in ways that are in the greatest harmony with our inner knowing and purpose. Sometimes, we can more easily recognize the times when we are *not* in harmony. We may feel dissatisfied, unhappy, unfulfilled. We just know that there is something else we should be doing.

What is calling is our *svadharma* referred to in Sloka 2.31. Our svadharma is a kind of predestined duty—the thing that calls us based on our interests, abilities and talents. It is our gift for the world.

Krishna reminds Arjuna of his svadharma as a warrior, *kshatriya*, and of his duty to restore righteousness to the kingdom. He tells him in Sloka 2.32 that in such a battle *the doors of heaven open*. Each time we act from a place of inner truth and knowing, we too are expressing our svadharma and experience a kind of heaven on earth. Arjuna is despondent because he knows he is a warrior, yet, he cannot seem to find the will to fight. He knows who he is and what he must do and still he cannot move forward.

And, sometimes, so it is with us.

In moments of doubt, we become Kauravas, desperately grasping for the winnings that we think will bring us happiness. As a Pandava, we find our authentic swing. Junah must decide what it is he wants most and so must we. Does he want to win a golf game or does he want to win at the game of life? It is our decision, as well. Do we align ourselves with the fleeting victories of the outer world or do we align ourselves with the inherent victory in our own true authentic swing? It is possible to "win" the golf game and, yet, lose at the game of life. Yet, it is impossible to win at the game of life and lose the golf game. So, which will it be?

Slokas 37-38

2.37 If you are killed you will win heaven, or if you are victorious you will have the world to enjoy. Therefore, stand up, Arjuna! Don't hesitate! Fight!

2.38   Joy and suffering, success and failure, victory and defeat: treat them all
       alike. Brace yourself for this battle. In this way you will avoid dishonor!

Krishna is telling Arjuna that he cannot lose the war with his inner demons.
Acting in accordance with the deepest impulse of his heart and releasing
all attachment to the outcome, Arjuna cannot lose. This is because the
"war" is not about a particular outcome but rather about overcoming the
illusionary fears of the ego so that we may become instruments for a
greater purpose.

And as such instruments, even if killed, we die a noble death. This is
why we really can't lose. When we walk our path in truth, we've already
won, regardless of outside circumstances or outcomes. Bagger Vance
"wins" when he plays his authentic swing in service to the greater good.

And, so do we.

In the next Slokas, Krishna begins to speak less of the philosophical and
more to the techniques for practical realization.

Sloka 39

2.39   This insight has been presented to you as a form of Sankhya philosophy.
       Now hear it in the form of yoga tradition. Disciplined by this insight,
       Arjuna, you will escape from the bonds of action.

In simplest terms, *Sankhya* philosophy is concerned with the wisdom of
the cosmos as expressed through the interplay of nature and spirit. *Yoga* is
the science offering techniques for the practical realization of such philosophical truths.

Sloka 40

2.40   Progress in yoga is never completely wasted and it is never
       unproductive. Even a little effort in this practice [dharma] saves
       you from the great terror of life.

Sloka 2.40 is comforting. *Even a little effort* saves us. This is because we
each have an impulse toward wholeness. It's why you're reading this book.
It's why we go to our helpers and healers. The truth is *we're not all happy
being sad* to paraphrase, in part, Swami Dayananda Saraswati's quote at the
beginning of this book. Psychologist Carl Jung called it the self-regulating
mechanism. I call it God.

Slokas 41–44

2.41 The insight that is based on firm resolve is uniquely special. Arjuna, men who have no resolve have poor insight that veers endlessly in all directions.

2.42 People who please themselves with debating the Vedas, they recite those florid Vedic chants, but they have no insight, while saying all the time that only the Vedas matter!

2.43 In their hearts they are driven by desire and eager for heaven. Their words promise rebirth as the fruit of their actions. Their talk is all about all of their elaborate rituals whose purpose is to gain pleasure and power.

2.44 They are obsessed with pleasure and power. The words of the Vedas deprive them of their good sense. They lack the insight that is based on firm resolve and they do not gain it even when engaged in intense concentration.

The antidote to fear is equanimity. Arjuna is stalled because he is averting what must be done. Yet, he also must release any desire for power or to win, (Slokas 2.43 and 2.44) or else, like in the TV show, he will simply mirror his enemy, the Kauravas. He must find the middle way to simply doing his duty, releasing all attachment to outcome and trusting that in doing so the greater good for all is won.

Slokas 45–46

2.45 The world of the Vedas is the natural world with its three qualities. Arjuna, live in the world that is beyond this one, free of its qualities and its dualities. Remain always within your true self, free from effort and comfort. Remain in your soul [Atman].

2.46 As useful as a water-tank is when there is flooding in all directions, that's how useful all the Vedas are to a Brahmin who has true insight.

The *Vedas*, of course, are the ancient scriptures of India. The *three qualities* referred to in Sloka 2.45 are the *gunas*, or energetic qualities of nature, *prakriti*. (Recall in "A Story of Yogic Wisdom" our discussion of prakriti as the transient, changing aspect of God. The gunas will be discussed in depth in later chapters.)

In Sloka 2.46, Krishna warns of confusing the scripture or ritual for true insight—for the *real* thing. I think of ritual as simply the context *through which* I may receive insight—and *through which* I may be informed. Informed by dancing a Psalm with a man with Cerebral Palsy in a wheelchair and his helper, informed by singing an old Christian hymn in a small Methodist Church in the deep South, informed by chanting the ancient Vedic mantras, informed by a cold shower at 3:30 AM to do yoga and chant the sun up, informed by sixty-two minutes with raised arms in White Tantric Yoga, informed by twirling with the Sufis, informed by time in the sweat lodge. *Everywhere* is God if we invite the ritual to *inform us.*

Slokas 47-53

2.47   Focus your mind on action alone, but never on the fruits of your actions. Your goal should never be the fruits of your actions, nor should you be attached to non-action.

2.48   Practice yoga and perform the actions that you are obliged to do, but, Arjuna, don't be attached to them. Treat success and failure alike. This kind of even-mindedness is called yoga.

2.49   Arjuna, action is far inferior to the yoga of insight. Seek refuge in insight. Those whose goal is the fruits of their actions wind up miserable.

2.50   A man who is committed to insight leaves behind both good actions and bad. Therefore commit yourself to yoga, for yoga is skillfulness in all action.

2.51   Those who are committed to insight, who are wise, renounce the fruit that is born of action. Freed from the bonds of rebirth, they go to a place where there is no misery.

2.52   When your insight transcends this jungle of delusion, then you will become indifferent both to what you've been taught by tradition and what you will be taught.

2.53   When your insight, which has been distracted by the traditional teachings, stands unwavering, motionless in concentration, then you will reach yoga.

True insight becomes ours when we keep our minds single-pointed and release attachment to the fruits of our actions. This is why Krishna's first practical instruction to Arjuna comes in Sloka 2.47: *Focus your mind on action alone, but never on the fruits of your actions.* Only with such a single-pointed mind can he rise above sentimental emotions to act with clarity.

In the Bible, this would be, "Seek ye first the kingdom of God and all will be handed unto you." The single-pointed mind enables us to see beyond the transient duality of black and white, joy or sadness, desiring or averting, winning or losing. Instead, our only single-pointed prayer is like that of Saint Francis, "Lord, Make Me an Instrument." We start to live the precepts only alluded to in scripture and become free to do the work that comes to us because we trust our place in the Divine plan.

But such sweet surrender only occurs when we focus our intention on the *process*—not the *outcome*—of our actions and when we *need nothing* in return for our efforts. To *need nothing*, no particular feedback from the outside, requires we rein in our attraction to the transient, changing world of sense experience and return to the eternal, unchanging, inner sanctuary where God in us resides. Such dispassionate non-attachment is *vairagya*. It's called Home. Only there can we trade in moments of fleeting happiness based on outside circumstances for the joy illuminated solely from within. Only there can we start to become our Self.

In the following Slokas, Krishna expounds on the importance of withdrawing the senses from all the sense objects—*like a tortoise that draws its legs into its shell* (Sloka 2.58).

Slokas 54–61

2.54   Krishna, How do you describe someone who is stable in this wisdom, who can stay fixed in concentration? How would such a person speak, how would he sit, how would he go about in the world?

The Blessed One spoke:

2.55   Arjuna, when one gives up all the desires that fill one's mind, when one is content with oneself in one's self [atman], then one is said to be stable in this wisdom.

2.56   When bad fortune no longer disturbs his mind, and when good fortune no longer excites him, then you could call this person a sage who is stable in this wisdom, one in whom longing and fear and anger have vanished.

2.57   When one feels no desire for any thing whatsoever, and no matter what good things or bad things happen to him, he doesn't delight in them nor hate them, such a person has wisdom that is stable.

2.58   When he withdraws his senses from all sensuous things, like a tortoise that draws its legs into its shell, then his wisdom is stable.

2.59 Sense objects withdraw from one who while still in the body gives up
      food. For him only the flavor, the trace of the flavor, lingers, and once
      he has seen the highest, that too leaves him.

2.60 Even an intelligent man who strives to control his senses can be
      tormented by them. They can attack him and violently seize his mind.

2.61 He should restrain all of his senses and committed [to yoga] he should
      sit, intent on me. If his senses are under control, then his wisdom will
      be stable.

. . . *he should sit, intent on me.* Only a single-pointed mind can hold such
intention. But simple desire is not enough. We must use discernment
or the *buddhi* aspect of our mind. A mind controlled by the world of the
senses is called the *manas* mind. *How much time we spending using either our
buddhi faculties or our manas mind determines how much free will we exercise.*
For example, if we allow our manas mind to rule, we lose all *viveka* or
discrimination, and do whatever the world of the senses dictates. We may
eat anything or as much as we want. We may choose to skip meditation
in favor of a "B" movie. We may spend much of our time focused on our
own desires and goals without regard for others.

Inevitably, over time, we may wonder why we still never seem to reach a
state of satisfaction. We may wonder why the happy moments slip away so
fast. But, we usually do not sit with discontentment for too long before we
are off in pursuit of the next thing that will satisfy our unending craving
for fulfillment. It never occurs to us to look inward for the eternal well of
contentment that is as close as our very breath.

However, if we are using buddhi to discern what is truly good for us,
we will try to eat moderately and in a healthy manner. We will create the
time for our spiritual practice. We will naturally look for ways to be of service. In short, by disciplining ourselves, we experience freedom from the
constant cravings for satisfaction because we are finally beginning to look
in the right place—within—to the blessings of each moment. Happiness
is not an achievement anymore. Happiness becomes the experience of
our being, because we have remembered our connection to the greatest
happiness of all.

*By not allowing ourselves to be controlled by the world of the senses, we become
free to actually enjoy the world more fully.*

Slokas 62–66

2.62 When a man meditates on sense objects, attachment to them develops in him, and this attachment produces desire in him, and this desire produces anger.

2.63 From this anger comes delusion and from this delusion comes the distortion of memory and this distortion of memory leads to the loss of insight. After that, one dies.

2.64 But when a man approaches sense objects with his own senses detached from desire and anger, that is, when his senses are controlled by his self [atman], then he is in control of himself and he finds peace.

2.65 In that peace, all of his sorrows vanish, for as soon as his thoughts become tranquil his insight becomes steady.

2.66 The undisciplined one who does practice yoga has no insight. The undisciplined one has no inner concentration, and lacking inner concentration he has no peace. And without peace how can such a one be happy?

Being attached to the world of the senses can bring about what I call the "I'll be happy when" syndrome. This is when we base our happiness upon what is happening outside of us. Some examples: King Duryodhana, leader of the Kauravas army, thinks he will be happy when he can rule the entire kingdom. We may think: I'll be happy when I get that degree . . . find the right partner . . . get over my fears . . . convince you I'm right . . . buy that new house . . . or find the right career. We are bombarded by this notion at every turn in our society. All advertising is based upon this premise. The trouble is that everything that comes from the world outside of us, including our very bodies, thoughts and feelings, is changing every second. So, soon, the original glow of getting "it" begins to fade and we're off in a search for the next thing to satisfy our never-ending craving for stimulation.

Slokas 67–69

2.67 For the senses wander, and when one lets the mind follow after them it carries away wisdom like a wind-blown ship on the waters.

2.68 Therefore, great warrior, the one who has withdrawn his senses entirely from the things of the senses has steadfast wisdom.

2.69   When it is night for all creatures, the one who is self-restrained is
       awake, and when others are awake, it is night for the sage who sees
       truly.

It is only when we use our discriminating intellect, buddhi, to shift our
focus inward that we become Pandavas and find the place of no change. At
home in this place, we may once again *enjoy all the stimulation of the sense
objects around us without needing them* to make us feel complete. Sloka 2.69
reminds us that such paradox is at the heart of the spiritual journey. The
happiness we had thought could only come from the outside was inside,
waiting, all the while.

Slokas 70–72

2.70   Just as the waters that enter the ocean do not fill it nor do they disturb
       its depths, so too is the peace of the one into whom all these desires
       pour. The man who is driven by desire does not know such peace.

2.71   The man who abandons all desires, who goes about free from cravings,
       for whom there is no talk of "mine!" or "me!" – he finds peace.

2.72   This, Arjuna, is a divine state. Having attained this, one is no longer
       confused. When one abides in this state, even at the moment of death,
       one attains divine serenity [brahmanirvana].

Krishna warns Arjuna that he must release all personal desire or sense of
"me" and "mine." Here we come to another paradox. It is our duty to show
up on the battlefield of life and live the will of our nature *and* it is our duty
to release all to Krishna or the Divine within.

It is all about us and not about us at all. We recognize those moments of
perfect balance between our will and Divine will because we could not be
more present yet unattached at the same time. In full equanimity, we discover
full love.

In letting go of our self, we suddenly find our Self.

Arjuna has asked Krishna to be his charioteer and yet he cannot hand
over the reins. There was once a sign in front of a church that said, "We
want God but only in an advisory capacity." And, yet, full victory is
ours—just waiting for us—if we could only let go and let God.

In Chapter 3, Krishna will begin offering practical advice on how we
may let go and let God to manifest our unique gift in service to all.

Key Points

1. Krishna's strong rebuke is our own inner knowing.
2. Asking for guidance—surrendering—allows for our own inner guidance, Krishna, to be heard.
3. Remembering that we are eternal—that we cannot kill nor be killed—allows us to rise above sentimentality to focus on the duty at hand.
4. Each time we act in accordance with the will of our nature, we create a little heaven on earth.
5. We can't lose the war!
6. No effort is ever lost.
7. To find peace, keep the mind single-pointed, centered in equanimity, and release all personal desire.
8. Don't confuse the letter of the scripture for the Truth.
9. Use discernment to control the senses and enjoy all.
10. Paradox is at the heart of the spiritual journey.
11. In letting go of self, we find our Self.

Terms

Atman (*Aht*-mahn) individual expression of the One

Svadharma (*Sva*-dar-mah) predestined duty

Kshatriya (*Kshut*-tree-yah) someone from the warrior cast

Sankhya (*Sun*-kyah) philosophy concerned with the interplay of nature and spirit.

Yoga (*Yo*-gah) the science of practical techniques for realization

Vedas (*Vay*-dahs) ancient scriptures of India

Gunas (*Goo*-nahs) energetic qualities of nature

Prakriti (*Prahk*-ri-ti) nature or creation

Vairagya (Veye-*rah*-gyah) dispassion; non-attachment

Buddhi (*Buh*-dee) discerning intellect

Manas (*Mah*-nahs) mind

Viveka (Vi-*vay*-kah) discrimination

Personal Reflection

1. If there is a part of us that knows exactly what we should be doing, who is it that's messing up?
2. What reaction comes when you think of "surrender"?

3. What shift starts to happen when you think of yourself as "eternal"?

4. Why is releasing personal attachment key to doing your duty?

5. Are you living your Svadharma?

6. What does "You can't lose the war!" mean to you?

7. Describe in your own words a "single-pointed mind."

8. Discuss the relationship between discipline and freedom.

9. How can you be totally present yet unattached at the same time?

10. So, what's wrong with being attached to someone or something anyway?

What We Must Do To Realize We Are Atman:
Offer Every Action as a Sacrifice in Service to the Greater Good

I have a duty to be holy where I am. You
have a duty to be holy where you are.
There is nothing extraordinary about
being holy. We were made for that.

—MOTHER TERESA

CHAPTER 3

Actions of Sacrifice

Each of us has a gift. This gift has been called by many names: svadharma, soul print, sacred contract, authentic swing. It is not so much something we do as much as it is an impulse we follow. It is our job to *follow* the impulse and then *release* the manifestation to the Divine. This is the *not about us at all* part just discussed. This is sacrifice.

Slokas 1-2

Arjuna spoke:

3.1   If you think that insight is more powerful than action, Krishna, then why do you urge me to engage in such a terrible action as this?

3.2   With words that seem very convoluted you have made my mind confused! Please tell me the one thing I need to know to attain the highest good.

Arjuna is seeking clarification from Krishna's earlier words in Sloka 2.49: *Arjuna, action is far inferior to the yoga of insight. Seek refuge in insight. Those whose goal is the fruits of their actions wind up miserable.* With true insight, we can joyously release the fruits of our actions and just watch in child-

37

like wonder at how the Potter may use the offering of our actions. It's so freeing to remember it's *not about us at all*.

Slokas 3-7

The Blessed One spoke:

3.3   O blameless one, long ago I explained the twofold basis of the highest good. For the followers of Sankhya philosophy it is by means of the yoga of knowledge. For the followers of yoga it is by means of the yoga of action.

3.4   A man does not go beyond action by avoiding action, nor does he achieve success by renunciation alone.

3.5   For no one exists even for a moment without performing actions. Even if unwillingly everyone must act, due to the forces of nature.

3.6   A man can control the senses by which he acts but if he sits still while recalling in his mind all of the attractions of the senses, then he fools himself. He is called a hypocrite.

3.7   But whoever controls his senses with his mind, and with all of his senses engages in the yoga of action, such a person is unattached, Arjuna. He distinguishes himself.

In Sloka 3.3, the *yoga of knowledge* is referring to the path of wisdom or *Jnana Yoga*. The *yoga of action* refers to *Karma Yoga*. What we think about we become. Thought creates action. Discernment keeps us on the path of wisdom—*Jnana Yoga*—and produces selfless action—*Karma Yoga*.

Earlier we discussed the importance of *needing nothing*. I first heard the phrase "Need nothing!" from the great teacher of Kundalini yoga, Yogi Bhajan. All action attached to personal need creates *karma*. Our personal agendas require a return on our investment. Action that is void of personal need and offered simply to serve a greater good creates dharma. The moment such an action is done it is also done for us. No replays are needed.

The choice is not whether or not to act. We cannot *not* act, as we are told in Sloka 3.5. Even inaction is action. The Buddhists call this the wisdom of no escape. So, if we cannot escape, it would seem prudent to go about the business of creating more dharma than karma. When we control the senses, release personal attachment and surrender the reins of our chariot to Krishna, we create dharma. When we fight for control, we create karma. Through the gift of free will, the choice is ours. Through the law of karma, we learn by the results.

Slokas 8–9

3.8　You should perform the actions that you are obliged to perform. Action is better than inaction. You cannot maintain your body's health. Without action it would fail.

3.9　This world is in bondage to action except when it is performed as a sacrifice. You should remain unattached, Arjuna, and continue to perform action that is intended as sacrifice.

In these two Slokas, Krishna counsels Arjuna on what he must do to be successful on the battlefield of life: do your duty and make every action a sacrifice. This is a simple and beautiful instruction on how to enter into the steps of will and surrender and dance with God. Let's look at this dance a little closer:

WILL:	SURRENDER:
Do your duty.	*Make every action a sacrifice.*
It's all about me showing up.	It's not about me at all.
I am enough.	I am nothing.
I follow the impulse of my heart.	I release the manifestation to God.
I work as if all depends upon me.	I pray as if all depends upon God.

Too much will without surrender may manifest a very productive life but one that feels empty. There may be a strong dependence upon outside validation and a constant striving for the next thing. Too much surrender without will may lead to wobbling, inaction and disappointment when life doesn't turn out as we'd hope.

In search of a harmonious balance between will and surrender, we seek to have our skills and actions used for a higher purpose while releasing any personal ownership. Instead of the constant striving for happiness, we seek truth and equanimity. Instead of seeking outside validation, we seek to follow an inner knowing. The last *work and pray* relationship is from John Wesley, who expressed an identical sentiment, encouraging us to work as if everything depends upon us and pray as if everything depends upon God.

But, as my Bhagavad Gita students have often heard me say, the best description of the will and surrender dance with God I have read actually came from the September 2002 edition of *O, The Oprah Magazine*. In her column *What I Know for Sure*, Oprah writes:

> The truth is that as much as you plan and dream and move forward in your life, you must remember that you are always acting in conjunction with the flow and energy of the universe. You move in the direction of your goal with all the force and verve you can muster—and then let go, releasing your plan to the power that's bigger than yourself and allowing your dream to unfold as its own masterpiece. Dream big—dream very big. Work hard—work very hard. And after you've done all you can, you stand, wait, and fully surrender.

. . . allowing your dream to unfold as its own masterpiece. No, it's not about us, at all. Thank God!

Slokas 10–16

3.10   Long ago Prajapati, the Lord of Creation, created all creatures along with sacrifice and said, "By means of it you will grow and multiply. Let sacrifice be your wish-fulfilling cow!

3.11   Make the gods flourish by means of it, and let the gods make you flourish as well! Make yourselves flourish for each other's sake. You will reach the highest good.

3.12   For the gods will give you the things that you desire because your sacrifices have made them flourish. Whoever enjoys their gifts without giving in return is little more than a thief."

3.13   Good men who eat the remnants of sacrifice are released from all guilt. But those who cook only for themselves are evil men who eat what is evil.

3.14   All creatures grow because of food. Food grows because of Parjanya, the God of Rain. Parjanya grows because of sacrifice. And sacrifice grows because of action.

3.15   Know that action arises from Brahman [the cosmic realm] and that Brahman arises from the imperishable [syllable OM]. Therefore the Brahman that pervades the universe is established permanently in sacrifice.

3.16 So the wheel is set in motion and whoever does not follow along with it, Arjuna, is sinful and addicted to sensual pleasures. He lives a pointless life.

The *wheel* in Sloka 3.16 is often referred to as the "revolving wheel" of sacrifice: sacrifice—action—God—sacrifice. In *God Talks with Arjuna: The Bhagavad Gita, Royal Science of God-Realization*, Paramahansa Yogonanda writes:

> He who does not heed the liberating laws laid down by his Creator misses the sole point of earthly existence. He who identifies himself with the senses is rooted in the soil of materialism. As a person who mounts a Ferris wheel can climb high and see a beautiful panorama, or climb down again, so a person who, instead of remaining stationary on the ground of materialism, climbs on the wheel of uplifting action can reach the high points in evolution; he is free to go to any world, whether the lower plane of earth or the rarefied regions of the devas.

Because actions of sacrifice are done with no desire for a return on our investment, we are completely fulfilled in the *very moment they are offered*. This is what is meant by truly living in the present moment.

Slokas 17–18

3.17 But the man who takes pleasure only in the self, and is satisfied only with the self and finds his contentment in the self alone, for him there is nothing to do!

3.18 For him there is no meaning whatsoever in what he has done nor in what he hasn't done. Nor does he depend on other creatures at all to give him meaning to his life.

If we are following the impulse of our heart, we will naturally look for ways to manifest our personal expression of dharma, our svadharma. The impulse will lead us in certain directions. I have noticed that when I have the courage to follow the inner impulse that the universe rallies to accommodate. Doors open. The phone rings. Opportunities arise. And, *why not?* Remember, when following our bliss we naturally serve the greater good for all. How beautiful is that?

But, living our svadharma is not just about how our inner impulse is manifested through conscious intention. It is also about being open to being an instrument of good in each moment because opportunities arise all the time for us to bring heaven to earth, often in ways we might not expect. This is what is meant by living a life of sacrifice. This is *yajna*.

One such moment came to me in the mid-eighties when I lived in Bangor, Maine. I was in the grocery store when I noticed a very old woman. She was hunched over so badly that her entire body from the waist up was parallel to the ground. As she hobbled along, I noticed that she could hardly lift her head enough to see where she was going. I felt for her but had a busy day ahead and went on about my way. After I checked out and was walking into the parking lot, I saw her again making her way up the street. She was holding two grocery bags and making her way along with a walking cane.

There was no question what I had to do. I approached her and offered her a ride home. I remember feeling surprised that she did not hesitate and, in fact, seemed quite glad to accept. I helped her into my car and drove her the few blocks to her apartment that was in an assisted-living complex. As I helped her out of the car, I noticed that her hair was falling forward over her eyes, so I carefully took one of the bobby pins holding her hair and used it to pin back her loose ends as best I could. As I finished, I looked up to see a policeman standing by his car just staring at us. He had seen me help her into my car and had followed us. What a smile he had on his face.

It was a small incident—not more than fifteen minutes out of my day and, yet, I can still remember the touch of her hair and her trusting smile. Most of all, I remember how it did not matter who she was, what kind of person she had been, what she believed or how rich or poor she might have been. I didn't even know her name and, yet, here she is still with me today.

So often our giving, while helpful, is safe, structured or conditional. We need to first see if someone "deserves" it according to our standards. Perhaps we'd like to know the other's national, political or religious persuasion. If all of the conditions are right, then we feel that giving or helping is justified. However, as I so clearly experienced that day, when we *give just to give* it changes us because we touch what we yearn to feel for one another.

For him there is no meaning whatsoever in what he has done nor in what he hasn't done (Sloka 3.18). Why? Because it's not about us at all. It's just God longing for God.

Slokas 19-21

3.19 Therefore, continue to do any action that you are obliged to do, but always without attachment. By continuing to act without attachment a man attains the highest good.

3.20 Janaka and the other ancient kings attained complete success by means of action alone. You too should act, while looking after only the care of the world.

3.21 Whatever the best among us does, the rest will also do. The world follows the standard which the best makes for himself.

When we align ourselves with our inner impulse and deepest truth, control the senses and release attachments, our actions become expressions of the Divine within—not the personality we more often think of as us. When it is the least personal, we have the greatest impact. This impact is felt by those around us because of the deep state of joy expressed when we are not in our own way. Others want to be in that joy as well.

And in the joy of God just longing for God, we discover that we are *both* the helper and helpee. I believe we are drawn to serve those who have the most to teach us. And, our "teacher" can feel the true motivation of our heart. This is why a saying I keep very close is from Australian Aboriginal Lila Watson, "If you've come to help me, you're wasting your time. But if you've come because your liberation is bound to mine, then let's begin our work."

In the previous story, we could say the elderly lady in Maine was the *helpee*. Ram Dass and Paul Gorman in their book, *How Can I Help?*, tell the story of another elderly person we might call the *helper* who so beautifully illustrates the *continue to do any action that you are obliged to do, but always without attachment* in Sloka 3.19.

> I'm ninety-two years old, all right. I get up every morning at seven AM. Each day I remind myself, "Wake up. Get up." I talk to my legs. "Legs, get moving. Legs, you're an antelope." It's a matter of mind over matter. You have to have the right spirit. And, I'm out on the

streets, seven-thirty AM sharp.

My job is I help get parked cars off the street so they can bring in the sanitation trucks . . . so when they show up, I go around blowing my whistle to get people to move their cars. I have a great time.

What can I tell you? I'm not a saint or a wise man. I'm not the Two-Thousand-Year-Old Man, I'm only the ninety-two-year-old man. Just a senior citizen. But what do I know that everybody doesn't know? We know. I just go out there in the morning and blow my whistle. That's what I do. You do what you do. Me, I have a great time. Wonderful fun. And when people see how much fun I'm having, they have to laugh. What else can they do? Then I hit them with it: "Move your car!"

I just go out there in the morning and blow my whistle. That's what I do. You do what you do. Me, I have a great time. Far from the doldrums of martyrdom, an action of true sacrifice lights the Soul and both helper and helpee dance.

Sloka 22–26

3.22 Arjuna, there is nothing whatsoever that I need to do in any of the three worlds [heaven, air, earth]. There is nothing to gain that I have not already gained, and yet I am still engaged in action.

3.23 For if I myself did not relentlessly engage in action at every moment, Arjuna, people everywhere would follow after my footsteps.

3.24 All these worlds would collapse if I myself did not perform my work [karma]. I would become an agent of caste confusion. I would kill these people.

3.25 Just as ignorant people act who are attached to their actions, so should the man of knowledge act, though without attachment, since he looks after the care of the world.

3.26 The man of knowledge should not cause conflict of understanding among the ignorant who are attached to action. Rather, behaving like one disciplined in yoga, he should let them take pleasure in all their actions.

What a sweet joy it is when we offer our actions for a greater purpose.

How infinitely more wondrous is the *it's not about us at all* part than the *it's all about us*. The first is a joy completely fulfilled in the moment. The second is a joy predicated upon what happens next. This is the essence of Sloka 3.25, or as Denis Waitley said, "Happy people plan actions. They don't plan results."

Sloka 3.26 warns of the temptation to tell the whole world about something we've found that is so sweet. Better, though, to just go about our business. If someone wants to know what the glow on our face is all about or what it is that enables us to navigate the storms of life without drowning, then it's appropriate to share. An old Shaman once said, "I never give advice until I am asked three times." Well, I can't say I always wait for three times but I do try to wait for at least one!

Slokas 27–29

3.27 Actions are performed at all times as a result of the three qualities of nature. The man whose self is deluded because of his egocentrism thinks "I am the actor."

3.28 But when he truly understands the difference between action and the qualities of nature, then, Arjuna, he thinks, "these qualities arise from other qualities." He is not attached to them.

3.29 People who are confused about the qualities of nature are attached to them and to the actions that follow from them. One who knows the entire story should not upset the slow-witted who know only a part.

Recall from the last chapter that the *qualities of nature*, referred to in these Slokas, are the *gunas*, the energetic qualities of nature, *prakriti*. They are the *rajasic guna* expressed as restlessness, the *tamasic guna* expressed as inertia and the *sattva guna* expressed as equanimity or balance. We will be exploring them in great detail in later chapters. For now, just the realization that "we," as Atman, are not born, act or die—only our body-mind is born, acts and dies—*through the expression of the gunas*—is important.

As Atman, we are unique expressions of Brahman. We journey through many lifetimes and abide in many body-minds. Through each lifetime, the Atman becomes imprinted with the memories and sense experience of that life. I think of the body-mind as a tool for manifesting so the Soul may experience itSelf. Without a body-mind, the Soul could not manifest. So, it is the body-mind, through the forces of nature, or prakriti, that does all the acting or creating. We, the Soul, or Atman, just abide within and observe all.

It's like distinguishing between a radio and the signal. The radio receives and transmits the signal but the radio is not the signal. The body-mind receives and transmits the Soul but the body-mind is not the Soul. To imagine that "we" are residing in a body-mind observing ourselves in the process of living creates an important distance from where we may observe, study and learn from our experience. We will talk much more about the distinction between the body-mind and the Soul, or Atman, in the next chapter.

Sloka 30

3.30   Surrender all your actions to me and fix your mind on your inmost self. Become free from desire and possessiveness. Cast off this fever and fight!

. . . *fix your mind on your inmost self*. Here, we are reminded that this great story is an allegory of the spiritual journey. When we surrender to the Divine impulse *within*, we are able to offer all our actions as sacrifice to those *without* and right then, in that present moment, we get a taste of freedom. And, we want more.

Now, nothing else can compare.

Sloka 31-34

3.31   Men who always follow this teaching of mine, confident in it and not disputing, are freed from their actions.

3.32   But those who dispute my teaching and do not follow it – know that they misunderstand all knowledge, they are senseless, they are lost!

3.33   Even a wise man behaves according to his own nature. All creatures follow their nature. One cannot stop that!

3.34   Passion and hatred await every single object of the senses. One should not come under the control of these two, for they are bandits lying in wait.

Passion means desire or running *to*. *Hatred* means aversion or running *from*. Both keep us out of the glorious freedom only found by being *in* the present moment.

Slokas 35

3.35 One's own duty [dharma] done poorly is better than another's duty
done well. It is better to die engaged in one's own duty. Taking on
another's duty is perilous.

Krishna assures Arjuna that it is better to do his own dharma imperfectly
than to do another's perfectly—better to die in his own dharma than to
die in another's. Anytime that we are not doing what is the calling of our
inner voice, we, too, die a little.

Most of us have at one time or another asked ourselves, "What am I
here for? What am I supposed to be doing?"

Sometimes, we have an idea of what it is that makes us feel most alive
but the details and necessities of everyday life somehow get ordered first on
our "to do" lists. We glance out the window as we sit in the board meeting
or out the car window on our way from the soccer field to the grocery store
and think, "One day, I'll find the time to do it." We may not even know
what "it" is. All we may have is a sort of yearning to feel or do something
that seems to elude us in the hectic pace of our day. That yearning is coming from the part of us that knows the gift we carry—our svadharma.

Gurumayi Chidvilasananda said, "Recognize that you have the courage
within you to fulfill the purpose of your birth. Summon forth the power
of your inner courage and live the life of your dreams." So, the question
becomes how to find out what our gift or duty is. Joseph Campbell told
his students to, "Follow your bliss." Rumi said, "Let yourself be silently
drawn by the stronger pull of what you truly love."

A good indication is to think of what it is we might be doing that would
cause us to totally lose track of time. Sometimes, it is a specific activity
such as painting, starting a business, writing or gardening. Sometimes, it
is more a trait or a quality that manifests throughout a host of activities.
For example, those of us just wanting to help or serve might find ourselves
as doctors, healers or clergy.

And, sometimes, we just offer an elderly lady a ride.

Slokas 36-43

Arjuna spoke:

3.36 Then what makes a man commit evil against his own will, Krishna, as if
driven to it by force?

The Blessed One spoke:

3.37   It is desire, it is anger, and it arises from the force of passion. It is an all-consuming mouth and a great evil. Know that this is the enemy!

3.38   As the fire is obscured by smoke and the mirror by stains, as the embryo is enveloped by the membrane, so this world is obscured by that desire.

3.39   And knowledge is obscured by it as well, that perpetual enemy of the wise man. Arjuna, it takes the form of desire and it is an insatiable fire.

3.40   The senses, the mind, insight – these are its foundation. By means of them desire confuses the embodied self and obscures knowledge.

3.41   Therefore, Arjuna, you must control the senses first, and then strike down that evil thing that destroys knowledge and discrimination.

3.42   They say that the senses are superior, but the mind is superior to the senses. And insight is superior to the mind. But still there is one who is superior to insight.

3.43   Thus gain insight into what is beyond insight, and find the stability of the self by means of the self. O Arjuna, strike the enemy. He takes the form of desire and he is formidable.

At the heart of all self-serving action is personal desire—desire to be perceived a certain way—desire to change someone or something—desire to control or coerce. Look a little closer and we find a need of some kind fueling the desire. Perhaps we need to look a certain way to hide insecurity. Perhaps we need to have someone love us to feel complete. Notice that all need arises from the Kaurava part of us—or more specifically from the rajasic guna. From this place, if we get what we want, we feel "good." If we don't, we feel angry or "bad." Desire and anger are like partners—one naturally comes with the other—enslaving us to particular outcomes in order to be happy.

How reassuring it is to know that it is possible to overcome personal desire and the anger it creates as we, the Soul, are the ruling force of the body-mind.

We are the signal. We are Atman.

In the following chapter, we'll explore how we begin to see ourselves and others differently when we remember that we are the signal, the Observer, Atman within.

Key Points

1. Need nothing and receive all. When we need something, we create karma. When we offer an action as sacrifice, we create dharma.
2. We cannot *not* act. All action speaks. We receive the results of our actions or inactions through the law of karma.
3. We are here to dance with God through will and surrender. We are enough and we are nothing.
4. The revolving wheel of sacrifice is *sacrifice—action—God—sacrifice*.
5. Our personal expression of dharma is called our svadharma.
6. A life of yajna recognizes that any moment can be used to bring heaven to earth.
7. When our actions are the least personal we have the greatest impact, bringing joy to all.
8. A best among us sets the example for others to follow.
9. Do not seek to change others. Instead, let's let our actions speak for themselves.
10. All action is done through prakriti by the forces of nature called the gunas. We, as Atman, observe all.
11. Passion and hatred keep us out of the present moment.
12. It is better to do our own dharma imperfectly than another's perfectly.
13. Key enemies on earth are personal desire and anger. Use the higher self, Atman, to control the lower self and destroy personal desire.

Terms

Jnana Yoga (*Jnah*-nah) the Path of Wisdom
Karma Yoga (*Kar*-mah) the Path of Action
Karma (*Kar*-mah) action and reaction
Yajna (*Yah*-jnah) sacrifice
Rajasic (Rah-*jah*-sik) restless, overactive guna
Tamasic (Tah-*mah*-sik) inert, underactive guna
Sattvic (*Saht*-vik) balanced guna

Personal Reflection

1. What does the word "sacrifice" mean to you?
2. Give an example of a karmic action and a dharmic action.

3. What does "we are the signal and the body-mind is the radio" say to you?
4. "It is better to do your own dharma imperfectly than another's perfectly." Why do you suppose "perfection" is *not* the guidepost?
5. Describe how desire and anger are related. Can you give an example?

What We Must Do To Realize We Are Atman:
Identify with the Observer Within

Open my eyes that I may see your love.
Open my ears that I may hear your love.
Open my heart that I may feel your love.
Open my life that I may be your love.

—MARK KELSO

CHAPTER 4

Seeing with New Eyes

In the last chapter, we saw that we are the signal. The body-mind is the radio. In the recent movie *What the Bleep!* this signal is called the *Observer*. When we are able to shift our identification to the Observer or Atman within, we realize that we are not the doer of anything—that it is our body-mind acting and creating. As unique expressions of Brahman, Atman within, we are the Infinite signal that brings the music, not the finite radio, here today and gone tomorrow.

With this shift in perception, we see with new eyes the signal vibrating throughout all creation, bringing forth all variations of harmonies, colors, textures, smells and tastes.

And though change is the nature of consciousness in prakriti, we now recognize the unchanging Source that sustains all. Not falling prey to *maya*, the illusion that the body-mind and the world of nature, prakriti, are what is real or eternal, we actually become free to enjoy the changes with less attachment and sentimentality.

We start to see that, just like the wildflowers of the field, though it appears we are separate, we are of the same Source. And, as we start to see that "I and my neighbor are truly One," we start to recognize what's the same in all of us.

We start to see God. Everywhere.

Slokas 1-3

The Blessed One spoke:

4.1   I taught this eternal yoga-tradition to Vivasvat [god of the sun]. Vivasvat taught it to Manu [the father of mankind]. And Manu taught it to Ikshvaku [first king].

4.2   The royal seers knew this tradition which was handed down from one to the other, but after a great length of time, Arjuna, it became lost.

4.3   This ancient yoga-tradition is what I teach to you today. You are my devotee and my friend. Indeed, this is the deepest of mysteries.

All spiritual traditions have a lineage through which the essence of the Divine is transmitted. To step into a divinely inspired lineage helps us to move *away* from the notion of us as the doers and *toward* becoming good transmitters of the One. Here, Krishna relays the lineage to Arjuna: beginning with *Vivasvat*, the sun God, to *Manu*, the father of humanity, to the great sage known as the first king, *Ikshvaku*.

Sloka 4

Arjuna spoke:

4.4   Your birth was not very long ago, whereas Vivasvat's was very long ago. How should I understand it when you say that you taught this teaching in the beginning?

How the mind likes to have all the facts in order! Like us, Arjuna forgets that, as Atman, he already has all the information he needs available to him, so he questions his access to the eternal knowing.

Slokas 5-8

The Blessed One spoke:

4.5   I have passed through many births, Arjuna, and so have you. But I recall them all, Arjuna, whereas you do not.

4.6   I am unborn and my soul [atman] is eternal, and I am the lord of all beings. Nevertheless, I take part in nature [prakriti] and I manifest myself by means of my own power [maya].

4.7 For whenever religious duty [dharma] wanes, Arjuna, and its opposite, chaos, waxes strong, I release myself into the world.

4.8 In age after age, I manifest myself in order to protect the virtuous, to destroy those who do harm, and to re-establish religious duty [dharma].

Krishna, or the Divine within, will not let us languish in our folly for long. Our suffering, eventually, causes us to heed the proverbial tapping on our shoulder—that impulse toward wholeness. We seek relief and help from our suffering because we yearn to have our challenges make sense and for the hard-won awareness to become a kind of compost from which a more rich and beautiful life may emerge.

We want to establish inner virtue and lead a righteous life because only then can we find the strength to rise each morning and continue to do our duty, offering our gifts to the greater good. So, again and again we appear in bodily form until we get it right.

Slokas 9–11

4.9 The one who truly knows that my birth and my action are divine, when he abandons the body at death, he does not return for another birth, Arjuna. He returns to me!

4.10 Many people have been purified by the fire of knowledge. They no longer experience passion or fear or anger. They belong to me and take their refuge in me. In the end they have all come to me.

4.11 Those who come to me, no matter how they do so – I grant them my grace. Arjuna, all men everywhere follow my path.

Sloka 4.11 assures us that what we *do* is not as important as *being* right in our own heart, as there are as many paths to God as there are souls. A saying that we use in our worship service programs at the Tree of Life Interfaith Fellowship is "Many are the ways we pray to one God." Or, as Sufi Murshid Samuel L. Lewis once said, "Unity, not uniformity."

Slokas 12–13

4.12 They hope for success in their actions, so they sacrifice here to the

gods, because here in the world of mankind success comes quickly
from acts of sacrifice.

4.13   I created the four classes of the world distinguishing them according
to their qualities and their actions. And though I am the creator of this
world, know that I am really the eternal non-creator.

. . . I am the creator, transient prakriti and *I am the eternal non-creator,
Brahman.* I am the impulse that brings forth the signal *and* the steady
hand that builds the radio. As Bawa said, "As flower and fragrance are
joined together, so our love and God's love should join." We are here to
experience the love that is us—body and Soul.

Slokas 14–18

4.14   Actions do not defile me, nor will you find in me any desire for the
fruits of action. One who understands this about me is not imprisoned
by his own actions.

4.15   Knowing this, the ancient sages performed the actions that they were
obliged to do, even as they eagerly strove toward liberation. And
therefore you too should perform the actions that you are obliged to
do, just as the ancient sages before you did!

4.16   What is action? What is not action? Even the sages were confused
about this. I will explain to you what action is since knowing this will
free you from your misery.

4.17   For you should understand what action is and distinguish it from wrong
action. And from these you must distinguish non-action. Surely the
path of action is hard to understand!

4.18   He who is able to see the non-action within action, and the action
within non-action, is truly full of wisdom among men. He performs all
of the actions that he is obliged to do, but is disciplined in yoga.

To create heaven on earth, we must see with new eyes. To see with new
eyes, we must differentiate between the transient and the eternal, between
the radio and the signal, between the one acting and the one observing. To
function as the Observer requires we be *totally present and totally detached* at
the same time. Only from this place do we see clearly and become able to
hold all that is happening without succumbing to the emotional reactions

that pull us out of the present moment and into the playpen. And, only from this place is it possible to see God in all—saint and sinner alike.

In *Dead Man Walking*, a Catholic sister, Helen Prejean, goes to pray with inmates on death row in Louisiana—inmates that have imposed great suffering on others. This is challenging, but I truly understand how this can happen. Years ago, when I was a counselor at our local community mental-health center, a four-year-old boy taught me all I needed to know about the difference between the mind and the soul, about seeing with new eyes, about being totally present—and about true healing.

I'll call him Jacob. I was a fairly new counselor and had not worked with many children. Each week when Jacob's foster care mother would drop him off he would stomp in, calling me names—most commonly, "Pig!" I tried all I could to connect with him. Nothing worked. I remember thinking that I was probably not cut out to work with children.

Then, as I discussed the situation with my supervisor, she asked me, "What are you doing with Jacob that you wouldn't think of doing with your adult clients?"

It was not a fun moment, but it opened me to allow for what was to become one of the most awareness-filled experiences of my lifetime. As we talked further, I came to understand what had been—and had not been—happening and why. The next week I was ready.

Jacob came in with his usual yelling, but this time I simply kneeled down so we could be eye to eye and said, "You're really mad, aren't you?"

He stopped in his tracks and looked at me suspiciously. This was new. I just patiently and thoughtfully repeated, "You're really mad."

And right before my eyes, he melted. He started to cry and said, "Is my mother coming back for me?"

"I don't know, Jacob," I said as I rocked him in the center of the floor.

"Am I bad?" he asked through tears.

"No Jacob. You're not bad." I answered. Knowing he liked to draw, I suggested he draw a picture. Over time, we created a game where each week he would name the feelings, draw, act with puppets and create little skits to help express what was happening for him.

Now, when Jacob asked me, "Am I bad?" could you imagine that I would say, "Well, if that's what you think and how you feel, I'm very sorry Jacob, but it must be true."

Sounds pretty ridiculous, right? Yet, so much of the time, most of us, because of our life experience, truly believe and feel that we are bad, not good enough, inadequate, and so on. And, because we believe and feel this way, we often manifest life circumstances to validate our beliefs. Psychologists call this the self-fulfilling prophesy.

Like Jacob, it is absolutely true that this is how we believe and feel and, just like with Jacob, *it is not true at all.*

Get this and it will make you free!

Our thoughts and feelings are a result of our conditioning. Change your thoughts and you change your life. This is why all spiritual practice is about cleansing the mind, as we'll explore in Chapter 6. But notice that the doorway into transforming the mind is self-acceptance. I had not been creating an atmosphere where this little boy felt *heard*. No wonder he was so mad at me!

It's easy for us to see beyond the false beliefs of a hurting four year old. It's more difficult with an inmate on death row. Of course, a small child is not bad but an inmate—well, that's another story. But, is it?

And, it's even more difficult with ourselves. Yet, like Jacob, when we dive deep into our emotional caves, we emerge stronger, freer and lighter. We begin to truly love our self for all of us. We start to unwrap gifts from all areas of our life experience. With less and less to hide, defend or project, we find our self more at peace in all sorts of situations. For, what is peace if not self-acceptance?

Swami Kripalu said, "Self-observation, without criticism, is the highest form of spiritual practice." This is our transient, finite human journey completely embraced and held by our eternal, infinite Self—Atman. Welcome Home.

To be able to differentiate between our body-mind human journey and the Observer, or Atman, is what is meant by being able *to see the non-action within action and the action within non-action*—Sloka 4.18. Who is acting? Again, the body-mind is acting through the forces of nature according to our thoughts and feelings. Regardless of our age, when our thoughts and feelings are controlling us and we are *re*acting to situations, disharmony results.

As we use discernment, or buddhi, to observe and harness the mind in spiritual practice, we begin to act more definitively, identifying more often with the inherent goodness within all people—so easily seen in a hurting child or not so easily seen in an inmate. In either case, however, it is still the transient, finite, body-mind through the forces of nature that believes, feels and acts. *We*, the eternal, infinite signal, Atman, observe.

I often tell my students, "Thank your mind for sharing and invite it to go sit on the couch. Invite the experience of the moment to inform and unfold you." We do have quite a nice couch for minds! This is one way to set the intention to shift perception in order to see—first our self and then others—with new eyes.

Slokas 19–24

4.19 A man whose endeavors are all free from the manipulations of desire sacrifices his actions in the fire of knowledge. The wise call him a learned man.

4.20 Giving up his attachment to the fruits of his actions, always content, dependent on nothing, even when he engages in action he isn't really acting at all.

4.21 When he is without hope, when he has restrained himself and his thoughts, when he has abandoned all of his possessions, when it is only his body that acts – then he does not accumulate guilt.

4.22 Content with whatever chance brings to him, he has passed beyond duality. He knows no envy. He is even-tempered whether in success or in failure. Even when he does act, he is not imprisoned by his actions!

4.23 When a man is unattached and free of all of this, when his thoughts are rooted firmly in knowledge, when he performs his actions in the spirit of sacrifice, his actions are completely dissolved!

4.24 The offering is this infinite Brahman. The oblation is this infinite Brahman. It is Brahman that pours the oblation into the fire of Brahman. One attains to Brahman by concentrating completely on the action of Brahman!

When we release attachment to our actions, need nothing and remain in equanimity, we are free and our actions are pure. We are not bound by our actions because we have no agenda to promote or point to prove. Our actions are simply offered to God as we joyously watch the dance of manifestations. We don't act *for* a particular outcome. We act *from* a particular intention. No rehearsing necessary. In this way, each moment is done for us.

We live more peacefully and we sleep more soundly.

Slokas 25–32

4.25   Some yogins engage only in sacrifices to the gods. Others offer up sacrifices by sacrificing into the fire of the infinite Brahman.

4.26   Other yogins offer the senses into the fire of self-restraint, restraining their hearing and other senses. Yet others offer sound [recitation] and other sense objects into the fire of the senses.

4.27   And others offer all of the actions of the senses, the actions of the breath and the other actions, into the fire of the yoga of self-control that is ignited by knowledge.

4.28   Some sacrifice material objects, others practice austerities, or yoga. Some sacrifice through their knowledge and their study of the Vedas – they are all devout men committed to keeping their sacred vows.

4.29   Others engage in the practice of breath-control [pranayama] by checking the course of the inhaled breath and the exhaled breath. Thus they offer the inhaled breath into the exhaled, and the exhaled breath into the inhaled.

4.30   Others refrain from eating, thus offering their breaths into the cosmic breaths [of Brahman]. All of these know the meaning of sacrifice. Sacrifice destroys impurities.

4.31   There are men who eat the remnants of the sacrifice, the nectar of immortality. They go to the eternal Brahman. Arjuna, what is this world, and the next world, to a man who does not sacrifice?

4.32   Thus the many forms of sacrifice are spread out before Brahman. Know that they are all born from action. Knowing this you will be free!

As we each express our svadharma, we begin to offer actions of sacrifice most natural to our nature according to our karma developed over many lifetimes. In Sloka 4.29, we see how those interested in the practice of breath-control, *prana-yama, offer the inhaled breath into the exhaled, and the exhaled breath into the inhaled.* Yogi Bhajan used to say, "The breath is the kiss of God." And, always with us, at any moment, we can pause and notice that *we are breathed* and sustained here by this kiss of God.

It is important to remember than no one's svadharma, or personal sacrifice, is more important or special than another's. True, some play a more visible role than others. Yet, *each is needed to complete the Divine plan* or as the Sufis say, "We don't get there until we all get there!" As we are One, how could it be otherwise?

Slokas 33–34

4.33 But, Arjuna, sacrifice in the pursuit of knowledge is higher than the sacrifice of material things. All action without exception culminates in knowledge.

4.34 Learn this, Arjuna, by submitting humbly to one's teachers, by asking them thoughtful questions, by serving them. They are men of knowledge and they have seen the truth. They will pass on their knowledge to you.

In Sloka 4.34 we are told to seek knowledge from those who have realized the truth. As I have studied the lives of our great spiritual teachers and saints, I am struck by how often they are quite ordinary—just like us. In the video *Mother Teresa*, Mother Teresa receives her "call within a call," as she put it, to serve the poorest of the poor. Some of her superiors did not feel her capable. One even proclaimed he had known her when she was a novice and "she could not even light the candles and you want to make her the head of a congregation? She's not able to do that!" Moses, who had speech difficulties, was ordered by God to go and represent his people before the pharaoh. Surely he must have felt that God had mixed up the assignments and given him the wrong one! And Mohammad was chosen to receive the Koran when he could barely write his name.

We are not given opportunities that have not been earned. So, when the call comes, and it often can in ways most unexpected, it is our duty, as Arjunas, Mother Teresas, Moseses and Mohammads, to be holy where we are—trust that we are enough—release attachment to the outcome—and surrender into the freedom that is true sacrifice.

Of course! Remember, in the end, it is not about us anyway. We're just here to perform a particular function or role.

Infinitely simple. Completely joyous.

Slokas 35–36

4.35 When you have learned this, Arjuna, you will never encounter delusion again. By means of this knowledge you will come to see that all beings are in yourself, and thus in me.

4.36 Even if you were the most sinful among all sinners, with the help of this ship of knowledge you will cross over all of this sorrow.

Sloka 4.36 is about grace. Sometimes we may think that there's just too much to overcome, work through, heal or forgive. Maybe we feel so much shame we can't imagine being worthy to rest on the Potter's wheel, much less to receive the touch of grace. We can't imagine that we are truly lovable. Maybe we feel like little Jacob in a grown-up body.

Yet, the great gift of this Song of God is that we can't lose the battle with our inner demons because, although we may believe we are lost, in Truth we are found—and, though we may believe we are blind, we see. Yet, "Amazing Grace! How Sweet the Sound" reminds us *how precious did that grace appear, the hour I first believed*. Our job is to keep our minds single-pointed on the sweet impulse within *and grace will lead us Home*.

Sloka 37–42

4.37   Just as fire when it is kindled reduces the firewood to ashes, so too, Arjuna, the fire of knowledge reduces all actions to ashes, in the very same way!

4.38   You will not find anywhere in this world a means of purification that is the equal of knowledge. A man who has been perfected by yoga, in time will find it in himself [in his atman].

4.39   A man of faith, intent only upon this knowledge, his senses well restrained, will obtain it, and once he has obtained it, he soon reaches supreme peace.

4.40   But a man who does not have this knowledge, and this faith, will perish, his soul filled with doubts. And filled with doubts as he is, there will be no joy for him either in this world or the next.

4.41   Arjuna, actions do not bind the man who renounces his actions through yoga, who severs doubt through knowledge, who is in full possession of himself [his atman].

4.42   Therefore, with this sword of knowledge, sever this doubt that rests in your heart, Arjuna, this doubt of yours that arises from ignorance. Stand up, then, and stand upon yoga!

When we use the keen blade of knowledge to sever any doubts about who we are, we see with new eyes and hear with new ears. We realize that we are just God being with God. And, as we look at our own lives and see the havoc created when the mind is not disciplined, we can better empathize when we see the same phenomenon happening in others. We're less quick to judge, yet more clear of mind, and can respond more appropriately.

Saint Augustine of Hippo said, "The whole point of this life is the healing of the heart's eye through which God is seen." Sooner or later we realize there is no enemy without—only all those false beliefs we carry within. And, just like with little Jacob, *they're not true at all.* Realizing this we come to a humble place with our head bowed and heart open.

What we have long been searching for *out there* was *right here* all along.

This awareness leads quite naturally to complete fullness, or renunciation, as we will see in chapter 5.

Key Points

1. By shifting our perception, we see with "new eyes." We are not fooled by maya. We can discern the transient, finite manifestations of nature, prakriti, from the infinite, eternal source, Brahman, that brings forth all.
2. Stepping into a spiritual lineage helps us to remember that we are not the doer—just the transmitter.
3. There are many paths to God.
4. We are the impulse that brings forth the signal *and* the steady hand that builds the radio.
5. With new eyes, we are *totally present and totally detached* at the same time. Finally, we recognize what's the same in all of us—saint or sinner alike.
6. It is true that we may think, feel and sense something due to past conditioning, *and* it's not true at all.
7. Being able to differentiate between our body-mind human journey and the Observer or Atman is what is meant by being able *to see the non-action within action and the action within non-action.*
8. We each offer our actions, svadharma, as sacrifice according to our karma. Each person's gift is equally needed to complete the Divine plan.
9. The keen blade of knowledge opens a space for a kind of grace to emerge. Seeing all in ourselves and all in others, we are less quick to judge and can respond in more appropriate and helpful ways.

Terms

Maya (*My*-yah) illusion

Vivasvat (Vee-*vas*-vaht) sun God

Manu (*Mah*-noo) father of humanity

Ikshvaku (*Eek*-sh-*vah*-koo) great sage

Prana (*Prah*-nah) vital energy or breath

Pranayama (*Pran*-nah-*yah*-mah) controlling or restraining vital energy or the breath

Personal Reflection

1. What part of you do you need to see with "new eyes"? Is there someone in your life you'd like to see with "new eyes"?

2. Has there been a time that you felt *totally present and totally detached at the same time?*

3. What belief or feeling do you hold from past conditioning that's *not true at all?*

4. Why do you suppose it requires the *keen blade* of knowledge to open a space for grace to occur?

What We Must Do To Realize We Are Atman:
Renounce All That Is Fleeting to Realize the Eternal

Renounce and enjoy!

−MAHATMA GANDHI

CHAPTER 5

Renounce and Be Free

When we realize that we carry a gift for the world only we can bring—that we have been given a body-mind through which to bring forth that gift—and by doing so we not only fulfill our destiny but serve the greater good for all—right there, in that moment, we realize that nothing else really matters. Heads bowed and hearts open, all we long for is to walk with our God. Nothing else will do now save the Potter Himself.

Renunciation used to mean give all away, leave society and begin a solitary journey. I believe it is a much greater challenge to stay here, serve others and live in community. I have always felt that if I can't walk with my God in the supermarket, I've missed the point.

Simply, to renounce is to remember the *it's not about me at all* part of the will and surrender dance with God.

Slokas 1-6

Arjuna spoke:

5.1 You praise the renunciation of actions, Krishna, and then again you praise yoga as a means of action. Please tell me with all certainty which one of these is the better one?

The Blessed One spoke:

5.2   Renunciation of action and the yoga of action both lead to the highest
       good, but of the two the yoga of action is better than the renunciation
       of action.

5.3   One who does not hate and who does not desire is understood to be
       a permanent renouncer. Because he is beyond dualisms, Arjuna, he is
       easily freed from his bondage.

5.4   It is the immature who declare that Sankhya philosophy and yoga
       are separate things. The learned don't say this. A man who is focused
       completely on either one will find the fruit of both.

5.5   The practitioners of yoga arrive at the same position as the
       practitioners of Sankhya philosophy reach. Whoever can see that
       Sankhya and yoga are a single unified thing sees correctly.

5.6   But, Arjuna, renunciation is difficult to attain without yogic discipline.
       A sage who is disciplined in yoga quickly reaches infinite Brahman.

Renunciation of action is the goal of Sankhya philosophy, and Jnana Yoga,
the path of wisdom, disciplines the mind to obtain such renunciation.
Karma Yoga, the path of action, challenges us to selfless service. Krishna
warns Arjuna, in Sloka 5.6, that the state of true renunciation, *sannyasa*,
which requires our motives for acting be pure, is particularly difficult to
reach without the ongoing purification of the mind through selfless action.
This is because it is very easy to hold an image of ourselves that may or
may not hold up when tested in the true light of daily experience.

The Buddha said, "Thousands of candles can be lit from a single candle
and the life of the candle will not be shortened. Happiness never decreases
by being shared." Yet, it has been my experience that nowhere are my
intentions and motivations more raw and visible than when I'm engaging
in selfless service. Five years ago, I started a foundation called The Gifts
of Grace. We are a charitable organization offering service to our community through volunteerism. I continue to learn the meaning of releasing
attachments to the fruits of my actions as I serve others.

All feels well when those I'm serving seem appropriately thankful
and appreciative. But, occasionally, someone is not—or does not appear
to be. Then, how do I feel? Does resentment creep in? Sometimes. Ah,
and what a great teacher resentment is! Right then and there I get to

learn—again—that the helping is not about *who I am helping at all*. In fact, it really has nothing to do with *them*.

It has to do with *me*. Am I really showing up with just the intent to serve with joy—to love my brother and sister—not because of who they are or aren't, what they have or don't have, what they have done or haven't done—but just because the God in me can do nothing else?

And, in such reflection, I remember where God is in selfless action. God is the longing that settles quietly in my heart, yearning to ease the pain of others. And, as I look into the eyes of suffering, it is God that is not concerned with religious or political persuasions or personal worthiness because it is God that loves my neighbor as myself.

Could this be the role of suffering? To awaken our longing—to be so pulled by the yearning to help that we forget to notice individual differences? Perhaps *truly seeing* suffering carves a place so deep in our heart that a love becomes possible that was not before. I just know that when I feel and respond to a need around me, *unencumbered by my own expectations*, Love sets me free. Again and again. This is, at once, the polishing, the cleansing, and the gift of Karma Yoga.

Slokas 7-13

5.7 Once he becomes disciplined in yoga, his self [atman] becomes purified, his self becomes controlled, and his senses become subdued. His self becomes united with the selves of all creatures. Whatever he does in this state does not stain him.

5.8 "I who am not doing anything" he should think to himself, the man who is disciplined in yoga, and who knows the true nature of things. Meanwhile, he sees, he hears, he touches, he smells, he eats, he goes, he sleeps, he breathes,

5.9 he talks, he gives, he takes, he opens his eyes, he shuts his eyes – but he holds firm to the thought, "it is merely the senses interacting with sense-objects."

5.10 He gives his actions over to infinite Brahman and abandons attachment. When he acts in this way, his guilt does not adhere to him, just as water does not adhere to the lotus-leaf.

5.11 Yogins perform actions with body and mind and insight, and with the senses as well, but since they have abandoned attachment, they perform these actions only for the purification of their selves.

5.12   The disciplined man abandons the fruits of his actions and thereby attains abiding peace. But the undisciplined man is attached to the fruits of his actions and is in bondage to the desire that causes them.

5.13   In his mind he renounces all actions. He sits easily in his body and in control, dwelling within that city of the nine gates, the body, neither acting nor causing others to.

. . . they perform these actions only for the purification of their selves (Sloka 5.11). We serve best when we need the least. It is only through renouncing attachment to the outcome of our actions that we begin to experience ourselves as Atman. It is only in these moments that we not only *believe* we are not the doer but clearly *experience* that we are not the doer. And, it is this *experience*, this Love, that informs us and sets us free.

Slokas 14–18

5.14   The lord does not engender the world's agency or actions or the perpetual union of the world's actions with their fruits. These arise autonomously, out of their own nature.

5.15   The ever-present lord does not take on the effects of anyone's misfortune nor anyone's good fortune. Knowledge is obscured by ignorance. All peoples are deluded by this.

5.16   But whenever this ignorance among men is destroyed by knowledge of the soul, then, like the sun, their knowledge illuminates that supreme realm of Brahman.

5.17   That is their insight, that is their true self. That is their foundation and their ultimate goal. They reach that state of no return where their sins are dispelled by knowledge.

5.18   Learned men look upon an educated and cultured Brahman just as they look upon a cow or an elephant or a dog or even a low-caste dog-eater.

Outward appearances become irrelevant as we perceive the same essence in a dog or a dog-eater (Sloka 5.18). Correctly identifying with what is the *same* in all, we observe but do not become involved with the differences. We experience great joy because no one or any thing has to be a certain way in order for us to be happy. It is from this place, we serve saint and sinner alike.

Slokas 19–24

5.19   This created world is conquered by those who maintain the mind in equanimity. And indeed for them the world of Brahman is a flawless equilibrium, and as a result they dwell in the infinite Brahman.

5.20   He should not take pleasure in getting what he wants, nor should he reject getting what he does not want. His insight is steady. He is not confused. He knows the infinite Brahman and he dwells in it.

5.21   When he is no longer attached to contact with external objects he finds his pleasure within himself. His self is disciplined by brahmayoga [yoga focused on Brahman] and he reaches a pleasure that is imperishable.

5.22   For the delights that arise from external objects are really wombs of misery. They all have a beginning and an end, Arjuna. A wise man takes no pleasure in them.

5.23   The man who is able to overcome the agitation that comes with desire and anger, here in this world, before he leaves the body – he is a disciplined man, he is a happy man.

5.24   Such a man contains his pleasure and his joy within himself. His light is within him and nowhere else. Such a man is a yogin who has become one with Brahman, he has reached the sublime peace of Brahman [brahminirvana].

Differentiating clearly between the transient and the eternal, the changing and the unchanging, we naturally hold our identification more often with the Atman—in our self and others. *It is only in this way that we can be in the midst of our own suffering and still remember our Divinity or withstand the suffering of others and still only see God.* This is what is meant in Sloka 5.24 by *His light is within him and nowhere else.* Such a person is illuminated solely from within and is called a *rishi.* The experience is called *moksha* or liberation.

In the video *Mother Teresa,* Mother Teresa picks up a dying man who smelled so bad no one can go near him. As she lifted him, he asked, "Why do you do this?" She answered, "Because I love you." She was able to see past the decaying vessel to, in her words, "Christ within." Mother Teresa often said, "We look but we don't see." With new eyes, we see. But we don't have to be a rishi, wait for optimal circumstances, or final liberation to glimpse this freedom. Everyday there are glimpses—if we have eyes to see.

Thirty years ago, I had a teacher who demonstrated this great truth. As a child, I loved to dance. When an auto accident at sixteen caused me to stop, I missed it terribly. Then, in my mid-twenties, I discovered a beginning adult ballet class just up the street from where I was working in Honolulu, Hawaii. Finding such a class was rare indeed, as most dance teachers would prefer working with children and teens interested in performing. But, there it was and I was thrilled.

My teacher's name was Jack Clause and he definitely did not look like a ballet teacher. He was rather short and stocky and had very little hair, but, his face—oh, that face with the glowing eyes—held me fast. I always knew something special was about to happen when he walked into the room. No chit-chat was allowed. No coming in late. Nothing less than full attention was accepted.

As we worked at the barre, he would come around to each of us and say, "Up . . . up!" and stand there until we were lifted and shining. But most importantly, he told us to be "beautiful" as we moved across the floor. Now, most beginning adult ballet students look anything but beautiful and graceful pirouetting across the floor!

Still, he would bellow at us, "Be beautiful! There are many technicians but very few dancers! Be a dancer!" After class, it was all I could do to remember it was not appropriate to *grande jette* down the sidewalks of Honolulu on my way to catch the last bus home!

After a little over a year of dancing, I left Hawaii to spend a year in Japan. It was during that time I realized the true gift of his teaching and it felt very important to say *thank you*. I anxiously waited for the day we would return home, as I knew there would be a brief layover in Honolulu. I would tell him then.

Finally, the day came when I found myself on the familiar sidewalk outside the old building. I hobbled up the stairs, as I was about eight months pregnant, and quite large. Breathlessly, I asked the girl at the desk how I might get in touch with Jack. She stared at me with a kind of awkward look and said, "You don't know?"

"Know what?" I asked.

"Jack died a few months ago," she said. "He had a heart ailment. He knew he could die at any time. You didn't know? Most people knew." All I could do was shake my head and make my way back down the stairs, stunned and sad.

In the days that followed, I began to realize the even greater gift I had received. I understood even more deeply why nothing less than *beautiful* was acceptable and why he wanted us to be *dancers*—not just technicians.

I am convinced that each of us carries our share of sorrow. Jack did. Sometimes it is a visible sorrow. Sometimes it is invisible and silent like Jack's. Yet, nonetheless, there it is. Sometimes we may feel that our sorrow is greater than others. We may not feel that others could ever understand what we have been through. This carries an added burden because it brings feelings of isolation.

In the book *Tuesdays with Morrie*, author Mitch Albom writes about his time with another who loved to dance, Morris (Morrie) Schwartz, and Morrie's struggle with Lou Gehrig's disease. Morrie's thoughtful reflection rings true here.

In an interview with Ted Koppel, he says, "Ted, this disease is knocking at my spirit. But it will not get my spirit. It'll get my body. It will *not* get my spirit." Toward the end, when those around him were expressing their frustration at the fact that he was not going to beat the disease—he was not going to win, Morrie says, "*Love wins. Love always wins.*"

Is there anyone who would not want to know how to do this? How is it that we are able to know joy in the midst of our sorrow? *It is only through dis-identifying with that which causes pain and identifying with that which cannot know suffering that this is possible.*

This is what is meant by renunciation. When we can draw our happiness from the deep still waters of inner silence, we are less affected by the changing tides of circumstance. When we experience the calm at our center, we can rest in the eye of the storm, safe and secure. Did Jack need a healthy heart to be happy? Did Morrie need to get well to shine? No. The Soul needs no particular set of circumstances. It only needs our permission.

However, it is also very important to note that Morrie allowed himself a certain amount of time each morning to vent his human anguish. Here again, as in the earlier story of Jacob, it is not about covering up, pushing away, or going around. It's about walking straight through our emotions because, inevitably, *what we resist persists*. Through self-acceptance of our human journey, we receive the gifts for compost, and future creations are enriched. Through continued self-acceptance, we learn to love ourselves, not *in spite of*, but *because of*.

I was not blessed to sit with Morrie. I was blessed to be with Jack and I'm sure he, too, had his difficult times. And, I am also sure that, when he was with us, there were no difficult times. Despite the realities of his physical condition, he shone and he made us shine. I believe that most of us would like to be more like Jack and Morrie. Most of us would say that we would gladly dis-identify with the pain in our lives if we only knew how.

Yet, is this true? It seems like we often become quite attached to the stories of our difficult experiences and may, in fact, have felt a certain way for so long that we have no idea who we might be without the struggle. So, instead of conceiving of the possibility that we could move through the suffering, receive what is there for us and move on, we try to escape. We numb out and set out to find that "something" that will fill the emptiness and make us happy.

This familiar strategy puts our emotional life on a kind of pendulum, swinging us back and forth from sad to happy and happy to sad. This is why *true renunciation means dis-identifying* with *both* the sorrow *and* the joy. Dis-identifying with the joy can be much more challenging as we all so want to feel good. After all, weren't we meant to be happy? Yes, but *without strings attached*. Each time we think that we need something from the outside world to be happy, a string is tied around us. We are less free.

Notice that whether we are renouncing sorrow or joy it is about renouncing the *need* to experience either. When we need nothing, there are no strings. We can move about the world and, yet, we're not *of* the world at all. We are free.

There is a passage in *Essential Sufism* from Attar that describes this search for balance and equanimity:

> A great king summoned his wise men. He ordered them, "Create for me a saying that will stabilize my inner state. When I am unhappy it will bring me joy, and when I am happy it will remind me of sadness. It cannot be too long, as I want to keep it with me always."
>
> The wise men consulted and contemplated deeply the king's command. Finally, they returned to the king bearing a small box. In it there was a ring, and inside the ring was inscribed the following words: "This too shall pass."

Both joy and sadness *pass.* Need one and you get the other. Embrace both, and you find joy, but not the joy predicated upon outside circumstances. This is the joy illuminated solely from within—the joy Gandhi was referring to when asked to describe the secret of his life in three words. He answered with a chuckle, "Renounce and enjoy!"

Slokas 25-29

5.25 Seers who destroy their sins, who cut through all doubt, who are masters of themselves, attain this sublime peace of Brahman, delighting in the welfare of all beings.

5.26 The sublime peace of Brahman is always present for those devoted men who have freed themselves from desire and anger, have tamed their minds, and have come to know themselves.

5.27 The sage shuns external objects and fixes his gaze between the eyebrows. He balances the inhaled breath with the exhaled breath as they pass through the nostrils.

5.28 His senses, his thoughts, and his insights are all restrained. This sage is committed to his liberation. In him desire, and fear, and anger are gone. He is what he always has been. He is free.

5.29 Know that it is I who am the enjoyer of sacrifices and penances. It is I who am the great lord of all worlds and the heart's friend of all beings. Know this and find peace.

He is what he has always been. He is free (Sloka 5.28). Remember little Jacob in the last chapter? Just because we may not feel, think or sense it, the Truth is we are already *free.* And, as we sit in the midst of our pain and suffering, there *joy* sits also. The means to realize this, our innate Divinity, is meditation. The place is the prayer mat.

In the next chapter, we will see just what we can do to make this realization a daily possibility. It's called *Sadhana,* spiritual practice.

Key Points

1. We discipline the mind with meditation, Jnana Yoga, and perform selfless action through Karma Yoga, harmonizing thought and action on the path to liberation.

2. Karma Yoga is necessary as it provides immediate feedback, revealing our true motivations.

3. Renouncing attachments to the fruits of our action creates the *experience* of our self as Atman. This is the Love that sets us free.

4. Suffering can only be endured and, in fact, serve us through increased awareness, when we identify with the part of us that cannot know suffering—the Observer or Atman within.

5. Identifying with Atman, we become illuminated solely from within.

6. True renunciation means dis-identifying with *both* the sorrow and the joy. This allows all to be embraced and held in equanimity.

Terms

Sannyasa (Sun-*yah*-sah) state of renunciation; pure of motive behind action

Rishi (*Ree*-she) sage

Moksha (*Mok*-sha) liberation

Sadhana (*Sah*-dah-nah) spiritual practice

Personal Reflection

1. What response comes when you think of serving without reward, acknowledgement or feedback?

2. Has there been a time when your efforts felt unappreciated and, if so, what did you learn?

3. How do you suppose the renunciation of attachment creates the *experience* of our self as Atman?

4. Reflect upon the notion of being able to stay illuminated solely from within in the midst of pain.

5. How is it that *walking through* the difficult emotions brings equanimity?

6. So, why is it necessary to give up *needing* to be happy?

What We Must Do To Realize We Are Atman:
Discipline and Refine the Mind through Meditation

Submit to daily practice. Your loyalty to
that is a ring on the door. Keep knocking
and the joy inside will eventually open a
window and look out to see who's there.

—FROM ILLUMINATED PRAYER,
THE FIVE-TIMES PRAYER OF THE SUFIS

CHAPTER 6

The Inner Sanctuary

By focusing and disciplining the mind, the practice of meditation slowly allows us to identify with the Observer, Atman within. Two stages of awareness emerge. First, by sitting and watching all the thoughts, feelings and sensations changing from moment to moment, at some point we ask our self, "Who's watching?" The answer to this question begins to open us to the *experience* of Atman. Second is the realization that it is in the full embrace of our human journey that we find equanimity, and experience the peace only self-acceptance can bring. Embracing all, everything becomes our teacher, so nothing, including ourselves, is a problem.

Slokas 1-4
The Blessed One spoke:

6.1 Whoever does not concern himself with the fruits of action and yet performs those actions that he is obliged to do is both a renouncer [sannyasi] and a yogin. Whoever merely neglects his ritual fire and his ritual obligations is not.

6.2 Arjuna, know that what people call renunciation is really yoga, for no one becomes a yogin who has not renounced personal intention.

6.3 For a sage who seeks to advance in yoga, action is said to be the

instrument, whereas for a sage who has advanced in yoga, serenity is
said to be the instrument.

6.4   One is said to be advanced in yoga when one has renounced all
        personal intention and when one is no longer attached to sense objects
        and actions.

Renouncing all personal intention immediately creates non-attachment to
outcome. This is because how we *are* creates the essence of what we *do*. It
is our intention that determines whether or not we create a karmic action
or a dharmic one—whether we create more bondage or become more free.
Medieval German mystic Meister Eckhart said, "People should think less
about what they ought to do and more about what they ought to be. If
only their living were good, their work would shine forth brightly." Let's
be good and do good.

Slokas 5-6

6.5   One should lift oneself [atman] up by means of the self [atman]. Do not
        degrade the self, for the self is one's only friend, and at the same time
        the self is one's only foe.

6.6   The self is one's friend when one has conquered the self by means of
        the self. But when one neglects the self, then, like an enemy at war,
        that very self will turn against him.

Eknath Easwaran writes in *Gandhi the Man*, "The principle of meditation
is that you become what you meditate on." Using buddhi, discernment, we
rise and take ourselves to our prayer mat. Using the manas mind, we sleep
in. It's our choice, and our fate, as the law of karma delivers the results of
our actions. Using buddhi, the mind becomes like a friend as we correctly
identify with the Observer, Atman, within. But, an uncontrolled mind
behaves like an enemy striving toward outward gratification of sense pleasures. Learning to befriend the mind is the whole purpose of meditation.

Slokas 7-10

6.7   A peaceful man who has mastered himself has a higher self that is
        deeply concentrated, whether in cold or in heat, in pleasure or in pain,
        whether in honor or in disgrace.

6.8   Such a man has a self that delights in knowledge and discrimination. He stands on the mountain top. He has conquered his senses. He is called a yogin because he is disciplined. Clay, rock, gold – for such a man, it's all the same.

6.9   He is distinguished among men because he regards them all as the same: a friend, an ally, a foreigner, a bystander, a neutral party, an enemy, a kinsman – whether good men or evil!

6.10   A yogin should always discipline himself. He should dwell in a remote place, alone, restraining his thoughts and himself, without hopes and without ambitions.

In honor or in disgrace, with ally or enemy . . . When the mind is disciplined, we remain peaceful. One of my favorite examples of not needing circumstances to be a certain way in order to be peaceful is a description of Gandhi's days in prison described, again by Eknath Easwaran, in *Gandhi the Man.* He writes, "He embraced the prospect of imprisonment with such joy and good humor that people all over the country began to laugh at their own fear." Continuing, he writes, "Gandhi was so detached from his physical environment that going to jail did not disrupt his work at all, and he drove some of his hardest bargains from behind jail walls."

He could give his full *attention* to the work at hand because his full *intention* was given to God. Notice that it's not the world that becomes different. Clearly, there is deep pain and suffering all around us. No, it is *we* that become different. Seeing clearly, we see the suffering all around, as did Gandhi, Mother Teresa, Dr. Martin Luther King, Jr., and others. *And*, because we don't need the world to be a particular way to be fulfilled, we naturally bring our happiness, illuminated solely from within, with us. This is true freedom – the joy that passes all understanding.

But, recall that simple desire is not enough. This is why Eknath Easwaran writes that the foundation of Gandhi's life was "to start each day before dawn with meditation and prayer, in which he found the strength to withstand the trials of his situation." It takes more than desire to discipline the mind. It takes the kiln. It takes Sadhana.

Slokas 11–15

6.11   He should prepare for himself a firm seat [asana] in a purified place that is neither too high nor too low, a seat that is covered by a sacred cloth, a deerskin, and kusha grass.

6.12   There he should fix his mind on a single object and restrain the activity
        of his thoughts and senses. Sitting down in that seat [also, posture:
        asana] he should practice yoga for the purification of the self.

6.13   He should be steadfast, holding his body, his head, and his neck straight
        and motionless. He should focus his gaze on the tip of his nose and
        keep his gaze from wandering.

6.14   With his self at peace and all fears gone, he should hold firm in his vow
        of celibacy. He should sit in full control of his mind, with his thoughts
        on me, disciplined, intent on me.

6.15   A yogin who disciplines himself vigilantly in this way, controlling his
        mind, attains the peace that surpasses serenity, the peace that rests in
        me.

For as long as I can remember, I have felt the Unseen Hand on my life.
And, through much experience, I have learned to trust It much more than
myself. Myself, with a little 's,' only has the vantage point of this particular
lifetime. My Self knows the bigger picture and has often graced me with
that which I could never have imagined—that which was not even *near*,
much less *on*, my radar. So, I trust the inductive nature of faith more than
the deductive nature of logic. Simply, I am in love.

But, it was not until I started meditating that, quite unexpectedly, I
began to *experience* my Self. Over time, I have learned that it is my job to
follow the deepest impulse of my heart and then to set my compass—or
tune the dial on the radio of my mind. Thinking again of the body-mind
as a radio, we get a lot of static if we're not tuned in to a frequency. But
not all frequencies serve to still and discipline the mind. Some are replay-
ing our old tapes, false beliefs, habitual fears and anxieties. Others are
forecasting our latest fantasy. Some frequencies feel "good" while others
feel "bad."

However, I as Atman, the Observer, can use buddhi, or the discerning
mind, to decide where the dial lands. I can choose the point of focus and,
in doing so, discipline the mind to serve me instead of enslave me. This is
why all forms of meditation use a point of focus, be it watching the breath,
a *mantra* (sound), a *yantra* (visual), or through conscious walking or movement. We use the buddhi aspect of our mind to practice *brahmacharya*, or
sense control, to return again—and again—to the point of focus. In this

way, we *practice staying in the present moment.* Back from my aching hip. Back from what happened yesterday. Back from my boredom. Back from a fantasy about tomorrow. Back from the parade of thoughts and feelings. Back *here now* to this breath, *this* sound current, *this* object, *this* touch of my foot to the floor, *this* movement.

Bringing the mind to stillness, if only for a brief moment, allows a kind of door to open, inviting us to *experience our self as consciousness, the Observer, Atman and not just our personality.* Slowly, in this way, our practice reveals glimpses of the inner sanctuary where God in us resides. Over time, as the mind rests more often in the present moment, we begin to see—ever so humbly—our bodies as a temple and the consciousness which sustains it as holy.

As Rumi so beautifully said, "There is a place where words are born of silence, a place where the whispers of the heart arise. There is a place where voices sing your beauty, a place where every breath carves your image in my soul." Such realization naturally leads to *nirvana* or full liberation.

As Kauravas on the battlefield of life, we rely on outside circumstances to determine our inner landscape. So, when things are going well, we feel *good.* And when things are not, we feel *bad.* As Pandava on the battlefield, we refine our minds to live more often in our inner sanctuary where we are able to receive the blessings in *all* circumstance. Resting in moments of equanimity, embracing all, we create the conditions to experience our self as Atman.

Slokas 16–17

6.16   Yoga is not the path for someone who eats too much, nor for someone who refuses to eat at all. Nor, Arjuna, is it the path for someone who sleeps too much, or someone who stays awake too much.

6.17   The yoga that destroys sorrow is the path for someone who is disciplined in his eating and in his playing, disciplined in his performance of the actions that he is obliged to do, disciplined also both in sleeping and in wakefulness.

Using discernment to still the mind and control the senses, we bring the body to equanimity. Now, *being* equanimity, our actions naturally reflect

MIND

Kauravas

Changing outer circumstances-conditions

Duality: "Good" thoughts, feelings, sensations

Kauravas

Changing outer circumstances-conditions

Duality: "Bad" thoughts, feelings, sensations

Pandava

Unchanging inner sanctuary

Equanimity: Embracing all in the present moment

An unrefined mind . . .

IDENTIFIES with the changing circumstances and conditions—sees only differences

RELIES upon external reinforcement—feedback

CREATES bondage—tossed about by the changing tides—swings on emotional pendulum
Feels "good" or "bad" based on circumstances

A refined mind . . .

IDENTIFIES with the unchanging essence—sees God everywhere

RELIES upon internal reflection from spiritual practice—inner guidance

CREATES freedom—finds peace in the storm—rests in devotion.
Feels equanimity in the present moment

this state of balance. Everything can be enjoyed in moderation without needing to under or over stimulate. Now, the mind and body become harmonized toward the ultimate goal of liberation.

Slokas 18-22

6.18 One is said to be disciplined in yoga when his craving for all of the pleasures of the world is gone, and when his thoughts are controlled and focused only on the self.

6.19 Like a lamp where there is no wind, he does not waver. This is the traditional metaphor for the yogin whose mind is restrained and who practices the yoga of the self.

6.20 When his thinking comes to rest, checked by the practice of yoga, and when one sees the self by means of the self alone, one takes pleasure only in the self.

6.21 The endless joy that is beyond the senses and can be perceived only with insight – when one knows this steadfastly one never wanders from this truth.

6.22 And when he has obtained this truth, he understands that there is nothing greater to be obtained than this. When he is steadfast in this truth, no sorrow, no matter how heavy to endure, disturbs him.

Sadhana, the daily spiritual practice of meditation, reveals to us this *Truth*. It is the greatest joy and the greatest challenge. It is not often the fun part, yet, it's what makes us free. It is not the road around or away but straight through. It invites our inner demons in to be transformed. Like the story of Jacob, we create a space where all of the emotions of our false beliefs may be felt and transformed. Many new to the practice may not realize that it can feel worse before it feels better. If we've spent a lot of time brushing things under the rug, well, we've got some serious housecleaning to do.

It's important to remember that all thoughts and the sounds they create are energy. This is why my practice of choice is mantra meditation. I call it my dial-up connection! I combine the sound current with intentional prayer to tune my radio dial and align with frequencies that deliver healing, strength, balance, self-acceptance and so on. I have, myself, experienced and observed through others, *so many extraordinary* experiences using intentional prayer with mantra that I am now documenting the process and examples for a future book.

For now, I'll share with you two techniques I have found very effective if your meditation focus of choice is mantra. First, remembering that all is energy or vibration, I know that all those demons, false beliefs (e.g. I'm not good enough; I'm not lovable; I don't know enough; I can't feel something or I'll die; No one will like me if they knew ...) are just dense forms of energy. By using a mantra, I use a higher energy vibration to act as a kind of detergent to cleanse the dirt or false beliefs of the more dense energy vibrations from my mind. *Notice nothing is added.* I am simply cleaning house to allow the beauty *that is already there* to shine through.

Secondly, when I start to experience strong emotions, I picture myself in a lifeboat of the mantra and imagine it carrying me over the stormy seas of my emotional life to the tranquil shore. My job is to stay in the lifeboat as I make my way through the storm. And, regardless of the quality of my experience, I always end with silent sitting. Chanting or sounding is very heart warming and wonderful. But, *we chant to hear in the silence that follows.* In the silence, having tuned in to the signal of equanimity, I am now ready to hear from my deepest truth. I am ready to listen.

Sadhana allows us to remember that the sun still exists on a cloudy day and that all weather patterns bring their own gifts in all seasons of our journey. So, we go *through.* Desiring nothing. Averting nothing. Simply, sensing and feeling our way *through what is.* And, we soon discover that the only real demon is fear, with a multitude of faces. But, with steady practice tuning our dial, we slowly become more light as we transform our dense places. This is what is meant by becoming enlightened. It's not that we become some perfect someone we may have imagined. It's about becoming our Self. It's not about more happy and less sad. It's about receiving the gifts of both.

And, suddenly, regardless of how we feel, all experience becomes our teacher as we sit at the feet of our life, ever so humbly, to be taught. This is coming to our prayer mat. This is Sadhana.

Slokas 23–28

6.23   He should know that this is what yoga is: it is to undo the bonds that bind us to sorrow. It should be practiced with determination and without the despair that troubles one's thoughts.

6.24 He should abandon all desires, without exception, that arise from self-interest. He should completely restrain the crowd of the senses with his mind.

6.25 Slowly but surely he should come to rest, with insight that is held firmly. He should direct his mind to the self. He should reflect upon nothing whatsoever.

6.26 Wherever the unstable wavering mind wanders off to, he should withdraw his mind from there and bring it under control within himself.

6.27 For supreme joy comes to the yogin whose mind is at peace. This yogin has pacified his passion, he has merged with Brahman, he is without stain.

6.28 In this way, constantly disciplining himself, the yogin has freed himself from sin stain. He easily attains the endless joy that comes from contact with Brahman.

Anyone who meditates regularly knows how difficult it is to harness the mind (Sloka 6.26). Jack Kornfield, in the video *The Inner Art of Meditation*, likens training the mind to house training a puppy. You don't beat the puppy or shame the puppy, but you do bring the puppy back to the newspaper again and again. This is steady practice or *abhyasa*. It's a good image to have when the normal exasperation begins to take hold. And, watching how we deal with challenge, impatience and frustration is also a part of learning how our mind plays. Cultivating non-attachment, vairagya, as we practice, on or off the mat, is done by holding our identification with the One rejoicing—regardless of what our ego is experiencing. With steady practice, abhyasa, and non-attachment, vairagya, we make our way toward victory.

And, then, after periods of seemingly endless practice, when we're no longer searching—simply sitting in the spacious fullness of what is—all we have so resisted and feared—all we have held so proud and dear—all of our searching—for one glorious moment, all evaporates, the door opens and *we are informed*—warmed by rays of the sun . . . filled with a Love we cannot describe. And nothing is the same. Nothing else of this world will satisfy anymore. Nothing save the Potter Himself.

And then, as we walk into our day, we notice the clouds returning—passing through. We observe more directly how our own inner life determines the weather. But, it's OK because now we have been given a drop of water in the desert and we know the spring is near.

Slokas 29–32

6.29 Having yoked himself by means of yoga, he sees the self, atman, that dwells in all beings and all beings within the self. He sees the same in all things.

6.30 Whoever sees me everywhere and sees everything in me will never be separated from me, nor will I be separated from him.

6.31 I dwell in all beings. The yogin who is aware of the oneness of life is devoted to me. Whatever happens to him happens within me.

6.32 Arjuna, whoever sees the identity in all beings by comparing them all to himself [or to the self, the atman] – whether there is joy or sorrow – I think of such a man as a highest yogin.

We have talked a lot about how meditation disciplines the mind to reveal the Atman within and how this experience begins to allow for seeing the same in others—*he sees the same in all things* (Sloka 6.29). And, yet, something equally wonderful is simultaneously happening in our human journey. I have noticed, as have others who meditate, a growing correlation between time spent with my own demons and less judgment of others. As I see *all* in myself, more often I find myself saying, "There, but for the Grace of God, go I." I begin to know more and more that I cannot hate you without feeling that hate poisoning me. And, I cannot love you without feeling that love freeing me. It's my choice. So, more and more, I work toward choosing love.

But, it is very important that we not fall prey to offering clichés or spiritual platitudes in an effort to gloss over our deep wounds. True forgiveness and deep healing takes time and, most of all, takes a willingness to hold a deep love for our self along the way. It is so easy to get lost in, "Why me?" Yet, the martyr route is always a dead end—in more ways than one. The only way to get found is to receive the lessons of our suffering so that our lives may blossom *because of* not *in spite of*.

Nowhere is this awareness tested more than when we perceive an injustice. Jack Kornfield, again from his video, *The Inner Art of Meditation*, relays an incident that occurred between one ex-prisoner-of-war who meets another ex-prisoner many years after their captivity.

"Have you forgiven your captors yet?"

And the second one said, "No never!"

And, the first looked at him quite kindly and said, "Well then, they still have you in prison don't they?"

Such forgiveness *does not* excuse the harm we do to one another. In fact, it is our duty, like Arjuna's, to stand up to wrongdoing, confront hurtful behavior and work to prevent such behavior from reoccurring. Such forgiveness *does* release the poisonous hatred and resentment within us so we may heal and be free.

Sadhana is the kiln. It is the burning away of all our painful conditioning, false beliefs, deeply held emotions and harmful habits. No, it is not the fun part. But, as Yogi Bhajan, once said, "First you make the habit and then the habit makes you." *Sat Nam.*

I believe a well known poem of Rumi's says it all. It's called "The Guest House."

> This being human is a guest house.
> Every morning a new arrival.
> A joy, a depression, a meanness.
> Some momentary awareness comes
> as an unexpected visitor.
> Welcome and entertain them all!
> Even if they're a cloud of sorrows
> who violently sweep your house
> empty of its furniture.
> Still, treat each guest honorably.
> He may be cleaning you out
> for some new delight.
> The dark thought, the shame, the malice,
> meet them at the door laughing,
> and invite them in.
> Be grateful for whoever comes,
> for each guest has been sent
> As a guide from beyond.

"He may be clearing you out for some new delight." It's the silver lining around the dark cloud—if we have eyes to see.

Slokas 33–36

Arjuna spoke:

6.33   You have explained yoga to me as equanimity and the identity of all
         things. But, Krishna, I cannot see how it can be firmly established,
         because of my mind's restlessness.

6.34   The mind is restless, Krishna. It is violent, strong, and stubborn. I think
         that restraining it is very difficult, like restraining the wind!

The Blessed One spoke:

6.35   No doubt, Arjuna! The mind is difficult to control and restless. But,
         Arjuna, practice and austerity can restrain it.

6.36   Yoga is difficult to practice for one who cannot control himself. That is
         my view as well. But a man who can control himself, and who strives,
         is capable of practicing yoga, by using the right means.

The key word in Sloka 6.35 is *practice*. Along with courage and discipline,
we need equal patience born out of love for ourselves. After all, it's not
about getting it perfect. We're already perfect! It's not about getting anything. We're already full! Yet, how hard it is to let go of . . . *if only this were
different or that were different* . . . How sure we are that the lack of peace
we feel is not about us but the conditions around us. Yet, over time, our
spiritual practice brings the insight necessary to begin transforming difficulty into freedom.

Right across the street from the Tree of Life Interfaith Fellowship is
the local fire department. When we first moved in and started offering
yoga classes, people asked how it was to be right across the street from the
fire department. Understanding the importance of cultivating a peaceful
inner garden irrespective of outside circumstances, suddenly I could see
that not only was there not a problem but, instead, a wonderful opportunity. Now every time the fire trucks go, we stop and send our prayers
for the ones in need and also for the helpers that go. It offers a wonderful
opportunity to remember our connection to all people known and not
known—and to love the one whose name we don't even know.

Slokas 37–44

Arjuna spoke:

6.37   Someone who does not strive but has faith, and whose mind frequently
         wanders from yogic practice, will not achieve success in yoga. Krishna,
         what path does he take?

6.38   Hasn't he fallen away from both yoga and self-control, and doesn't he
       die like a cloud cut in two? Krishna, he has no foundation. On the path
       that leads to Brahman, he is utterly deluded.

6.39   Krishna, you can cut through this doubt of mine completely. There is
       no one but you who can cut through this doubt!

The Blessed One spoke:

6.40   Arjuna, my friend, neither in this world nor in the next does anyone
       perish, for anyone who has done some measure of good cannot possibly
       take the wrong path!

6.41   He goes to the worlds that he has made with his good actions and he
       dwells in them for endless years. Then the man who has strayed away
       from yoga is reborn into a house of the pure and the blessed.

6.42   Or he is born instead into a family of enlightened yogins, for such a
       birth is even harder to obtain in this world.

6.43   There he obtains the kind of understanding that he had gained from his
       previous life. And then, Arjuna, he strives further toward perfection.

6.44   For he is carried along, beyond his own control, by the power of his
       previous practice. Anyone who merely desires to know yoga transcends
       the Vedic recitations about Brahman.

Sometimes it is difficult to understand *why* we have been born into a particular family, into difficult circumstances or with challenging personal
conditions. Yet, just as I only have the vantage point of this particular
lifetime when it comes to receiving the so-called blessings, so too do I only
have the vantage point of this particular lifetime when it comes to receiving the so-called lessons. Ultimately, in the crucible of self-acceptance,
they are one in the same.

It is true, like most, I would not have asked for my challenges. And, yet,
it is equally true, I could not be writing this book had I not had them. I
am able to serve now, as mentioned earlier, not *in spite of* but *because of*.
And, I notice the deeper my wrinkles and the greyer my hair, the lighter
my Soul.

Slokas 45-47

6.45   When he strives with great effort, the yogin becomes purified of his
       faults, and through the course of many births he becomes perfected.
       Then finally he takes the highest path.

6.46   The yogin is considered to be superior to ascetics who practice austerity, superior to men of knowledge, and superior also to men of action. Therefore, Arjuna, become a yogin!

6.47   But among all yogins whatsoever, the one who places his faith in me, who devotes himself to me, who has gone to me with his inmost self – I judge him to be the most disciplined of all!

Here we are reminded again that we cannot lose the war. Sooner or later, the darkness of our false beliefs will be brought into the light of day. Becoming clear about who *we are not* opens the door to who *we are*. This is the most precious gift of all as we begin to realize that our deepest longing can now be satisfied. All the while we have been searching and searching, only to discover that the very searcher is God. That, *Tat*, who has been watching is the One, *Atman*.

That, who has been watching, is our Self.

Welcome Home.

> *Be still and know that I am God.*
>
> **—THE BIBLE**

Key Points

1. The practice of meditation brings the awareness of the Observer, or Atman, within, and the realization that equanimity and peace come in the full embrace of our human journey.

2. Renouncing all personal intention immediately creates non-attachment to outcome.

3. We become what we meditate on.

4. We use our buddhi faculty to practice brahmacharya or sense control. We turn our intention inward using a point of focus.

5. Meditation allows for the experience of our self as consciousness, Atman, not just personality. Such realization naturally leads to nirvana, or full liberation.

6. Sadhana allows for the full embrace of our human journey. Through this embrace, we transform the energies of our false beliefs and move toward enlightenment.

7. Through steady practice, abhyasa, and non-attachment, vairagya, we make our way toward victory.

8. In Sadhana, we receive the blessings of Oneness with Atman and the lessons of our human journey. Here, we see our self in all beings and all beings in our self.

9. The limited vantage point of any particular lifetime can conceal the full understanding of our blessings and our challenges.

10. We cannot lose the war because the very searcher is God. Welcome Home.

Terms

Mantra (*Mahn*-trah) sound current
Yantra (*Yahn*-trah) visual
Brahmacharya (*Brah*-mah-*char*-yah) sense control
Nirvana (Near-*vah*-nah) full liberation
Abhyasa (Ah-b*yah*-sah) steady practice

Personal Reflection

1. Do you currently have a Sadhana practice? If so, what has been your experience? Blessings? Challenges?

2. If you do not currently have a Sadhana practice and would like to begin one, write a prayer or intention for your practice.

3. Why do you suppose we cannot *will* our enlightened moments but can create the condition to *allow* them?

4. What response happens when you contemplate yourself in all beings and all beings in yourself? How does this begin to shift how you look at yourself and how you look at others?

Bhakti Yoga

The Path of Devotion

What is to be *realized*
about the nature
of Brahman

तस्मात्सर्वेषु कालेषु
मामनुस्मर युध्य च
मय्यर्पितमनोबुद्धिर्
मामेवैष्यस्यसंशयः Sloka 8.7

Overview of Chapters 7–12

Chapter 7: The Heart of Devotion
True Essence of Devotion Within

Krishna reminds Arjuna that it is only through the quality of his faith and devotion that oneness with Brahman can occur. And, with such faith, we trade in the *emotion* of changing moods for the *devotion* of eternal bliss.

Chapter 8: Going Home
Eternal – Is Never Born nor Dies

Brahman is never born and never dies—is beyond time and space—so may only be experienced in the eternal present moment. Krishna assures Arjuna that if he can think only of Brahman at the moment of physical death that he will come directly to Him.

Chapter 9: The Source and the Seed
Not in Us – We Are in Brahman

We are used to saying that God is "within us." However, Krishna tells Arjuna that, in fact, we are "in God." Though Brahman creates and sustains all in the great womb of prakriti, Brahman, eternally infinite, is contained by nothing.

Chapter 10: Ordinary Divinity
Compassion in the Heart of All Creation

Brahman is the Source that brings forth all that exists. He dwells in the heart and from there removes darkness with the great light of wisdom. Krishna offers many examples of the manifestations of Brahman.

Chapter 11: Ripened Fruit
Righteousness That Defeats Ignorance

The fruit falls from the tree in its own time. We cannot force our spiritual development. Through "true seeing," darshan, we see all aspects of prakriti—all aspects of ourselves. Only through steady practice and constant devotion do we move closer to Brahman—closer to our Self.

Chapter 12: The True Devotee
Devotion

We are called to be true devotees—not true intellectuals. It is the *experience* of our God that *informs* us. Lastly, Krishna lists the qualities of the true devotee.

God, or Brahman, is known through the quality of our *experience* of Him in the eternal present moment. At one such moment, the moment of physical death, we have an opportunity to return directly to our Source if we can train the mind to hold who we truly are in that critical moment. As true devotees, we begin to realize that we *live in God* and we start to see God in all creation. We become more patient with ourselves as we journey toward liberation and more and more become the Love that is us.

What Is To Be Realized about the Nature of Brahman:
True Essence of Devotion Within

*For those who have come to grow, the
whole world is a garden. For those who
wish to remain in the dream, the whole
world is a stage. For those who have come
to learn, the whole world is a university.
For those who have come to know God,
the whole world is a prayer mat.*

—BAWA MUHAIYADDEN

CHAPTER 7

The Heart of Devotion

We are called to be true devotees—not true intellectuals. Knowledge is
the first step and a good one. With knowledge, awareness increases and
shame often decreases. But thinking, talking and understanding are not
enough. We can have the most honored degree in theological studies—the
finest library, and be known for our eloquence in speaking about esoteric
matters—and still have never had an *experience* of our God.

I have found that the essence of God must be experienced and then it
is *this experience that informs me*. Such an experience naturally replaces the
emotion of changing moods and needs for the *devotion* of eternal bliss. And,
it is just a taste of this *experience* that gives us the courage to step off the
edge, without first seeing the safety net, and fly.

Slokas 1–3

The Blessed One spoke:

7.1   Focus your mind on me, Arjuna, rely on me, and commit yourself to
       yoga. Hear how you will come to know me, completely, without doubt.

7.2   I will tell you completely what knowledge is, and discrimination also.
       And once you have known this, there will be nothing more to know.

7.3   Among thousands of men only one may strive for success, and among
       those who strive thus and succeed, perhaps only one will truly know
       me.

Once we have the *experience* of the Divine, Brahman, within, there is nothing else to know. This does not mean that we stop studying, learning and growing. It just means that we've experienced a glimpse of *what truly matters*—a glimpse of *freedom*—and, like the sip of water in the desert, we ache for more.

Swami Satchidananda says in his video, *Meditation*, that it is fine to know things but better to know the "real thing." When you know the "real thing," you know everything. He says, for example, that he does not always know the answer to a question when asked but he trusts that the answer will come through to him. He says sometimes, "as you are hearing it, I am hearing it. As you are clapping, I too am clapping." What a beautiful balance of trust and non-attachment. Through meditation, we become so tuned to the signal, that *all* is available to us. Through devotion, the humble heart can take no credit—only clap with joy.

Slokas 4–7

7.4   This my physical nature consists of eight parts: earth, water, fire and
       air; and then space and mind, and intelligence and ego-sense.

7.5   But this is my lower nature. You should know that I have a higher
       nature as well, Arjuna. It is the life-force that sustains this world.

7.6   It is the womb of all beings. Consider this well, Arjuna. I am the origin
       of this entire world, and I am its dissolution as well.

7.7   There is nothing whatsoever beyond me, Arjuna! All this world is
       woven on me like rows of pearls on a thread.

In Sloka 7.4, Krishna refers to eight aspects of prakriti. Five are the subtle, vibratory elements: *earth, water, fire, air and space.* Two are the perceptive cognitive processes: *mind* referring to manas, the sensory mind, and *intelligence* to buddhi, discernment. And, the eighth aspect is the *ego-sense.* The *ego-sense* is called *ahamkara,* referring to each individual as a singular perceiving entity—or what distinguishes each wildflower in the field from the others. The eight aspects of prakriti, discussed in Sloka 7.4, are the gross aspects of nature expressed in the physical universe. They are often referred to as the lower nature of Brahman, or *apara-prakriti*.

In Sloka 7.5, Krishna introduces another *higher nature* of prakriti, relating to the higher nature of Brahman. This *higher nature* of Brahman refers to the *jiva*, the consciousness of the Soul identified with its incarnate or manifested state, expressed in the astral and causal universes, or *para-prakriti*.

Both aspects of prakriti bring forth the changing, transient aspect of Brahman, creating and dissolving all that is. Beyond both aspects of prakriti, is the unchanging, eternal aspect of Brahman, forever observing with pure neutrality.

Slokas 8–13

7.8   I am the taste, the essence [rasa], in the waters, Arjuna. I am the light in the sun and the moon. I am the sacred OM in all of the Vedas. I am sound in space. I am the manhood in men.

7.9   I am the sweet scent of the earth as well, and I am the radiance in fire, the life in all beings, and I am the ascetic heat in holy men.

7.10   Know, Arjuna, that I am the eternal seed in all beings. I am the insight of the insightful. I am the brilliance of brilliant men.

7.11   I am also the strength of strong men, the strength that is free from desire and passion. And I am that desire in all beings, Arjuna, that does not resist duty [dharma]!

7.12   There are states of clarity, states of passion, and states of inertia. Know that they come only from me. But I am not in them. They are in me!

7.13   These states consist of the three qualities [gunas] of nature. The entire world is deluded by these qualities. The world does not recognize that I am beyond qualities and eternal.

There are many sweet and glorious aspects of prakriti expressed through the energetic qualities of nature, the gunas. Recall from Chapter 3, the *three qualities* referred to in Sloka 7.13 are: *rajasic*, restlessness; *tamasic*, inertia; and, *sattvic*, equanimity or balance. In Chapter 3, we learned that we, as Atman, are not born, act or die—only our body-mind is born, acts and dies—through the expression of the gunas. Here, Krishna is stressing the importance of not confusing the changing, transient expression of God, prakriti expressed through the gunas, with the unchanging, eternal expression, Brahman.

And, why is this important? We are told in the next two Slokas.

Slokas 14–15

7.14 This my veil of illusion [maya] is woven from these strands of nature. It is divine and difficult to grasp. But those who take refuge in me can pass through this veil of illusion.

7.15 Men who do not take refuge in me do great harm. They are deluded. They are the worst kind of men. The veil of illusion has robbed them of true knowledge and they descend to demonic behavior.

In the broadest sense, *demonic behavior* is any behavior that brings harm—to our self or to others. Such behavior is done out of ignorance because we have momentarily forgotten our oneness with all, momentarily forgotten that what we do to another we do to our self. When we lash out, we are the first to feel the sting. Even, if due to painful conditioning, our empathetic feeling sense has become numb, such action is still recorded for later resolution. This is the law of karma.

Sloka 16

7.16 Arjuna, there are four types of virtuous men who do take refuge in me. One comes to me when in distress. There is the seeker of wisdom as well. There is the one who prays to me for wealth and success. And there is the man of knowledge.

Sloka 7.16 speaks to our motivation for living a prayerful and spiritual life. Certainly it is wonderful to be relieved of distress when we've received a spiritual two-by-four. Wisdom, related to understanding, is fine and there's nothing innately wrong with wealth and success. But the distress will not make sense, the understanding won't sustain a more challenging argument, and all that wealth buys and success brings won't last.

If we're wandering in the desert, we may as well search for the "real thing," where only the eternal waters flow. We may as well seek to be a person of knowledge, a devotee.

Slokas 17-19

7.17 Among them, the always disciplined man of knowledge is distinguished by his devotion to me alone. I am especially dear to the man of knowledge, and he is to me.

7.18 All of these are noble men, but I think of the man of knowledge as my very self. For with his disciplined self he resorts to me as the highest path.

7.19 At the end of many births the man of knowledge prays to me, saying to himself, "Krishna is all!" Such a great soul is hard to find.

The person of true knowledge, or insight, *is distinguished by his devotion to me alone* (Sloka 7.17). Simply, those of true devotion excel because they love God most. Loving God most, they need the least, for all else is secondary. In the Bible, this is expressed in Matthew 16:26, *For what is a man profited, if he shall gain the whole world and lose his own soul?*

Slokas 20-24

7.20 All of these desires take away their knowledge, and as a result people pray to other gods. They commit themselves to this or that ritual restriction but it is their own nature that restricts them.

7.21 I will give unshakable faith to any devotee who wishes to worship god in any form, as long as he worships with fervent faith.

7.22 When he has gained discipline he seeks to propitiate his god by means of his faith. He thus obtains his desires from that god, but it is I who have granted them.

7.23 But such men have little wisdom and the fruit of their actions is limited. Thus those who worship the gods go to the gods, whereas those who are devoted to me come to me.

7.24 Men who lack insight think that I, the unmanifest one, have become manifest in a particular form. They do not know that higher state of mine which is perfect and unchanging.

If our faith, *shraddha*, is pure and fervent, the form of our worship becomes secondary, for it is the eternal Brahman who grants our desires *through all* forms of worship. With true insight, we begin to recognize the *unmanifested one* expressing through all manifestations.

One of the most beautiful examples I know of recognizing the

unmanifested one, through the manifestation of creation, is the life of
George Washington Carver. In the article, "The Man Who Talks with
the Flowers," condensed from the book of the same title by Glenn Clark,
George Washington Carver is asked how it is he was able to discover 300
new uses for the peanut and 150 new uses for the sweet potato.

Like our discussion of Gandhi in the last chapter, his foundation was
daily spiritual practice:

> There is literally nothing that I ever wanted to do that I asked the
> blessed Creator to help me do that I have not been able to accom-
> plish. It's all very simple if one knows how to talk with the creator.
>   . . . All my life I have risen regularly at four o'clock and have
> gone into the woods and talked with God. There He gives me my
> orders for the day. Alone there with things I love most I gather
> specimens and study the great lessons Nature is so eager to teach
> us all. When people are still asleep I hear God best and learn my
> plan.

In describing his workshop, he said,

> No books are ever brought here. What is the need of books?
>   . . . Here I talk to the peanut and the sweet potato and the
> clays of the hills and they talk back to me. Here great wonders are
> brought forth.

When asked how he did it, he replied,

> You have to love it enough. Anything will give up its secrets if you
> love it enough. Not only have I found that when I talk to the little
> flower or to the little peanut they will give up their secrets . . . but
> I have also found that when I silently commune with people they
> give up their secrets also—if you love them enough.

And in summary, he says,

> It is not we little men that do the work but our blessed Creator
> working through us.

Faith is not about the *emotion* of our changing moods and needs from which we may tend to ask, plead or beg. Faith is about the *devotion* of our eternal Self—so neutral, so free from need, so able to *really see*—that total loving becomes possible. From this neutral, unencumbered place, the fog of wanting ourselves, another or something to be a certain way clears, and the truth of *what is* comes into focus.

This is why true seeing is true love. This is why true creating, transforming or healing only occurs in the sweet embrace of unconditional love. Only here, do we feel safe enough to give up our secrets.

Slokas 25-28

7.25   I am not revealed to everyone. I am veiled by the illusion [maya] of my yogic power. Deluded as it is, the world does not recognize that indeed I am unborn and unchanging.

7.26   I know the things of the past and I know the things of the present and, Arjuna, I also know the things of the future. But no one knows me!

7.27   Arjuna, all beings at birth enter into this grand delusion, because they are deluded by the dualism that arises from loathing and desire.

7.28   But those who have put an end to their sins, these men who perform acts of merit, they free themselves from the delusions of duality, and they worship me, firm in their vows.

To free ourselves from the *delusions of duality*, we must awaken from the spell of maya. It's important to understand that the nature of prakriti is duality. In fact, we come to know things through their opposite. We can only know light in relation to dark, sweet in relation to sour, up in relation to down.

However, if we forget the One essence behind all the expressions of duality, we get into trouble. In this light, someone committing an evil act, for example, can easily become "bad" instead of the action. Suddenly, instead of saying, "You have committed an evil *act* for which there are consequences," we say *"you* are evil." Or, seeing someone perform a helpful action, we may think, they are "good."

All conditions, judgments and actions, "bad" or "good," arise from the law of karma, experiences that have conditioned our body-mind and from the choices we've made—all parts of prakriti. The Soul, Atman, is the impartial Observer—the *devotion that is the same within all.*

To love sinner and saint alike, we must break from the spell of maya and *see* past the "bad" and "good" actions. We must *love enough* to *see* the Truth.

And, suddenly, *there* is God.

Slokas 29–30

7.29   Those who restrain themselves, resorting to me for liberation from old age and death, know Brahman completely, and its relation to the self, and the full world of action.

7.30   Those who have disciplined their thoughts will know me in all of my aspects – even at the moment of death – as I relate to creatures, to the gods, and to sacrifice!

These final two Slokas introduce the following chapter, reminding us of the importance of staying conscious at the time of so-called death.

Key Points

1. We are called to be true devotees, not true intellectuals.
2. An *experience* of our God *informs* us. Such an experience naturally replaces the *emotion* of changing moods and needs for the *devotion* of eternal bliss.
3. There are two aspects of the changing, transient expression of God, prakriti: apara-prakriti expressed in the physical universe and para-prakriti expressed in the astral and causal universes.
4. Those of true knowledge, or insight, worship because they love God most.
5. Shraddha, faith, enables us to *really see*, so total loving becomes possible.
6. We are able to rise above the *delusions of duality, maya,* when we can see the eternal — the unchanging essence behind all creation — beyond the opposites in duality.

Terms

Ahamkara (Ah-hahm-*kah*-rah) each individual; a singular perceiving entity

Apara-prakriti (*Ah*-par-rah-*prak*-ri-tee) prakriti expressed in the physical universe

Jiva (*Jee*-vah) the consciousness of the Soul identified with its incarnate state

Para-prakriti (*Pah*-rah-*prak*-ri-tee) prakriti expressed in the astral and causal universes

Shraddha (Shrah-*dah*) sincere belief—faith

Personal Reflection

1. If we are called to be devotees as opposed to intellectuals, what would you say is the role of the intellect in the spiritual journey?
2. Describe in your own words the "real thing."
3. Give an example of a time when you acted from emotion and another example of a time you acted with devotion. How were you informed?
4. What does faith, shraddha, mean to you? Describe that in which you have faith.
5. Can you remember a time when you were able to *truly see* beyond a challenging situation and respond—to God?

What Is To Be Realized about the Nature of Brahman:
Eternal – Is Never Born nor Dies

From joy I came, for joy I live, and in
sacred joy shall I melt again!

— PARAMAHANSA YOGANANDA

CHAPTER 8

Going Home

Death. It is said to be the number one fear of most people. Recall that Krishna begins his counsel to Arjuna by reminding him who *he is*, the eternal Atman, never born nor dies, so that he may *see* clearly, and rise to do his duty. Remembering who *he is*, whether or not his physical body is killed in battle becomes immaterial, for not to do his duty has a consequence greater than death.

And, so it is on our battlefield of life.

Remembering, we, like Arjuna, can align with the eternal expression of God within and rise up with courageous joy to do our duty in service to the greater good. Remembering, victory on the battlefield of life is the only possibility.

Slokas 1-2

Arjuna spoke:

8.1 What is this infinite Brahman? What does it have to do with the self? What has it to do with action, Krishna? What does it have to do with beings in general? And what does it have to do with the gods?

103

8.2   What is it, and how does it relate to sacrifice, Krishna, here in this
       body? And how exactly are men of self-restraint to know you at the
       moment of death?

Arjuna continues to have many questions—and continues to stall. He
knows what needs to be done, yet, still cannot quite muster the courage
to rise up. Are we so different? Do we not know a difficult truth sometimes
long before we're able to face it directly? Do we not get busy in our own
way to avoid the discomfort? And yet, our deeper knowing will not let us
go. The impulse toward wholeness will keep tapping us on the shoulder
until we show up. *This is how much we are loved.* We can turn away, shrink
away, even run away, but we *can't get away* from the truth.

But, let's look at his questions. In Sloka 8.1, Arjuna wants to know how
Brahman relates to the *self*, here referring to the supreme self, *adhyatman.*
He also wants to know what Brahman has to do with *beings in general,*
referring to the earthly realm, *adhibhuta,* and to the *gods,* the kingdom of
light, *adhidaiva.* In Sloka 8.2, Arjuna wants to know how Brahman relates
to the nature of sacrifice, *adhiyajna.*

His last question, however, is paramount: *And how exactly are men of
self-restraint to know you at the moment of death?* The focus of this chapter
is devoted to Krishna's answer.

Slokas 3–4

The Blessed One spoke:

8.3   The supreme Braman is imperishable. It is said to relate to the self as its
       inherent nature. It is the creative impulse that causes the origin of all
       beings. As such, it is also known as action.

8.4   Brahman relates to beings in general insofar as they come into being
       and perish by means of it. The individual spirit [purusha] is that
       Brahman in us which has to do with the gods. And with regard to
       sacrifice, I am the form of Brahman that dwells in the body.

Like a patient father, Krishna answers Arjuna's questions. *Purusha,* in Sloka
8.4, refers to the aspect of Brahman that is the essence behind the changing forms in nature. It is the nature of Brahman that is expressed through
prakriti and the gunas.

Slokas 5–10

8.5   When at the moment of death one abandons the body, holding in mind
       me alone, one passes and enters my state of being. About this there is
       no doubt.

8.6   Whatever state of being one holds in mind, when at the moment of
       death one leaves the body, that is the state that he returns to. Arjuna,
       that is the state that he has always dwelled in.

8.7   Therefore, at all times you should hold me in memory, and fight! Fix
       your mind and your understanding on me. Without doubt you will
       come to me.

8.8   When one meditates with one's mind disciplined by the practice of
       yoga, pursuing nothing else, then, Arjuna, one comes to that highest
       divine spirit within us all [purusha].

8.9   One should hold in memory the ancient poet, the lord who is finer than
       an atom, the lord who ordains all things, the lord of incomprehensible
       form with the radiance of the sun who is beyond darkness.

8.10   At the moment of death, with an unwavering mind, one should be
       disciplined by means of devotion and the power of yoga. One should
       direct one's breath completely onto the middle point between the
       brows. By doing so, one attains to this supreme divine spirit.

Krishna tells Arjuna, if he can only think of Purusha at the time of physical death, he will be able to direct his breath, *prana*, to the middle point between the brows, and realize God. But, the trouble is, in the midst of an emotionally charged situation, particularly our death, it is extremely difficult, if not impossible, to summon that which has not *already been made a part of our experience through regular practice*. Again, simple desire is not enough.

Take, for example, someone who suffers from acute anxiety or panic attacks. How effective is it to repeat "I am peaceful" once the symptoms have begun? Not just ineffective, but downright impossible! But, imagine that a person who has such symptoms resolves to practice diaphragmatic breathing on a daily basis to instill a different response to the anxiety producing situations. With the ongoing daily practice, it becomes *possible* to respond in a new way when trouble approaches.

Similarly, through our daily spiritual practice, Sadhana, we *practice* creating the conditions to experience life *and* death more consciously.

Slokas 11-16

8.11   What students of the Vedas call the imperishable, what ascetics who have renounced passion enter into, what those who live the celibate life seek – I will tell you briefly about that very place.

8.12   One should control all of the doors [entrances] of the body, and keep one's mind within one's heart. One should establish one's breath within the head, and remain fixed in yogic concentration.

8.13   OM. One should utter the one imperishable syllable which is Brahman. One should hold me firm in memory. When he abandons his body and departs from this life, such a man takes the highest path.

8.14   For a man who always remembers me, who keeps his thoughts always on nothing other than me, for an ever disciplined yogin like this I am easy to reach.

8.15   Those great souls who have attained the highest perfection come to me, Arjuna. They do not experience rebirth – that impermanent home of sorrow.

8.16   From out of the realm of Brahman all these worlds unfold over and over again. But, Arjuna, whoever comes to me instead will never experience rebirth.

Yoga practitioners of all traditions will recognize OM in Sloka 8.13. At the time of physical death, as we direct the breath, prana, to the middle point between the brows, we are to utter OM. OM, also written as *Aum*, refers to the cosmic sound vibration, the universal mantra, which includes all other sounds. Meditating on OM reveals the true essence of our connection with the Divine.

In *God Talks with Arjuna: The Bhagavad Gita, Royal Science of God Realization*, Paramahansa Yogananda writes:

> Gabriel's trumpet is the sound of the Cosmic Aum that ushers man from the physical body at death . . . By practice of non-attachment the yogi dissolves all the inclinations and desires of the heart and remains in continuous ecstasy with the Aum vibration, the expression of God in creation. When death arrives, the yogi finds Gabriel's trumpet, issuing from the Cosmic Aum, ushering him into the transcendental spheres of God.

The great fear surrounding death would seem to be the belief that it is *we* who are dying. In order to transcend such fear and walk consciously into the arms of death, a deep knowing must prevail that it is not we who are dying—but our body-mind—and that, being eternal, our Soul will either continue its journey to the next incarnation or go home to Brahman, or God.

I don't think there is a greater privilege than to witness the passing of a Soul. I was with my mother when she passed and will always feel very blessed to have been able to witness this journey. Although I had been to funerals and had seen clearly that the deceased person was not there, to watch a passing took this awareness to a much deeper level. Clearly, my mom was there, then lifted out of her body and was gone. Only her empty shell remained. I had prayed for her safe passage and was grateful her death was peaceful.

Now that both of my parents have passed, I am acutely aware that, in the natural order of things, I am next up. However, the most unexpected and wondrous thing has happened as a result of this unavoidable realization. I am now very conscious that there are *only so many days left*. Of course, no matter how old we are, there are always *only so many days left*. The difference is now I *really* get it and, thankfully, far from creating fear and anxiety, this deep awareness actually serves to make each day a little sweeter.

Gerald G. Jampolsky, MD, who worked with children facing death and their families in a center he created called The Center for Attitudinal Healing, writes in his book *Teach Only Love: The Seven Principles of Attitudinal Love:*

> Without a change in perception about what we are, anxiety will continue to underlie all we think and do as we anticipate the approach of our final annihilation. Somehow we must begin to recognize that we live now and eternally as love. I believe we are in this world only to learn and teach love. The lengths of our stay vary, but what each of us gives and is given is the same: love.

And, later he writes:

As long as our bodies are alive, our job is to use them as a means of allowing our love to extend in a form others can recognize and receive. It is what we all do with our hearts that affects others most deeply. It is not the movements of our body or the words within our mind that transmit love. We love from heart to heart.

We love, touch and heal one another with that which cannot be described—yet, is instantly known—the devotion of Brahman—the Love of God.

Later, he shares a story about one of the children at the Center:

The first of the Center's children to die was Greg Harrison. He was eleven years old. When there were no more new drugs to be administered and it appeared he didn't have much more time left, Greg was asked by the other children in his group, "What do you think it will be like to die?" I know I will never forget his answer. He said, "I think that when you die, you just discard your body, which was never real in the first place. Then you are in heaven, at one with all souls. And sometimes you come back to earth and act as a guardian angel to somebody. I think that's what I would like to do."

Slokas 17-19

8.17 When people come to know that a day of Brahman revolves through a thousand ages, and that a night of Brahman also lasts a thousand ages – then they will truly know about days and nights.

8.18 At the dawn of a day of Brahman all manifest things arise from the unmanifest, and at the fall of its night they dissolve back into that, what is known as the unmanifest.

8.19 This same vast host of beings arises again and again, and then unwillingly dissolves at nightfall. And then it all arises again, Arjuna, at the next dawn of day.

The beautiful description of birth, death, and rebirth from eleven-year-old Greg Harrison is echoed here. *At the dawn of a day of Brahman*, we *arise*, born into manifestation, and at the *fall of its night*, we die or *dissolve* back into the unmanifested state, only to *arise again*. Simply, from God we come and to God we return.

Slokas 20-22

8.20 Beyond all that, there is another state, an eternal unmanifest state that is beyond that unmanifest world. Whereas all beings perish, this [the unmanifest, Krishna himself] does not die.

8.21 It is said that this unmanifest being is imperishable, and men say that he is the supreme path. Once they have reached him, they do not return. This is my highest dwelling.

8.22 But, Arjuna, this highest person [purusha] can be reached through devotion to him alone. In him all beings rest. By him all this was made.

And still, beyond all the cycles of creating and dissolving is the eternal and everlasting One, here referred to as *Purusha, reached through devotion to him alone. In him all beings rest.*

One of my favorite Christian hymns is "Oh God, You Search Me," taken from the 139th Psalm in the Bible. It says, in part:

> Oh, God, you search me and you know me.
> All my thoughts lie open to your gaze.
> When I walk or lie down you are before me.
> Ever the maker and keeper of my days.
>
> You know my resting and my rising.
> You discern my purpose from afar.
> And with love everlasting you besiege me.
> In every moment of life or death you are.

In devotion, we come to rest in God. And, *besieged* by *love everlasting*, we walk free with the *maker and keeper of our days.*

Slokas 23-28

8.23 Yogins when they die sometimes return to the world and sometimes they don't return. Arjuna, I will tell you about these times.

8.24   People who know Brahman reach Brahman, when they die at the
following times: when there is fire, or light, or daytime, or the moonlit
fortnight, or the six months of the sun's northern course.

8.25   But a yogin reaches the light of the moon and returns, when he dies at
these times: when there is smoke, or nighttime, or the dark moonless
fortnight, or the six months of the sun's southern course.

8.26   Indeed, these two courses – the light one and the dark – are thought to
be permanent in this world. By means of the one, one does not return
to this world. By means of the other, one returns again.

8.27   By knowing these two paths a yogin will never become deluded.
Therefore, Arjuna, become disciplined in yoga at all times!

8.28   Whatever reward for merit has been taught in the past with regard to
the Vedas, to sacrifices, to austerities, as well as the giving of gifts – the
yogin overcomes all of this. Having gained this knowledge, the yogin
reaches the realm that is both first and last.

Different interpretations are offered in various commentaries on these
mysterious Slokas. Generally, it is thought that one who aligns with
Divine Consciousness at the time of death follows the northern course of
the sun and goes to God. One who does not, follows the southern passage
to rebirth.

Ultimately, to know if we are truly unattached to the fruits of our
actions, it's good to notice if it's equally OK to stay or go. This is what
is meant by Sloka 8.28. We can perform many wonderful acts. We can
study scripture. We can live simply and offer much. But, beyond all these
acts, there must be complete freedom to stay or go at any moment. Why?
Because the *only true goal here is to be present as long as necessary to perform
the function for which we have come.*

This is another expression of the *it's not about us at all.* It has nothing
to do with us as individuals. We are simply here to perform a particular
function to serve the greater good. That is all. Remembering this, our
intention stays clear. Our only desire is to be a fully cooperative and
supremely honed instrument of the Divine and then, when our work is
done, to leave gracefully and joyfully.

Instead of wondering, "How much time do I have left?" ask, "What can
I do this very moment to serve with joy?" and all else will suddenly and
effortlessly make sense. You will be made to fulfill your purpose and all

around you will be served in the most perfect way. Sure, there will come a time when your body will fall away—but you will never die.

And, hold close the words of Richard Bach, "What the caterpillar calls the end of the world, the master calls a butterfly."

Death is the master illusion of prakriti. Let us be too busy loving, to die!

In the following chapter we'll discover why we could never die—we live in God.

Key Points

1. Arjuna continues to have many questions. He is still stalling.
2. What we are thinking about at the time of bodily death determines our experience and destiny.
3. At the moment of death, to return to God, direct the breath, prana, to the middle point between the eyebrows and utter OM.
4. There are *only so many days left*.
5. "Day" and "night" refers to the natural cycle of creation and desolation and re-creation—from God we come and to God we return.
6. When we remember that *we* are never born and never die—that we have come for a particular purpose—to get something done—we remember that *it's not about us at all*. With this awareness, we can come and go less encumbered.

Terms

Adhyatman (*Ah*-dyaht-mahn) supreme self
Adhibhuta (*Ah*-dee-*boo*-tah) earthly realm
Adhidaiva (*Ah*-dee-*dive*-ah) kingdom of Light
Adhiyajna (*Ah*-dee-*yah*-shnah) the nature of self-sacrifice
Purusha (*Pu*-roo-shah) essence behind the changing forms in nature
OM (*Oh*-m or *Au*-m) cosmic sound vibration

Personal Reflection

1. What are your thoughts about death?
2. Write your epitaph.

What Is To Be Realized about the Nature of Brahman:
Not in Us—We Are in Brahman

*All know that the drop merges into
the ocean but few know that the
ocean merges into the drop.*

—KABIR

CHAPTER 9

The Source and the Seed

We are used to saying that God is within. However, Krishna tells Arjuna the greatest of secrets: that *we*, in fact, *are in God*. Though Brahman creates and sustains all in the great womb of prakriti, Brahman, eternally infinite, is contained by nothing.

Simply, there is *only God*—the *maker* and *keeper* of our days.

Slokas 1-2

The Blessed One spoke:

9.1 So then, I will teach this greatest of secrets to you, since you do not dispute what I have said so far. When you have understood the wisdom that comes with knowledge you will be freed from misfortune.

9.2 This is the knowledge of kings, the secret of kings. It is the highest means of purification. It is readily accessible. It conforms to dharma [law, duty]. It is easy to accomplish, and also everlasting!

Knowledge, in Sloka 9.1, refers to the personal realization born of daily practice. It is here that we *experience* this *maker* and *keeper* of our days. And, the wisdom born of such experience begins freeing us from misfortune, from being on-going problems to ourselves. With personal realization, wisdom is no longer an intellectual exercise. It becomes as concrete as the pulse of our heartbeat, and as sustaining as the rhythm of our breath—yet, equally mysterious.

Who beats our heart when we are sleeping? Who breathes us when we are busy? While the rational mind likes to feel in control, truly it is a mystery that has *loved us into birth* as Bernadette Farrell sings in "God Beyond All Names." Yet, in Sloka 9.2, we are told that this *everlasting* mystery is *readily accessible* and *easy to accomplish*. But, like Arjuna, it often seems easier to hold on to our fear than to *let go and let God.*

To truly begin to comprehend that we are finite, mutable expressions of an Infinite creator requires that we relinquish the illusion of control. At first this can feel like we are losing our self. After all, we have been given an ego sense, ahamkara, a body-mind as a tool for manifesting, and free will. We are told that, with each thought, we chisel out our destiny. How is it that we can settle into the notion that we are just instruments of Divine providence? Sloka 9.3 answers this question.

Sloka 3

9.3   Arjuna, men who do not place their faith in this dharma do not return to me. Instead they turn back upon the endless cycle of death and rebirth.

It is only by placing our faith, shraddha, in this dharma, truth, that we truly begin to *live the mystery* and dance with God.

Slokas 4–6

9.4   I am woven into all of this world, but my form remains unmanifest. All beings find their support in me, whereas I do not at all depend on them.

9.5   And yet beings do not find their support in me. Behold the regal force of my yoga! My self brings all beings to life, and supports all beings, but does not dwell in them.

9.6   Just as the great wind that goes everywhere dwells eternally in the ether, so all being dwells in me. Ponder this, Arjuna!

Thirteenth century Beguine mystic, Mechtild of Magdenburg said, "The day of my spiritual awakening was the day I saw and knew I saw God in all things and all things in God."

. . . and all things in God. We are used to saying that *God is in us.* Yet, here, and in Sloka 9.5, we learn the greatest of secrets: it is *we who live in the heart of God.* And a profound shift happens. We are used to thinking of *ourselves* like instruments bringing forth the Song of God. Yet, does an instrument contain the song? No. It simply *allows* for the expression of the song. Do we contain God? No. Yet, we *allow* for the expression of God. With this shift, we know that it is not about *us*, ourselves, at all.

We are simply the instruments, *through which* our glorious maker and keeper plays.

The ego definitely does not like this, for it defines itself through what it thinks are its unique characteristics—not *that which is the same in all of us.* To lose a grip on these special qualities would mean death. So, the ego desperately holds on for dear life. Little does it know that to *let go* and *let God* is to truly live. But, letting go requires a leap of faith *into the truth*, expressed in this Sufi tale . . .

A stream was working itself across the country, experiencing little difficulty. It ran around the rocks and through the mountains. Then it arrived at the desert. Just as it had crossed every other barrier, the stream tried to cross this one. But it found that as fast as it ran into the sand the water disappeared. After many attempts it became very discouraged. It appeared that there was no way it could continue the journey.

Then a voice came in the wind. "If you stay the way you are you cannot cross the sands. You cannot become more than a quagmire. To go further, you will have to lose yourself."

"But if I lose myself," the stream cried, "I will never know what I'm supposed to be."

"Oh, on the contrary," said the voice, "if you lose yourself you will become more than you ever dreamed you could be."

So the stream surrendered to the dying sun. And the clouds into which it was formed were carried by the raging wind for many miles. Once it crossed the desert, the stream poured down from the skies, fresh and clean and full of energy that comes from storms.

Slokas 7–10

9.7   At the end of every eon [kalpa], all these beings return again to the nature [prakriti] that belongs to me. And at the beginning of the next eon I send them forth again.

9.8   Relying on my own nature alone, I send forth again and again this vast host of beings, not by the force of their will but by the force of nature [prakriti].

9.9   But these actions do not bind me down, Arjuna. I am seated here [that is, involved in the ceremonies: karma here in the sense of ritual action] but actually I am like one seated apart, detached from all of these actions.

9.10 Nature gives birth to what moves and what does not move – while I oversee it all! Arjuna, the world turns and turns in this way – while this [Krishna pointing to himself] is the cause!

As the Observer, Atman, in our meditations, we experience that we are the neutral witness watching all our thoughts, feelings and sensations come and go—changing moment to moment. So too, collectively, is Brahman, within all, the neutral witness of all creation. A popular image used to illustrate this esoteric truth is a film projector projecting a movie onto a screen. The light delivers and sustains the changing images on the screen, but is not, in any way, involved with them. And, just as we have learned, it is not *we* who act, but the energetic forces of nature through prakriti, so too, does *Brahman send forth again and again the vast host of beings* (Sloka 9.8) while *seated apart, detached from all these actions* (Sloka 9.9).

And, how does this awareness inform our daily life? Remember our discussion on duality in the last chapter? If we have had the *experience* of our self as the Observer, Atman, in daily practice, and realize that what we are experiencing is *that which also brings forth all others*, then, not only can we begin to observe our own folly with increased neutrality, but, also, the folly of others. Such awareness creates the possibility that we can respond appropriately, for example, to a hurtful behavior, from the neutrality of equanimity instead of from the reactions of the moment.

This is Arjuna's challenge. And, ours as well.

This continued awareness now makes loving our neighbor a *concrete reality* born of *experience* of the eternal, indwelling, devotion of God—not

of the here-today-gone-tomorrow emotions brought forth by outer circumstance. Now, when I say, "I and my neighbor are one," it is not just a
lovely sentiment but a *concrete experience*. Now, I *know* who I am—who my
neighbor is—and, that *we are One and the same*.

And, we are *besieged* by *Love everlasting*.

Slokas 11–14

9.11   Deluded men dismiss me when I take on a human body. They do not
        recognize my higher state, as the great lord of all beings.

9.12   Their hopes are sheer folly. Their actions are sheer folly. Their wisdom
        is sheer folly. They have no insight whatsoever. They surrender
        themselves to a delusory nature that is full of demons and devils.

9.13   But great souls surrender instead to a divine nature, Arjuna, to me!
        They worship me, thinking of nothing else. For they know the eternal
        source of all beings!

9.14   Ever singing my praises, ever striving toward me, firm in their
        vows, ever paying homage to me with devotion [bhakti], ever
        disciplined – thus do they worship me!

But the great souls surrender instead to a divine nature, Arjuna, to me (Sloka
9.13). When we *know who we are*, we move into the mystery of offering up
our best while letting go of the outcome—from needing to control the
creation to allowing the creation to inform us—from having to hold fast
to simply being held.

One of the most inspirational stories of complete abandonment of one's
life creation to the Unseen Hand, is the story of the beginning of Mother
Teresa's work. The following passage is taken from *Mother Teresa: The
Authorized Biography* by Navin Chawla.

> When she set foot in Motijhil, she did not feel that it was neces-
> sary to carry out a survey or to make a plan or raise funds. She
> simply saw that there was need for a school. The fact that there
> was no building, no chairs or tables did not deter her. On a small
> open patch among the shanties, she began to scratch the Bengali
> alphabet with a stick on the ground. A few children appeared and
> with each passing day more and more children joined. In a spirit of

community participation someone donated a chair or two, a bench and blackboard. Within a few days, the little school had become a reality.

What? No business plan? No well-organized fund-raising campaign? No money? Impossible! Not at all . . . *if you know you live in the heart of God.*

Sloka 15

9.15   Yet others make offerings to me with offerings of knowledge. Thus they worship me – I who face in all directions – as having one form, having several, having many!

When we know who *we* are, suddenly, all forms, each clearly different and facing in all directions, look the same. Although, sometimes they are pretty and sometimes ugly. Sometimes helpful and sometimes hurtful. When we know who *we* are, we know, also, who the other is—and, all we see is God. Simply, we see beyond the changing, transient, expression of God, prakriti, to behold *Brahman, Tat, that which is the same in all.* This is why Jesus was a great teacher of inclusion. His ministry on earth included all those whom we might ordinarily avoid or even discard. This is how he challenged us to love our neighbor as our self.

Slokas 16–18

9.16   I am this ritual. I am this sacrifice. I am the libation for the dead and the healing herb. I am this mantra and I am this ghee. I am the ritual fire and its oblation.

9.17   I am the father of this world and its mother. I am its guardian and its grandfather. I am all that is to be known. I am the purifier and the sacred syllable OM. I am also the Rigveda and the Samaveda and the Yajurveda.

9.18   I am the way and the support, the lord and the witness. I am your dwelling, your refuge, and your heart's friend. I am the world's origin and its dissolution, its stability, its treasure, its imperishable seed.

I am the way and the support (Sloka 9.18). In the Bible, this is expressed in John 14:6, *I am the way, the truth, and the life.* And, with God as our *heart's friend*, how could there be enemies?

Slokas 19–22

9.19   I radiate this heat. I withhold the rain and then I release it. I am immortality and mortality both. Arjuna, I am both being and non-being.

9.20   Those who study the three Vedas, those who drink the soma, those who purify themselves of sin – they all direct their sacrifices to me, seeking a path to heaven. They reach the blessed world of Indra, lord of the gods, and in that heaven they partake of the heavenly pleasures of the gods.

9.21   And having thus enjoyed this heavenly world at length, having exhausted their merit, they return to the world of mortals. Thus those who observe the duties [dharmas] of the three Vedas win only what comes and goes. Their desire is desire itself.

9.22   But those people who devote themselves to me, thinking of nothing else whatsoever, once they have become constant in their discipline – I bring them success and peace [this is a pun: yoga-kshema here = "success and peace," but it implies "yoga and peace"].

For those who *know* they live *in* God, there is no possibility of starvation, on any level, because, for them, all of life is a banquet. They *partake of the heavenly pleasures of the gods* (Sloka 9.20) and are brought *success and peace* (Sloka 9.22).

A wonderful example of such concrete *surrender* is demonstrated in the story "Two Penniless Boys in Brindaban" in *Autobiography of a Yogi*, by Paramahansa Yogananda. Yogananda, called Mukunda in the story, wants nothing more than to lead a spiritual life, but his older brother, Ananta, is intent on persuading him to follow a more traditional path to gain financial security. Exasperated, his older brother, says, "How foolish, you are throwing away your life!" And the following conversation ensues, ending in a challenge, or test, that Mukunda must pass in order to convince his brother of his sincerity. Mukunda says,

> "I am conscious of my dependence on God."
>
> "Words are cheap! Life has shielded you thus far. What a plight if you were forced to look to the Invisible Hand for your food and shelter! You would soon be begging on the streets."
>
> "Never! I would not put faith in passers-by rather than in God!

He can devise for His devotee a thousand resources besides the begging bowl."

"More rhetoric! Suppose I suggest that your vaunted philosophy be put to a test in this tangible world?"

"I would agree! Do you confine God to a speculative world?"

"We shall see; today you shall have opportunity either to enlarge or to confirm my own views." Ananta paused for a dramatic moment, then spoke slowly and seriously.

"I propose that I send you and your follow disciple Jitendra this morning to the nearby city of Brindaban. You must not take a single rupee; you must not beg, either for food or money; you must not reveal your predicament to anyone; you must not go without your meals; and you must not be stranded in Brindaban. If you return to my bungalow here before twelve o'clock tonight, without having broken any rule of the test, I shall be the most astonished man in Agra!"

"I accept the challenge."

Through a series of events, they were, of course, not just fed a meal, but enjoyed a banquet filled with delicacies as they "had never before tasted." And, a young man showed them the city and provided them with the means to return home, "a bundle of rupee notes and two tickets, just purchased, to Agra."

Surprising? Not at all, *if you know you live in the heart of God.*

Slokas 23–25

9.23 And even the devotees of other gods, who worship in good faith – in the end, with their sacrifices they worship me, Arjuna, even if they do not observe the traditional rites.

9.24 For I am the recipient and the lord of all sacrificial offerings, but those who sacrifice to others do not recognize me in my essence, and so they fall from their heavens.

9.25 Men who offer their vows to the gods go to the gods. Those who offer their vows to the fathers go to the fathers. Those who sacrifice to ghosts go to the ghosts. In the same way, those who worship me come to me.

... those who worship me come to me (Sloka 9.25). Let's go for the "real thing."

Slokas 26-27

9.26 A leaf, or a flower, a fruit, or water, whatever one offers to me with devotion [bhakti] – I accept it, because it is a gift of devotion, because it is offered from the self.

9.27 Whatever you do – whatever you eat, whatever offering you make, whatever you give, whatever austerity you perform – Arjuna, do it all as an offering to me!

Austerity in Sloka 9.27 refers to our suffering or *tapas*. And, nowhere is our devotion greater than when we offer our suffering to God. When we offer our suffering, or tapas, we are following the impulse toward wholeness. We sit in our pain—tapas—totally present—yet, witnessing with non-attachment—becoming porcelain in the heat of the kiln, receiving the results of our actions, needing nothing but our God.

Slokas 28-29

9.28 In this way you will be freed both from the bonds and also from the fruits of your actions, whether good or bad. Train yourself in the yoga of renunciation. Freed thereby, you will come to me.

9.29 Among all beings I am always the same. No one is hateful to me. No one is especially dear. But if they worship me with utter devotion, they will be in me, and I will be in them.

As God is the same toward all beings so is every action we offer to God the same, if it is offered with devotion. Mother Teresa said, "Once you give it to God, it becomes infinite." It is only our job to make the offering. God does the rest.

Slokas 30-33

9.30 No matter how badly a man has lived his life, if he worships me and worships nothing else, let him be considered upright and wise [sadhu], for he has come to recognize what is right.

9.31 He quickly commits himself to duty and righteousness [dharma], and he

enters into eternal peace [shanti]. Arjuna, understand this well: no one
who is devoted to me is ever lost to me.

9.32   For, Arjuna, no matter how low their birth may be – whether they are
women, or villagers, or low-caste slaves – those who rely on me all
attain to the final goal.

9.33   How much more is this true, then, for virtuous priests [brahmins] or
devoted royal sages! Arjuna, having entered into this fleeting, joyless
world, devote yourself to me!

A Native American shaman once said, "We earn our way." Who has not,
from lack of awareness, committed acts of harm against others? Who has
not been harmed by others? Making sense, gleaning awareness, assuming
responsibility for our part in the human drama, is the substance of wisdom.
And, these Slokas assure us that, if we take refuge in Brahman, no matter
where we have been or what we have done, it is still possible to reach the
supreme goal of final liberation. It is the blessing in karma and the gift
in grace.

Sloka 34

9.34   To me should your mind be directed, to me your devotion aimed, to me
should you make your sacrifices! Pay your homage to me! Disciplining
yourself in this way, you will come to me. I will be your final refuge!

This final Sloka is a perfect summary of Krishna's council to Arjuna.

To me should your mind be directed —Keep your mind single-pointed.
To me your devotion aimed —Keep your heart devoted.
To me should you make your sacrifices —Offer your actions up.
Pay your homage to me —Bow your ego down.

Challenging? Sometimes.
Impossible? Not at all, if *you know you live in the heart of God.*
In the following chapter, we'll see just a glimpse of the heaven on earth,
in which we live.

Key Points

1. God is not in us. We are in God.
2. To find our self, we must lose our self. This requires a leap of faith, *shraddha, into the truth.*
3. Brahman is the neutral witness of all creation.
4. When I have the *experience* of myself as the Observer, Atman, in daily practice, and I realize that what I am experiencing is also that which brings forth all others, then my awareness of my oneness with all life becomes a *concrete experience.*
5. When we surrender to our Divine nature, our security is complete.
6. When we offer our suffering, or tapas, to God we are following the impulse toward wholeness. We become porcelain in the heat of the kiln needing nothing but our God.
7. No matter how evil, hurtful or unconscious we have been, with firm resolve and pure devotion we can be transformed. This is the blessing in karma and the gift in grace.

Terms

Tapas (*Tah*-pas) suffering — burning — spiritual austerities

Personal Reflection

1. Write the "greatest of secrets" in your own words.
2. How strong or weak is shraddha in you at this time? Do you recognize occurrences which affect the quality of your sincere belief?
3. How do you understand the notion of losing your self to find your Self?
4. When was a time you experienced life as a banquet? And, when was a time you found yourself starving? Can you say how each of these experiences informed you?
5. What does it say to you to *offer your suffering to God?*
6. How do you interpret the notion of grace?

What Is To Be Realized about the Nature of Brahman:
Compassion in the Heart of All Creation

It is better to see God in everything
than to try and figure it out.

—NEEM KAROLI BABA

CHAPTER 10

Ordinary Divinity

As God, Brahman, is the Source of all, it is not a matter of *getting* God from the outside but *allowing* God to emerge from the inside. Using buddhi, or discriminating intellect, we step into tapas, the fire, to become holy ash—to burn away the rust—allowing our innate beauty to shine. Here, darkness is removed with the great light of wisdom, *jnanam.* Here all is extraordinarily ordinary.

Slokas 1–5

The Blessed One spoke:

10.1 Once more, Arjuna, listen to my supreme word, which I will here declare to you, since it pleases you to hear it, and since my desire is for your welfare.

10.2 The hosts of the gods do not know my origins at all, nor do the great seers, for I am the source of these gods and great seers.

10.3 A man who knows that I am unborn and without beginning, the great lord of all worlds, is free from all delusions and among mortals is released from all evils.

10.4 Insight, knowledge, freedom from delusion; patience, truth, self-control,

and peace; pleasure and pain, coming into being and passing away; also
fear and fearlessness;

10.5   Non-violence, equanimity, contentment; austerity, generosity, glory
and shame – all of these conditions that all beings experience, in all of
their varieties, arise from me alone.

Within the transient expression of God, prakriti, all is allowed, because
this is the schoolhouse for Souls. Duality being the nature of prakriti, we
are provided with constant choice, creating an optimum environment for
learning. This is why we see the dualities of *pleasure and pain*, *fear and
fearlessness* and *glory and shame* listed in Slokas 10.4 and 10.5. Those who
have studied Patanjali's "Eight Limbs of Yoga" will recognize truth, *satyam*,
in Sloka 10.4, and non-violence, *ahimsa*, in Sloka 10.5, as the first two of
five *Yamas*, or restraints, of the first limb.

Satyam and ahimsa, truth and non-violence, have a special relationship
when viewed within the context of what I call our *emotional feedback loop*.
Pause and remember a time when you were not honest with yourself or
another and, in the moment, *you knew*. Can you remember how it felt in
your body? In my experience, it has felt like a constriction or tightening
in my solar plexus. It doesn't feel good. My body immediately registers
my dishonesty with myself. Simply, when I am not truthful, I do harm to
myself as I also do harm to others. This is why the Buddha said, "If you
truly loved yourself you could never hurt another." And, whether consciously or unconsciously, I create all this misery via the most precious gift
of all – free will. I choose to pick up the boomerang. I choose to throw it.
And the law of karma returns it to me in straight order. This is the rod in
the 23rd Psalm.

Now, pause and remember a time when, though difficult, you spoke a
great truth to yourself or another – perhaps something you'd been avoiding or a secret you'd been hiding. Though emotionally difficult, such
moments have opened my solar plexus and have left me breathing more
freely. When I am being *true*, I love and serve myself as I also love and
serve others. The truth may or may not *feel good*, to us or to the other,
yet, it is always *freeing*. This truth is the eternal *devotion* of God, not the
transient *emotion* of the moment.

In order to live more often in *devotion*, it is important to be in touch with our *emotional feedback loop* so we may transform the harm and injury we do to our self and to others. I know that my not-so-fun moments of hurt-filled *r*eactions are my greatest teachers—hands down—because they show me clearly where it is I need to work. What anger needs to be confessed? What hurt needs to be healed? What fear needs to be faced?

And, as we are willing to sit with our darkness, the fear, the hurt and pain dissipate like clouds clearing, and right *there*, the Light shines, *as it always has*. This is grace.

Walking through valleys of my shadow or darkness, I have found myself humble, empty and, oh so grateful to, finally, rest on holy ground. Here, the Light of all lights warms me. Here, I am supported and carried. Here, I remember, *I live in the heart of God*.

Sloka 6

10.6 The seven great seers of ancient times and the four ancestors of man originated in me, born from my mind. All of these beings in the world are their descendents.

Seers, here, refers to *rishis*. In *The Living Gita: The Complete Bhagavad Gita and Commentary*, Swami Satchidananda writes, "The seven rishis represent the seven planes of consciousness." At the highest level are the *devas*, the gods. These devas are part of creation, and as such, are not the Absolute Supreme Godhead. There are also different levels of higher and lower gods. He goes on to explain that the second level is the human level, the third level is the animal level, the fourth, the birds, the fifth, the reptiles, the sixth, the aquatic creatures, and the seventh level is the inanimate or stationary.

The *four ancestors* Swami Satchidananda describes as *manus*, or law-givers. They are the ancient founders of humanity, aspects of the Absolute God, functioning to create and give order to the different levels of creation.

Sloka 7

10.7 Whoever comes to know this power [vibhuti] of mine and the disciplined use [yoga] of it, as it truly is, will thus come to discipline himself with unwavering yoga. There is no doubt about this.

Vibhuti means dissolving power or holy ash. In the crucible of self-acceptance, we transform emotion to devotion, dissolving into the One.

Slokas 8–10

10.8 I am the origin of all this and from me all this unfolds. Men of insight who have realized this therefore worship me, filled as they are with my presence.

10.9 Their thoughts are on me. Their life-breaths [pranas] go from them to me. They enlighten each other about me and they constantly tell the traditional tales about me. Such things please and comfort them.

10.10 Because they worship me with unfailing discipline and with love, I give to them this yoga of insight by which they will come to me.

Because they worship me with unfailing discipline and with love (Sloka 10.10). One of the most heartfelt expressions of worshiping with unfailing discipline and love is the following excerpt from the CD *Truth is the Only Profound—Meditative Readings from the Wisdom-Teaching of Ruchira Avatar Adi Da Samraj*, track 6, "The Essence of Devotion":

If there is not the quality of heartfelt devotion to Me—the Radiant Self,
then even intelligent understanding of the teaching
commitment to discipline and compassionate service of others
cannot cleanse and relieve the Soul of its urges
toward fulfillment in the phenomenal realms—high or low.

How can I be loved
if the hair does not stand on end when there is contemplation of me?
How can I be loved
if the heart does not melt in my presence?
How can I be loved
if tears of joy do not pass freely from the eyes
when I am standing there?

If I am Love,
then the entire body-mind is filled by that Love.
If my devotee is filled by Me through Love Communion,

his voice often falters and chokes with the emotion of Love.
Because he always dwells in contemplation of me at the heart,
he often weeps—and suddenly laughs.
He sings aloud. He always speaks of Me. He dances with joy.
Even all his movements are a dance of joy in Love.

Gold can be made pure only through submission to fire.
Just so, the Soul is purified and liberated from its deep urges
only when it submits to self-transcendent Love Communion with me.
Such a devotee is awakened through essential unity with Me
and his ecstatic presence serves the purification of the entire world.

Awakened, our mind is still and our heart wide open. We sing aloud and
dance with joy. And, the devas sing.

Sloka 11

10.11 So out of compassion for them, I destroy that darkness of theirs that is
born of ignorance, with the shining light of knowledge. All the while I
remain within myself, in my true state.

Sloka 10.11 is a key Sloka. It is only with the heart, *compassion*, born of the
devotion of the One, we *shine the light of knowledge*. Such light *destroys that
darkness born of ignorance*. The manas mind tends to get stuck in layers of
story and explanation. The devotional heart cuts through the emotional
story like a laser. The clouds of fear dissipate and the sun shines through.
This is Truth. This is wisdom.

And it frees everyone in sight.

Slokas 12–18

Arjuna spoke:

10.12 You are the supreme Brahman, the supreme foundation; and the
supreme purifier as well. You are the human spirit [purusha] eternal and
divine; the unborn primordial god and lord;

10.13 All of the seers say this of you, and the divine sage Narada too, and
Asita Devala, and Vyasa also. And now you yourself tell me that this
is so.

10.14   All of this that you have told me, Krishna, I accept it as true. Indeed,
        neither the gods nor the demons know, Lord, your manifest form.

10.15   O best of spirits, you alone know yourself [atman] by means of your
        self alone! O source and lord of all beings! O god of gods, lord of the
        world!

10.16   Please explain to me completely these divine powers of the self, the
        very powers by means of which you dwell in these worlds, pervading
        them.

10.17   Here I am meditating incessantly on you, great yogin! How should I
        understand you? And what are the many states of being, Lord, in which
        I should conceive of you?

10.18   Krishna, tell me more, and in full detail, of your yoga and its powers, for
        I have not had enough of listening to the nectar of your words!

Arjuna is still stalling with all his questions. Krishna continues to show
tolerance and patience and accommodates. Sometimes, things need to be
cultivated in order to come to full bloom. We will discuss this in depth in
the next chapter.

Krishna begins his listing of manifestations in Sloka 10.20 with *I am
the self, Atman, that resides in the heart of all creatures.* Here, again, is the
eternal sun behind all our changing weather patterns, the Observer, witness, devotion of all, *us.*

Krishna offers a long list, yet, just a sampling, of his manifestations.
They speak for themselves. Please see *Terms* for help with pronunciation.

Slokas 19–41

The Blessed Lord spoke:

10.19   Come, then, and I will tell you about the divine powers of my self,
        starting from the most important ones. But as for full detail concerning
        me, Arjuna, there is no end!

10.20   I am the self [atman] that resides in the heart of all beings. I am their
        beginning and their middle and their end.

10.21   Among the gods of heaven I am Vishnu. Among the celestial lights I am
        the radiant sun. I am lightning among the gods of the storm. And I am
        the moon among the stars.

10.22   Among the Vedas I am the Samaveda [the book of songs]. Among the gods I am Indra, their king. Among the senses I am the mind and among the sentient I am consciousness.

10.23 Among the terrifying deities I am gentle Shiva, and among demons and devils I am the lord of wealth. Among the bright gods of space I am Agni, god of fire, and among great mountains I am Meru.

10.24 Arjuna, know that I am the foremost among domestic priests, Brihaspati. Among generals I am Skanda, the god of war, and I am the ocean among the waters.

10.25 Among the great seers I am Bhrigu, and among words I am the sacred syllable OM. Among sacrifices I am the chanted prayer [japa]. Among mountain ranges I am the Himalaya.

10.26 Among all trees, I am the sacred fig tree, and among the divine seers I am Narada. Among the celestial musicians I am Chitraratha, their chief, and among perfected saints I am Kapila.

10.27 Among horses know that I am Indra's stallion, born of immortality. Among elephants I am Indra's elephant, and among all men I am king.

10.28 Among weapons I am the vajra, Indra's thunderbolt, and among milk-cows I am the wish-granting Cow-of-Plenty, and as for procreation I am Kandarpa, the god of love. I am prince Vasuki among snakes.

10.29 I am Ananta, the cosmic water-snake, and Varuna, lord of the gods of the sea. And I am Aryaman, lord of the ancestors, and I am also the lord of the dead, Yama, chief among those who lead to the otherworld.

10.30 Among demons I am Prahlada, the pious. Among record-keepers I am time. Among wild beasts I am the lion, their king, and among birds I am Vishnu's Garuda.

10.31 Among the things that purify I am the purifying wind. Among men bearing arms I am Rama. Among sea-monsters I am the crocodile, and among rivers I am the Ganges.

10.32 Arjuna, I am the beginning and the end of all created worlds, and their middle as well. Among sciences I am the science of the self, and I am the argument among those who argue.

10.33 Among syllables I am the syllable A. Among word combinations I am the couple [pair]. I am also imperishable time, the creator facing in all directions.

10.34 And I am death that carries all away, and also the birth of those who will be born. Among feminine nouns [also feminine qualities] I am Fame and Fortune and Speech; Memory also, and Wisdom and Stability and Patience.

10.35   Among the Vedic chants I am the high chant. Among the meters I am the gayatri meter. Among the months I am Margashirsha [the first month], and among the seasons I am the flower-bearer, spring.

10.36   Among gamblers who cheat I am the game of dice. Among the glorious I am glory. I am the conquest and I am the exertion and I am the courage of the courageous.

10.37   Among the clan of the Vrishnis I am Krishna, among the Pandavas I am Arjuna. Among the holy hermits I am Vyasa, and among the ancient poets I am Ushanas.

10.38   I am the rod of the punishers. I am the policy of the politicians. I am also the silence of secret doctrines. And I am the wisdom that wise men know.

10.39   And beyond that, I am the seed of all beings, Arjuna. Nothing – neither what moves nor what does not move – could exist without me.

10.40   Arjuna, there is no end to my divine powers. But I have shown you the extent of my power by using a few examples.

10.41   Understand that whatever displays divine power, or great beauty, or enormous vigor, arises from but a small portion of my glory.

Sloka 10.35 references the *gayatri* meter or mantra. About six years ago, I studied Thomas Ashley-Farrand's *MANTRA: Sacred Words of Power* and was completely captivated by the long version of this "mother" of all mantras. The vast majority of people who chant this mantra chant the short version, but he chants the long version in his course as this was the version first taught to him. I started a 40-day practice, chanting a minimum of 108 times a day—often with many more repetitions. Close to a year later, it still was not done with me! I simply could not stop. Impossible.

Important to the discussion here is that this mantra is the perfect and complete dial-up connection to the One. Thomas Ashley-Farrand explains that there are seven *lokas*, or luminous spheres, corresponding to each of the seven subtle nerve or energy centers of the body, the *chakras*. Each loka can be summarized in a single vibration which is invoked by a syllable. To intone the syllable is to bring the vibration of that sphere into oneself. (The lokas are referred to in Chapter 18, Sloka 18.71 as the *luminous worlds*.)

The Sanskrit syllables of the Gayatri mantra contain the essential vibrations of all seven lokas and, according to Thomas Ashley-Farrand, can be generally translated, "O self-effulgent light that has given birth to all the lokas, who is worthy of worship and appears through the orbit of the sun, illumine our intellect."

Both the long and the short form of the Gayatri mantra are presented below. Please see *Terms* for help with pronunciation.*

LONG FORM:

Om Bhuh Om Bhuvaha Om Swaha

Om Maha Om Janaha Om Tapaha Om Satyam

Om Tat Savitur Varenyam

Bhargo Devasya Dhimahi

Dhiyo Yo Naha Prachodayat

SHORT FORM:

Om Bhuh Bhuvaha Swaha

Om Tat Savitur Varenyam

Bhargo Devasya Dhimahi

Dhiyo Yo Naha Prachodayat

Chanting this mantra opens us to the *experience* of the One—to the *experience* of our Self.

Sloka 42

10.42   But what use is it to you, Arjuna, to know all of this? With one small portion of myself I have propped up this entire world, and still I stand here.

Krishna is letting Arjuna know that he's approaching full bloom! Sometimes others need to hold for us—see in us—that which we're not yet able to hold and see for ourselves. It's a beautiful gift. It's what I held for Jacob. It's what God holds for us.

And, we are held, until ready, as we will see in the following chapter.

Key Points

1. We "allow" the experience of God. There is nothing to "get."
2. We step into tapas, the fire, to become holy ash—to burn away the rust—allowing our innate beauty to shine through.

---

* The general translation offered above is suitable for our purpose here. A translation of the specific phrases may be found in Thomas Ashley-Farrand's *MANTRA: Sacred Words of Power.*

3. The relationship between satyam and ahimsa assures we cannot be untruthful or hurt one another without it manifesting in us.

4. The *emotional feedback loop* is a key element in recognizing where it is we need to work.

5. God is compassion—*the true self in the heart of all creatures.* This is why the devotional heart can see right through the emotional story.

6. The Gayatri Mantra is called the "mother" of all mantras. It is our perfect and complete dial-up connection to the One.

7. Although Arjuna knows all he needs to know, he still continues to question. More cultivation, or readiness, is needed.

8. Krishna is patient and holds for Arjuna what he is not yet ready to hold for himself. And, so it is with us, when *we hold our selves* with compassionate patience.

Terms

Satyam (*Saht*-yahm) truth

Ahimsa (Ah-*him*-sah) non-violence

Yamas (*Yah*-mahs) restraints in Patanjali's "Eight Limbs of Yoga"

Manus (*Mah*-noos) law-givers

THE SAMPLING OF MANIFESTATIONS — SLOKAS 10.21–41

Vishnu (*Vish*-new) sustainer in the Hindu masculine trinity

Samaveda (*Sah*-mah-*vay*-dah) one of the four Vedas written for liturgical purposes

Indra (*In*-drah) king of the Gods

Shiva (*Shi*-vah) transformer or destroyer in the Hindu masculine trinity

Agni (*Ahg*-nee) god of fire

Meru (*May*-roo) sacred Mt. Meru; highest place of divine consciousness in the body

Brihaspati (Bree-*hahs*-pah-tee) priest of the devas

Skanda (*Skahn*-dah) god of war

Bhrigu (*Bree*-goo) rishi who dwells constantly on the super-consciousness plane

Japa (*Jah*-pah) mantra repetition

Narada (*Nah*-rah-dah) a great sage

Chitraratha (*Chit*-rah-*rah*-tah) chief of celestial musicians
Kapila (*Kah*-pi-lah) founder of Samkhya philosophy; a great sage
Vajra (*Vah*-jrah) heavenly thunder bolt
Kandarpa (Kahn-*dar*-pah) god of romantic love
Vasuki (Vah-*soo*-kee) king of snakes
Ananta (Ah-*nahn*-tah) five-headed king of water snakes
Varuna (*Vah*-roo-nah) lord of the gods of the sea
Aryaman (*Are*-yah-mahn) lord of the ancestors
Yama (*Yah*-mah) lord of death
Prahlada (*Prah*-lah-dah) the pious demon
Garuda (*Gar-roo*-dah) half-man, half-bird carrier of Vishnu
Rama (*Rah*-mah) an incarnation of Vishnu
Ganges (*Gahn*-jees) sacred river Ganges
Gayatri (*Gah*-yah-tree) mother of all mantras; most sacred verse of
   Rig Veda
Margashirsha (*Mar*-gah-*sheer*-sh-ah) month in the beginning of the
   Hindu calendar
Vrishnis (V*rish*-nees) clan of Krishna
Vyasa (V*yah*-sah) author of the *Mahabharata*
Ushana (*Oo*-shah-nah) poet with great intuitive power

INTRODUCTORY TERMS AND THE GAYATRI MANTRA
   Gayatri (*Gah*-yah-tree) mother of all mantras
   Lokas (*Low*-kahs) luminous spheres
   Chakras (*Chah*-krahs) subtle nerve or energy centers of the body

The accents in the following mantra may vary with the actual chanting:

Om (*Oh*-m or *Au*-m) **Bhuh** (Boo)
Om Bhuvaha (*Boo*-vah-ha)
Om Swaha (Swah-ha)
Om Maha (*Mah*-ha)
Om Janaha (*Jah*-nah-ha)
Om Tapaha (*Tah*-pah-ha)
Om Satyam (*Sah*-tyam)
Om Tat Savitur Varenyam (Taht *Sah*-vee-toor Var-*ayn*-yam)
Bhargo Devasya Dhimahi (*Bar*-go Day-*vah*-sya *Dee*-mah-hee)
Dhiyo Yo Naha Prachodayat (Dee-yo Yo Nah-ha Prah-*cho*-day-yaht)

Personal Reflection

1. Describe the relationship between satyam and ahimsa in your own words.

2. If God is the *true self in the heart of all creatures,* where does evil come from?

3. Describe a time when some darkness of ignorance within you was removed by the great light of wisdom.

4. What parts within yourself are you currently cultivating?

What Is To Be Realized about the Nature of Brahman:
Righteousness That Defeats Ignorance

To everything there is a season and a
time to every purpose under heaven.

—ECCLESIASTES 3 :1

CHAPTER II

Ripened Fruit

The fruit falls from the tree in its own time. No matter how much the desiring mind may want enlightenment, we cannot force spiritual development. This is because, as we have seen, there is nothing to *get*, only something to *allow*. Remember, we don't have to create the sun. It's already there. It *is* our job to remove the self-imposed clouds.

Slokas 1-4
Arjuna spoke:

11.1 You have explained this sublime secret doctrine concerning the self, as a kindness to me. Your words have freed me from my delusion.

11.2 I have heard in detail of the arising and the passing away of all beings. Krishna, your eyes are like lotus petals and your greatness is unending!

11.3 I want to see you as you have described yourself, Krishna, as the lord of the world and the supreme person.

11.4 If you think that it is possible for me to see you as you really are, Lord and Master of yoga, then please show your eternal self to me!

Arjuna acknowledges understanding the most profound mysteries. Yet, his understanding falls short of delivering the deeper mystery of *experience*. So,

he asks to *see* the *lord of the world* (Sloka 11.3). We sense a hint of reserva-
tion in the request in Sloka 11.4, as Arjuna wonders if Krishna deems it
possible for him to see the eternal self.

It is this deeper knowing, often appearing in the form of self-question-
ing, that is informing Arjuna and can inform us as well. How often *after* we
have received, unceremoniously, the unexpected spiritual two-by-four do
we say, "I *knew* that was coming." We know but we don't know. But truth
will always find its expression. It's why we can't lose the war.

We want enlightenment. We don't want the work. We fall prey to the
wanting mind that moves us out of the eternal moment into our latest
fantasy. Arjuna's deeper knowing tries to inform him that he is asking
for something prematurely. That he's plucking the fruit before its time.
But, the wanting mind tricks him, convincing him there's a shortcut to
Nirvana—that he can become a beautiful pot off the Potter's wheel without enduring the fire of the kiln—that he can reach the summit without
the climb. Do we not all wish it so?

This is why our daily spiritual practice is so crucial to our journey
Home. It is the precious time of day we give ourselves to tune the dial on
the radio of our minds, away from all the mind-chatter static, to the clear
signal of Truth.

Slokas 5–8

The Blessed One spoke:

11.5   Arjuna, look at the forms that I take, hundreds of them and thousands
       of them! So many divine forms! So many colors and so many shapes!

11.6   Look at them all: gods of heaven, gods of light, terrifying gods; the
       celestial twins and the storm gods. Look at these wonders, Arjuna, so
       many, never seen before!

11.7   Look now at this whole world, here in one place, both what moves and
       what does not move, all of it here in my body, Arjuna! And whatever
       else you wish to see!

11.8   But you cannot see me with your own eye alone. Here, I give you a
       divine eye. Now look at my majestic yoga!

Arjuna needs glasses to perceive this *majestic* vision (Sloka 11.8). His sight
is not yet matured to behold the vision he's asked to be shown. He's not
yet ready to see all parts of *himself,* the light *and* the dark. So, Krishna gives
him a *divine eye,* or spiritual sight.

Yogi Bhajan said, "A person of God consciousness can display his entire personality before the world without fear." Why? Because enlightenment is nothing more than the full embrace of all of our parts—the light *and* the dark. Only then, are we free from the mental, emotional and energetic chains of hiding. Only then, are we free to be our Self.

Slokas 9–14

Sanjaya spoke:

11.9   O my king, thus he spoke, Krishna, the great lord of yoga, and also Vishnu! And he unveiled his supreme majestic form to Arjuna.

11.10 Krishna in this form was a great wonder to see, with many mouths and many eyes, with many divine ornaments, and many divine weapons raised up in his arms.

11.11 Divine also were the garlands and the robes that he wore. Divine were the perfumes and the ointments. His divinity was an endless profusion of wonders. And in every direction were his faces turned!

11.12 If the light of a thousand suns were to arise in heaven suddenly – as at the dawn of a new age – it would be something like the radiance of this great soul!

11.13 There Arjuna saw the entire world, the whole world in all of its infinite manifestations, drawn together as one in the body of the god of gods.

11.14 And so, thus seized with wonder, the hair on his body bristling with ecstasy, Arjuna joined his hands together in reverence, bowed his head to the god, and said . . .

And, *Arjuna bowed his head* and so do we in moments of *ecstasy* (Sloka 11.14). And, as his vision sharpens, he first beholds the more splendid aspects of Krishna, the Divine personified.

Slokas 15–19

Arjuna spoke:

11.15 I see all of the gods within your body, O god of gods! I see the whole array of beings – the lord Brahma sitting on his lotus seat, all of the seers, and the celestial serpents!

11.16 Countless arms, countless bellies, countless mouths and eyes – I see you everywhere in this infinite variety of forms! I see no ending to you, and no middle, and no beginning. You are the lord of all things and the form of all things!

11.17 I see you here, wearing your crown, bearing your mace and your discus.
I see you full of light, your radiance pouring forth in all directions. I
see you everywhere, but it is a sight that is hard to bear. Immeasurable
light of flames and fires and suns and lightning!

11.18 You are the imperishable, the supreme, the goal of all knowledge. You
are the world's finest treasure-house. You are the unfailing guardian of
unchanging dharma. I now understand: you are the eternal spirit in man.

11.19 I now see that you are without beginning or middle or end, that your
power is infinite, that your arms are beyond number, that the sun
and the moon are your eyes. I now see that your mouth is a blazing
sacrificial fire and that your radiance burns all this world.

Arjuna is given the gift of seeing the entire manifold universe. The
Splendor of all that is splendid. The Doer in all that is done. The silent
Impulse birthing each breath. The Message in silence. The Awe beyond
knowing. The supreme Self, great exalted one, or *Mahatman.* And all he
can do is fall in adoration before the Lord.

It is so sweet to have moments of total immersion in that which is
just not possible to describe. And, what an adventure life becomes when we
truly experience being guided and unfolded to our greatest joy in the
service of all. How tempting it is to think we must be on the right track
to enlightenment in moments when it all feels and seems *so good.* But the
mind easily confuses *emotion* with *devotion,* so when it feels *good,* it thinks
it's getting spiritual.

Steven Levine has a great description of this in his book *A Gradual
Awakening.* He writes, "I used to think that peak experiences were a sign
of attainment. I'd have some new experience and sometime later have
some other insight, and think, 'Oh, it's really paying off. I'm getting closer
now!'" But, later he writes, " . . . it turns out there are hundreds and hundreds of so-called 'peak experiences.' And they're all just experiences."

Getting spiritual has nothing to do with feeling any particular emotion.
The litmus test is being able to hold the full range of our experience—the
joy *and* the sorrow—within the crucible of devotion. Here, is where we
learn to sit at the feet of our life and be taught. Here, we understand that
time in the kiln makes what, at first, seems sour, later sweet. Here, the soul
rejoices as the ego cries. Here, we can humbly receive the staff that guides
and the rod that disciplines because the Lord is the Shepherd of our days.

Arjuna is ready for the staff, but not the rod.

Slokas 20-22

11.20   For you alone pervade this space between heaven and earth and all of
        the directions in it. The three worlds gaze upon this your wondrous
        and terrible body, Krishna, and they tremble!

11.21   For these multitudes of gods enter you. Some of them are terrified.
        They hold their hands in reverence to you and they sing your praises.
        Multitudes of seers and perfected sages chant to you in copious rounds
        of recitation.

11.22   Terrifying gods and heavenly gods, bright gods and perfected gods;
        universal gods, the divine twins, storm gods and ancestral spirits; hosts
        of celestial musicians, sprites, demons and saints – they all look upon
        you now and are seized with wonder.

But, the vision continues, coming into full focus. And, the rod descends.
Arjuna sees the war in all its color and horror.

Slokas 23-31

11.23   Krishna, when the worlds see this massive form of yours, with its many
        mouths and eyes, with its many arms and legs and feet, its many bellies
        and terrible tusks – they look and they tremble, as I do now!

11.24   I see your body as it touches the clouds, shining a rainbow of colors,
        your large gaping mouth, your wide flaming eyes. In my inmost self I
        tremble. I cannot find my resolve, Krishna. I cannot find peace.

11.25   I see your mouths and your wide gaping tusks which look to me like the
        fires at the end of time. I am disoriented now and I can find no shelter.
        Krishna, lord of the gods and the world's repose, have mercy!

11.26   And now all of those sons of Dhritarashtra, together with their host
        of kings, Bhishma, Drona, and Karna, the son of the charioteer, are
        here – and our best warriors are as well.

11.27   They rush headlong past your gaping, terrifying tusks into your
        countless mouths. Some of them seem to hang lifeless, caught between
        your teeth, with their heads crushed.

11.28   Like the countless river torrents that flow back toward the sea, those
        heroes in the worlds of men pour into your blazing mouths.

11.29   Like the moths that rush frantically to the burning flame, and to their

> destruction, so these worlds rush in a frenzy into your mouths, to their
> destruction also.
>
> 11.30 Vishnu, you devour everything, all these worlds, licking at them with
> your flaming tongues. You fill the whole world with your brilliancies. O
> your terrible flames, how they burn!
>
> 11.31 Tell me, who are you, O lord of such terrible form? Let me pay homage
> to you. O best of gods, have mercy! I wish to know you as you were in
> the beginning, because I do not understand your present course.

Each morning, when we get up for spiritual practice, we, too, begin to
unveil all our not-so-pretty parts. Here, we begin the practice of offering
ourselves, *darshan*, the blessing of true seeing. And, as our sight develops,
we start to cut through the illusions we have so dearly held about who
we think we are and about how we want others to be. And seeing *what is*,
the desiring mind has nothing to hold onto. Slowly, we begin to rest in
moments of equanimity.

And, in such moments, God within *and* without, is revealed.

But the desiring mind is not so easily tamed and our deep yearning can
easily lead us astray, wanting that which has not yet been cultivated. This
one I know well. Many years ago, like most, I began my spiritual journey
in firm pursuit of a spiritual teacher. I was very interested in the Native
American culture at the time and felt I had some potential for being a
healer, so I decided I should be a shaman. No matter that there was little
to no evidence to support such a notion. No matter that, at that time, I
had never been in a sweat lodge, endured a vision quest nor even been
out in the woods overnight alone. Still, I just knew I was to be a shaman
and that was that.

About that time, I read a wonderful book called *Native Healer, Initiation
into an Ancient Art* by Medicine Grizzlybear Lake. In all of my readings,
nothing had moved me like his words. I just knew I had met my teacher.
So, I wrote him and asked if he would consider being my spiritual teacher.
I was, however, careful to point out that, while I was totally motivated to
be his student, I could only be available to do assignments part-time, as
I still had young children at home and had to work to help support my
family!

What a chuckle he must have had receiving a letter from someone
applying for the job of part-time shaman! How kind he was even to

respond and kinder still was his reply. He shared with me all the years he had lived around his teacher before his actual training began and about the many years of study and training that followed. He referred me to some local resources and wished me well on my journey. I was not happy. Yet, over the years, I have grown to have many a chuckle at myself remembering this incident.

I wasn't even spiritually mature enough to warrant a good scolding! Gratefully, I was spared the worst. He could have sent me into the woods for a week or given me some assignment that would have left me feeling, as Arjuna, in Sloka 11.27, like I, too, was rushing headlong into the *terrifying tusks* of death!

Today, I continue to appreciate the role of a true spiritual teacher. It is their job to reveal us to ourselves and to help us enter the shadows of our fear so we may be transformed. They love us most because they need us least.

Slokas 32-34

The Blessed One spoke:

11.32   I am time, the agent of the world's destruction, now grown old and set in motion to destroy the worlds. Even without you, all of these warriors arrayed in opposing battle-formation will cease to exist

11.33   Therefore, rise up and seek your glory! Conquer your enemies and enjoy successful kingship! In fact, I have slain them all already long ago. Simply be the instrument by my side!

11.34   Drona and Bhishma and Jayadratha, and Karna as well – and all of the other war heroes – have been killed by me already, so now you should kill them. Don't waver! Fight! And you will defeat your rivals in this war!

One of my favorite sayings from the Bible is Romans 8:28: *And we know that all things work together for good to them that love God, to them that are called according to [his] purpose.* If we remember that the law of karma is taking care of everything, we can trust Krishna's words, in Sloka 11.33, that the enemy warriors have already been slain. This means that darkness can only manifest darkness. Arjuna, pure in heart and desiring only to do his duty for God's purpose, can only win. So, why not stand up and be famous? It's perfectly fine as long as we remember the *it's not about us* part.

Sometimes, we're more afraid of our light than our shadow. This is expressed in the 1994 inaugural speech by Nelson Mandela:

> Our deepest fear is not that we are inadequate. Our deepest fear is that we are powerful beyond measure. It is our light, not our darkness, that most frightens us. We ask ourselves, "Who am I to be brilliant, gorgeous, talented and fabulous?" Actually, who are you not to be? You are a child of God. Your playing small doesn't serve the world. There's nothing enlightened about shrinking so that other people won't feel insecure around you. We were born to make manifest the glory of God that is within us. It's not just in some of us; it's in everyone. And as we let our own light shine, we unconsciously give other people permission to do the same. As we are liberated from our own fear, our presence liberates others.

When Krishna is our charioteer, we rise in full glory and bow in sweet gratitude.

Slokas 35-40

Sanjaya spoke:

11.35 Arjuna listened to Krishna's words. Trembling beneath his crown, he brought his hands together in homage and bowed, and again he spoke to Krishna. He stammered, overwhelmed by fear.

Arjuna spoke:

11.36 It is fitting, Krishna, that the world rejoices and devotes itself to praising you. The frightened demons flee in all directions. All of the hosts of perfected sages also pay homage.

11.37 And why shouldn't they pay homage to you, great soul – a creator more worthy than Brahman itself? You are the infinite lord of the gods and the world's resting place. You are the imperishable, both what exists and what does not exist, and beyond them both.

11.38 You are the first among all gods, the ancient spirit. You are the final resting place of all things. You are both the knower and the known and the world's supreme foundation. Krishna, you reach everywhere into all of this world!

11.39 You are the god of the wind, and you are death. You are fire, and the god of the waters and of the moon. You are the lord of creation, the grandfather of creation. Homage to you, a thousand homages to you! Homage and again homage to you!

11.40 Homage before you and homage behind you, let there be homage to you, the all, on all sides! O Krishna, endless hero, your striving power is unmeasured. You embrace all of it, and indeed you are all of it!

Arjuna pays deep homage to his Lord. Humility is the only authentic response when we come face to face with our shadows. We're not so cocky anymore. And, as we learn to love and forgive ourselves, we naturally open to love and forgiving others the same.

We start to recognize *the first among all gods, the ancient spirit* (Sloka 11.38), the original, primal, eternal expression of God, *Adideva*, animating all the forces of nature as well as the human face. There is God in the wind, *Vayu*, fire, *Agni*, and water, *Varuna*.

And, there is God bagging our groceries.

Slokas 41-42

11.41 Whatever I may have said impulsively, thinking "this is my friend," addressing you "Hello Krishna, hello Yadava, hello my friend!" unaware as I was of your true greatness, whether out of carelessness or affection,

11.42 And if while joking I have said something offensive, while relaxing or resting or sitting or eating with you – whether alone or publicly – immeasurable Krishna, I seek your forgiveness.

Confidence is not cockiness. Confidence is equanimity.

Slokas 43-46

11.43 You are the father of the world of the things that move and the things that do not move. You are the world's guru, the best and most revered. Krishna, there is no one equal to you in the three worlds – so how could there be one greater?

11.44 Therefore I bow down and I prostrate this body. I seek grace from you, a lord to be revered above all others. Like a father to a son, like a friend to a friend, like a lover to the beloved – please, god, bear with me!

11.45 I have seen what no one else has seen before, and I am exhilarated, but my mind is shaken with fear. Krishna, please show me once again that body that I know so well. Lord of the gods, the world's refuge, be gracious!

11.46   I wish to see you again as you used to be, wearing your crown, bearing your mace and your discus. O Krishna of the thousand arms, true body of all this world, return to that four-armed body that I know so well!

And, how we, too, would just like to feel *normal* again, quickly, when we have come face-to-face with one of our not-so-pretty parts. It's just the law of karma giving us the results of our actions—conscious *and* unconscious. The Sikhs have a great song for remembering, in these difficult times, that the Soul *is* rejoicing as the ego cries. It's called *Captain Karma*. In part, it sounds like this:

> They call him Captain Karma, he's the Lord's own right-hand man.
> He never spares the rod when you mess up on the job,
> he's the one who gets you canned.
> Now you just can't stop that old cosmic cop when the warrant's out on you,
> There's no place you can hide, the man's a bona fide
> detective for the Wha Guroo.

> Well, it ain't so weird, you see, the way it's geared
> is what you owes is what you pays.
> So don't blame this guy when trouble comes from the sky.
> He just does what the Lord wills.
> The Guru's your protector when you meet the Collector,
> say "Sat Naam" and pay your bill.

Recall from Chapter 2, *this* is why Krishna is smiling!

Slokas 47-51

The Blessed One spoke:

11.47   As a kindness to you, Arjuna, and as an expression of my yogic power, I have revealed this my supreme form to you. It is radiant, universal, endless, and primordial, and with the exception of you alone, no one has ever seen it before.

11.48   I can be seen in this form, in the world of men, only by you, Arjuna, hero of the Kurus! The Vedas will not help, nor will sacrifices, nor will much studying or gift-giving. The performance of ritual will not help, nor will terrible austerities!

11.49 Do not waver. Do not be confused. Now you have seen this my
terrifying form – for such it is! But let go of this fear. Put your mind at
ease. Look again at this body of mine that you know so well.

Sanjaya spoke:

11.50 Krishna spoke these words to Arjuna, and revealed himself again in his
familiar form. And by returning to this gentle form again the great soul
gave that frightened man a moment to regain his breath.

Arjuna spoke:

11.51 Krishna, once again I can see this human, this gentle, form of yours.
Now I am settled down, in control of my thoughts. I am back to my
normal state.

Sloka 11.48 reminds us that we can sacrifice, study, give to others, perform
ritual, even engage in austerities, yet, none of these things will gain us the
vision of the Lord of Lords. This is because the door to the full embrace
of all our parts, the light *and* the dark, is only found in equanimity—in our
daily meditation practice. And, remember, Arjuna represents equanimity.
This is why only he can receive the vision.

Nothing replaces our time in the kiln. Nothing.

Slokas 52–55

The Blessed One spoke:

11.52 The gods themselves constantly yearn for a view of this body of mine
which you have now seen. Indeed, it is a body that is very hard to look
on.

11.53 I am not to be seen in this form, and as you have now seen me, through
the study of the Vedas, nor through the practice of austerities. Nor is
gift-giving of any use. Nor is sacrifice.

11.54 It is only through devotion [bhakti] that I can be known in this way.
Only through devotion to me alone can I be known, and seen as I really
am, and entered into.

11.55 Whoever performs his actions for my sake, whoever makes me his
highest goal, whoever devotes himself to me, without attachment and
without hostility toward anyone, Arjuna, such a man comes to me.

*Only through devotion to "me" alone can I be known, and seen as I really am,
and entered into* (Sloka 11.54). Is it possible that we could love *"ourselves"*
enough?

Let this be our only desire. It is, after all, our only *true* security. It's what makes everything else make sense. And, when all falls away, it's all that *really* matters.

In the following chapter, Krishna reveals to Arjuna the description of the true devotee.

Key Points

1. Enlightenment is not something we *get*. It's something we *allow*.
2. The *desiring* mind can lead us astray—wanting the fruit before it is ripe.
3. Enlightenment is nothing more or nothing less than the full embrace of *all* our parts.
4. Getting spiritual is about *devotion*—not *emotion*.
5. We are meant to be bold, beautiful and triumphant!
6. Only the humble response is authentic before the Lord.
7. The door to the majestic vision is only found in equanimity—in our daily meditation practice.
8. It's really about loving *ourselves*—enough.

Terms

Mahatman (Mah-*haht*-mahn) great exalted one
Darshan (*Dar*-shahn) true seeing or blessing
Adideva (Ah-dee-*day*-vah) the original One; Primal God
Vayu (*Veye*-yoo) god of wind

Personal Reflection

1. Recall a time when you *knew*, but did not know.
2. Has there been a "fruit" you plucked before its time?
3. What reaction do you have to being *powerful beyond measure?*
4. Can you recall a time when humility opened you to new awareness?
5. How challenging is it for you to love yourself—enough?

What Is To Be Realized about the Nature of Brahman:
Devotion

The devotee who with pure devotion
and faith seeks the unconditional love
of God, and who brings his actions into
harmony with divine law, will surely
receive the purifying, mitigating touch
of God.

— PARAMAHANSA YOGONANDA

CHAPTER 12

The True Devotee

The true devotee lives from the heart and sees the heart in all things. It is not an *emotional* place of ego and personal need. It is a *devotional* place of truth and freedom. And, more often, we start to see the sacred where once we only saw the mundane.

We start to see our neighbor as our self—and Love becomes the only possibility.

Slokas 1-5

Arjuna spoke:

12.1 There are some who are constantly disciplined, devotees who worship you. And there are others who devote themselves to the imperishable, the unmanifest. Which of these have the best knowledge of yoga?

The Blessed One spoke:

12.2 I consider them to be the best disciplined who focus their minds on me, who, constant in their discipline, worship me with the greatest faith.

12.3 But those who worship the imperishable, the unmanifest which is beyond words, which is found everywhere and is inconceivable, sublime, unmoving and firm,

12.4   who have gained complete control over the senses and equanimity
       toward all beings, rejoicing in the welfare of all beings, they also attain
       to me.

12.5   There is greater distress for those who have set their thoughts on the
       unmanifest, because it is difficult for those who are embodied to reach
       a goal that is indeed unmanifest.

If someone came to you and said, "Tell me about love," what would you
say? You might try to describe it. Explain the various types. Discuss the
many aspects and expressions. But, in the end, all your words would fall
short, seem incomplete or inadequate, because nothing can quite capture
the *experience* of love. This is why we need prakriti, the world of the senses,
to *experience* ourselves as manifestations of the Divine. And, through this
experience, we come to realize we always have been, are and always will
be, *Tat, that which we seek.* This is why Krishna tells Arjuna that those
who worship the unmanifested expression of the Divine choose the more
difficult way.

Slokas 6–12

12.6   But those who surrender all of their actions to me and who are focused
       on me alone, who meditate on me with yoga, and worship me,

12.7   I will lift them up out of the ocean of the cycle of death and rebirth,
       Arjuna, once they have set their thoughts on me.

12.8   Keep your mind fixed on me. Make your intelligence enter into me.
       Thus you will come to dwell in me, without question.

12.9   But if you cannot concentrate your thoughts firmly on me, then, Arjuna,
       try to reach me through the diligent practice of yoga.

12.10 And if you are incapable of this sort of practice then make it your goal
       to perform action for my sake. If you perform your ritual and social
       actions for my sake you will find success!

12.11 And if you are unable to do even that, then simply resort to me in yoga.
       Renounce the fruit of all of your actions. Restrain yourself, and act!

12.12 For, in fact, wisdom is better than practice, and meditation is better
       than wisdom. Renouncing the fruit of action is better than meditation,
       for from renunciation peace follows immediately.

Here, we are given clear instruction on how to proceed. *Keep your mind fixed on me* (Sloka 12.8). By tuning the dial on the radio of our minds, we keep ourselves tuned into the truth signal. Here, we invite the devotion within to shine through, transforming our dark places, leaving us just a little more light. But, most of us are still on the road to becoming accomplished trainers of our wayward minds. So, we need *diligent practice of yoga* (Sloka 12.9), or Sadhana. If spiritual practice is new to you, or if you're having trouble sustaining your commitment, I'd recommend committing to one 40-day practice at a time. It's a reasonable starting place. Who knows? Maybe a practice will catch you much like I was caught by the Gayatri Mantra. It's very sweet to get caught.

But, if a daily commitment seems a little more than you're able to do right now, just start by dedicating your day, a part of your day, or just one activity, to God. Try to remember the *it's not about me* part and you'll notice the wanting mind releasing personal expectations. I experience this as a kind of exhale. A calm settles, and peace, *shanti*, follows. This is how we practice *renunciation* (Slokas 12.11–12). And, it is a *practice*, one moment, one breath, at a time.

Ultimately, it is this practice, cultivated on our prayer mat and carried out into our day, that enables us to say, "OK, God, I am ready to offer my gifts in service to the greater good. I remember that *I am enough and I am nothing*. Thank you for this opportunity to be your instrument!" This is *tyaga*, renunciation that releases identification with the fruits of our actions. It's what's left at the end of the exhale.

Slokas 13–20

12.13   Let there be no hatred in you. Offer friendship and compassion to all living things. Give up thoughts of "I" and "mine." Accept both pleasure and sorrow alike, and endure all things with patience.

12.14   The yogin who is always content and self-restrained and firm in his resolve, and who directs his mind and his awareness [buddhi] upon me—he is my devotee and he is dear to me.

12.15   The world does not tremble in fear before him, nor does he tremble in fear before the world. He has freed himself from the disturbances of joy or impatience or fear, and so he is dear to me.

12.16 He is indifferent to circumstance. He is pure and capable. He is a detached witness, untroubled by events. He does not initiate new engagements – he is my devotee and he is dear to me.

12.17 He does not delight in things nor does he loathe them. He knows neither anguish nor longing. Indifferent to good fortune and to bad fortune alike, he is a man of devotion and he is dear to me.

12.18 In the presence of an enemy or a friend, he is impartial to both, just as he is in the presence of honor or dishonor, or heat or cold, or pleasure or sorrow. He is impartial and unattached.

12.19 A silent sage for whom blame and praise are the same, content with whatever happens, homeless, but firm in his mind, he is a man of devotion and he is dear to me.

12.20 In fact all who worship this divine nectar of dharma which I have now declared to you, all who have placed their faith in this teaching, all such devotees for whom I am the supreme goal are dear to me – even more!

These last Slokas tell us in clear, simple, terms exactly how we need to be and what it is we need to do. It's all here. Notice how many of the instructions require that we rise above duality:

Sloka 12.13: *Accept both pleasure and sorrow.* We receive the gifts of both.

Sloka 12.15: *He has freed himself from the disturbances of joy or impatience or fear.* We trade in fleeting emotional joy for eternal devotional joy.

Sloka 12.17: *Indifferent to good fortune and to bad fortune alike.* We carry our inner riches within us.

Sloka 12.18: *Impartial to enemy or friend, honor or dishonor, heat or cold, pleasure or sorrow.* We rest in equanimity.

Sloka 12.19: *and, for whom blame and praise are the same.* We sit humbly at the feet of our life to be taught.

This is how we become true devotees. It is how we become heaven on earth. But, again, just wanting is not enough. We are required to walk in faith with our God, *indifferent to circumstance; untroubled by events* (Sloka 12.16), particularly when we are unable to see the rationale for events or the *why* in the bigger picture. In these times, we are called to trust most of all that *all does work for good for those who love God.* And, more and more, we witness how it really is *not about us at all.*

A few years ago, I had an experience that provided just a glimpse into how our *maker and keeper,* the blessed Potter, shapes and molds our days for His purpose.

I am an interfaith minister and, for many years, have practiced mantra meditation using a rosary I bought at the Chimayo mission in New Mexico. I bought it because it had a picture of Mother Teresa on it and I am fond of calling it my Mother Teresa rosary. Although I am not a Catholic, her life has always been an inspiration to me and was the impulse for the creation of my foundation The Gifts of Grace. The rosary is *never* far away from me and I consider it my most treasured spiritual object.

One morning, I went to retrieve it from my prayer bowl to begin my meditation. It wasn't there. Instantly, I remembered it had been on my lap in the car the day before and I knew it had probably fallen out in the snow during one of my stops. I drove into town and retraced my steps. I checked around each spot where I had parked and up and down the sidewalks. No rosary. Then, I tried praying, fervently. Still, no rosary.

After a couple of weeks, I accepted that it was probably not going to return. As I could see no good reason why such an object would go missing, I truly felt that someone must have needed it more than I did. I told myself I would see if I could purchase another one during our next trip to New Mexico.

And life went on.

A short time later, I ran into my landlord, Dick MacDonald, who owns a business, Dick's Barber Shop, downstairs in the same building where my office was located. We had lunch and he told me about his daughter, who had come into some very difficult times with her health and her job. He was very worried about her.

And, life went on.

Then, one day in the spring—it was late on a Friday afternoon and I remember being very tired and just wanting to go home—Dick came up to my office to check the air-conditioner. As we talked, he noticed the Mother Teresa tapestry on my wall.

He said, "You know, just before the holidays, a woman brought a rosary into my shop she'd found in the snow outside. It had a picture of Mother

Teresa on it." Instantly, I started jumping up and down hugging him. I scarcely noticed the blank stare on his face.

He said, "I called everyone I knew, but I didn't call you because I didn't think you were Catholic. But, you remember my daughter? Well, I'm not a praying man, but, I do believe in God. So, I decided to pray for my daughter with the rosary. Well, since then, she's gone into remission and she's gotten a new job."

He paused a moment and said, "See you lost it because I needed it and now it's time for you to have it back."

We are not called to be successful.
We're called to be faithful.

−MOTHER TERESA

Key Points

1. The ego feels emotion based on need. The heart that belongs to God lives in the devotion of truth and freedom.
2. We need prakriti in order to experience and realize our divinity.
3. Discipline the mind with daily spiritual practice, Sadhana. If a daily practice is challenging, try offering your day or just one activity to God.
4. Release identification with the fruits of your actions and shanti, peace, instantly follows. This is tyaga, renunciation.
5. To live *in God* means to trust the greater plan of which we are only a part—that all truly does work for good for those who love God.

Terms

Shanti (*Shahn*-tee) peace

Tyaga (T*yah*-gah) renunciation of identification with the fruits of our actions

Personal Reflection

1. We are told that Brahman is devotion, yet Krishna's first instruction to Arjuna is about the mind—keep your mind single-pointed. Comment on the relationship between devotion and the mind.

2. Recall when seeing with the eyes of devotion transformed a difficult or challenging time.
3. Considering the description of the true devotee (Slokas 12.13–19),
   which attributes feel familiar to you and which seem like they may
   be out of reach?
4. Recall a time when you were asked to trust that *all works for good for
   those who love God.*

Jnana Yoga
The Path of Wisdom

How we *experience*

the relationship between

Atman and Brahman

ज्योतषिामपि
तज्ज्योतसि्तमसः परम ुच्यत े
ज्ञानं ज्ञ ेयं ज्ञानगम्यं
ह ृद सिर्वस्य वष्िठतिम् Sloka 13.17

How We Experience the Relationship between Atman and Brahman

Overview of Chapters 13-18

Chapter 13: Two Birds
We Are the Knower of the Field
   Krishna explains the relationship between the eternal, unmanifested Brahman, Knower, and all the transient manifestations of prakriti, the field. As the Knower of the field, we stay clear about *who we are* and are less likely to become personally entangled with the events in the field.

Chapter 14: May the Pendulum Rest
We Experience God through Creation's Energetic Qualities – The Gunas
   The energetic qualities of prakriti are responsible for all the changes and modifications in the field. These energetic expressions are rajas, expressed when the mind is overactive; tamas, expressed when the mind is dull; and, sattva, expressed when the mind is in equanimity.

Chapter 15: Plant Roots in Heaven
We Discern the Truth Veiled by Maya
   In order to end the cycle of birth and death, we must cut down the eternal Asvattha tree (upside-down tree) with the sharp sword of non-attachment. This means we must release attachment to the world of the senses and identify with that part of us which is eternal. As this happens, we often begin to see things as opposite from before.

Chapter 16: The Gift of Imperfection
We Choose to Develop Divine or Demonic Habits

Endowed with the gift of free will, we are free to plant and manifest anything we want in this field of prakriti. We can manifest the darkest of the dark to the lightest of the light. Regardless, according to the law of karma, we reap what we sow. However, of all mental states, we must be most wary of lust, anger and greed, as these are the gates to self-destruction.

Chapter 17: Make Me an Instrument
We Manifest According to Our Faith

The quality of our faith, shraddha, will determine how the energetic qualities of prakriti—the gunas—will be expressed through us. Krishna offers concrete instruction on how to become divine instruments—manifesting in partnership with Brahman.

Chapter 18: Rise Up!
We Choose Right Action Leading to Moksha or Liberation

Similar to Chapter 2, many of the key concepts of the Bhagavad Gita are summarized in this chapter. In addition, Krishna expounds on the *trinity* of action and how the gunas impact our understanding, will and happiness. Finally, Krishna tells Arjuna that He has shared his most profound wisdom but continues to acknowledge Arjuna's free will—*Consider it fully. And then do what you wish.*

We are each manifestations of Brahman, the Knower of the field. We are made to act by the gunas, the qualities of nature in prakriti. Realizing *who we are*, we are able to release attachment to the world of the senses and discern Truth from maya. We recognize that, through the gift of free will, we may manifest all qualities, from the darkest of the dark to the lightest of the light. Yet, according to the law of karma, we will reap what we sow. The quality of our faith becomes the cornerstone of our days as we find ourselves being used as instruments in everyday life. And, more often, we *rise up!*

How We Experience the Relationship Between Atman and Brahman:
We Are the Knower of the Field

> *Two birds*
> *inseparable companions*
> *perch on the same tree.*
> *One eats the fruits,*
> *the other looks on.*
> *The first bird is our individual self*
> *feeding on the pleasures and*
> *pains of this world.*
> *The other is the universal Self*
> *silently witnessing it all.*
>
> **—MUNDAYA UPANISHAD**

CHAPTER 13

Two Birds

Imagine you are a farmer. For many years you harvest your crops without incident. You've learned what to do to be successful. Then one year, for no apparent reason, disaster strikes and your crop is lost. Now what? You could blame yourself. Your inner dialogue might go something like: "I must be a terrible farmer." Or worse, "Boy, I'm a failure." You could get angry at life in general, or blame God. "Why me? I've been a good person, worked hard, played by the rules. It's not fair."

Or, you could say, "OK, I wonder what happened here? What is different from years past? What do I have control over and what do I not? Sure feels bad, but I know there's something I can learn from all this. And, maybe, if I can figure out what happened, it'll make me a better farmer."

Notice how blame and judgment of yourself, or God, gets you nowhere, only more of the same. And, over time, you become a very good martyr. Despair is inevitable because you have entangled your life experience, what's happened with your crop, with your self worth, with you. Because the crop has gone bad, you think you've gone bad. When you're able to sit back, gain a little distance, observe, feel all that is there for you *and* resolve to learn from the experience, you remember that you are just a farmer looking out over the *field. You no longer confuse what's happened in the field with yourself.* You become the *knower of the field.*

Slokas 1–6

The Blessed One spoke:

13.1   Arjuna, this body of yours is known as the field, and one who knows it as such is called the knower of the field. This is what those who have studied this doctrine say.

13.2   And know also, Arjuna, that in all fields I alone am the knower of the field. Knowledge of both of these – both the field and the knower of the field – that I consider true knowledge.

13.3   Hear from me briefly what this field is, and what its features and its variations are, and where it comes from, and who the knower of the field is, and what his powers are.

13.4   It has been sung in many ways by the ancient seers and in various meters and on many occasions, and in the words of the sutras [sayings] on Brahman. It has been extensively argued and it has now become settled doctrine.

13.5   There are the gross elements, the ego-sense, consciousness, unmanifest nature, the eleven senses, and the five sense-realms,

13.6   There are desire and loathing, pleasure and pain, the bodily aggregates, awareness, steadfastness: this is a brief description of the field and its variations.

In Chapter 6, we introduced the notion of *who's watching* during meditation. Who is watching the thoughts and feelings passing by, changing moment to moment? Who knows that my hip hurt yesterday but not today? If I *were* my thoughts, feelings and sensations in my body, how could I be observing them?

Returning to our example of the farmer and the crops, we can analyze a little deeper, expanding the field of crops to also include our own bodies and minds. Now, as the *knower of the field, kshetrajna,* I can look out at the crops *and* observe my reactions, notice my thoughts and feelings, name and embrace the full range of human emotions passing through.

From this vantage point, *I can remain totally present to what is happening in the moment without personally identifying with any of it.* By not becoming personally entangled, I am free to learn from the experience. Now, the situation can be received as necessary compost for my flowering. Now, I become the lotus, drawing myself up from the depths of the murky waters, to blossom beautifully above.

Let's look more closely at the aspects that make up this field, Slokas 13.5 and 13.6, so we may better differentiate those aspects of *our self* which are transient, the field, from that which is eternal, the knower. This will help us to determine just *who* to put in charge of our chariot on this battle-field of life to stay free of entanglement.

In Chapter 7, we identified eight aspects of prakriti, the transient aspect of God, expressed through the field. The eight include the *five subtle, vibratory elements*: earth, water, fire, air and ether; the two perceptive cognitive processes: manas, sense mind, and buddhi, discernment; and ahamkara, the singular perceiving identity.

However, in addition to these eight aspects of prakriti, Sankhya philosophy identifies sixteen more aspects, for a total of twenty-four, which, collectively, bring forth all the variations in the field of prakriti, the transient expression of God. These are alluded to in Sloka 13.5. Recall from Chapter 2, Sankhya philosophy is concerned with how the eternal, unmanifested One, Spirit, comes to be differentiated and expressed throughout all the transient manifestations, or Nature. Simply, the twenty-four principles are responsible for bringing forth all creation—the field.

The additional sixteen aspects include: *chitta*, feeling; the five *instruments of sense perception:* the ear, skin, eye, tongue and nose; the five *instruments of action:* mouth-speech, hands, feet, organ of excretion and organ of procreation; and, the five *pranas*, life forces, which, together with the subtle vibratory elements, bring forth the *sense objects:* flesh, blood, heat, air and bodily ether.

Sloka 13.6, describes the qualities arising from the field due to our human experience: *desire and loathing, pleasure and pain.* Finally, we have *awareness*, or consciousness, *steadfastness*, or will, and, the actual body, holding all together.

Behold the field!

Yet, remember, like the farmer, the eternal aspect of God, the Knower, stands *in* the field, but is not *of* the field. *The Knower, observes the entire field of the cosmos, just as we, individual expressions of the Knower, observe the field of our personal experience.*

Before having the experience of observing and asking, "Who's watching?" during meditation, we might have read this exhaustive list of aspects bringing forth all the cosmos, including our very own bodies, and wonder, "What else could there possibly be?" But, having sat on our cushions, we know just a little about the mystery. We know a little about the *knower*, the most precious *beyond all aspects*—playfully hiding, yet loving us most.

And, exhaustive analysis yields to humble wonder.

And, suddenly, we hear a child's voice:

> As long as we go on feeling this mystery, we feel free and full and happy and we feel and act free and full and happy to others. This is the secret of being happy from the time you are small until the time you are old.
>
> If you will remember every day to feel the mystery and if you will remember that you are more than what you look like and if you will remember to "be" the mystery itself, then you will be happy. Every day.
>
> And all kinds of wonderful happenings will come up for you. You will feel happy and you will always help and love others—even those who are having trouble feeling happy and are even trying to make you forget the mystery.

This excerpt is taken from the CD *Truth is the Only Profound: Meditative Readings from the Wisdom-Teaching of Ruchira Avatar Adi Da Samraj*, track 5, "What To Remember To Be Happy," in which Adi Da's words are spoken by a child. Beautiful.

Right where we sit, right now, each of us is an expression of *both* aspects of God: the eternal Knower, and the one creating through the transient field. We, the Knower, have come into being, into this field, for the purpose of experiencing and realizing our Divinity. But, to do so, we must learn how to stay untangled. We must decide who will drive our chariot. Will it be the manas, sense mind, or buddhi, discernment? Sorrow or joy?

Slokas 7–11

13.7   Knowledge is said to consist in the absence of pride and deceit, of non-violence and patience and upright honesty, of service to one's teacher, purity, stability and self-control,

13.8   dispassion with regard to sense-objects, and the absence of an ego-sense. There should also be an accurate perception of the misfortunes that inevitably come with birth and death, and old age and disease and sorrow,

13.9   the absence of attachment or affection toward a son or a wife or a home, and all the rest; the constant practice of equanimity, whether events are wished for or not wished for,

13.10   and there should be undeviating devotion, along with yoga focused on me alone, a preference for solitary places, and a distaste for large crowds.

13.11   Finally there should be constant attention to knowledge of the self, and a perception of the purpose of the knowledge of reality – all of this is called true knowledge. What differs from this is just ignorance.

True knowledge (Sloka 13.11) is a clear understanding that we can choose to live our life as the Knower of the field in any moment—that we have the complete knowledge of how to go from sorrow to joy—from being lost to being found.

From the vantage point of the Knower, we develop a critical distance from which to observe and study the workings of the field. We start to transcend duality as we get that good times are no better than bad times when all is received as necessary to our growth. The times of pruning may not feel as good as the leisurely days but they are, in fact, just as critical to our ongoing health. How free we start to feel when, one by one, we let go of our conditions to be happy. As personal attachments wane, a certain dispassion, vairagya, grows, and our ego feeling of separateness, ahamkara, lessens.

Sure, as a farmer, I would not choose to have my crops fail. Yet, when I am clear about *who I am*—the Knower of the field—the Observer of all, I am less likely to allow the ebb and flow of outside circumstances to become entangled with my inner life. After all, they are just that—circumstances subject to the changing nature of prakriti. I on the other hand, am an expression of that which is eternal. I am already full and complete, whether I have a record crop or a failed crop.

And with the gift of free will, *each moment*, it is my choice—to follow the manas mind and stay entangled, *r*eacting to life's circumstances, or shift to discernment, buddhi, and act with clarity. This is nicely illustrated in the following Native American story:

> A grandson told of his anger at a schoolmate who had done him an injustice. The grandfather said, "Let me tell you a story. I too have felt a great hate for those that have taken so much with no sorrow for what they do. But, hate wears you down and does not hurt the enemy. It is like taking poison and wishing your enemy would die. I have struggled with these feelings many times. It is as if there are two wolves inside of me. One is good and does no harm. He lives in harmony with all around him and does not take offense when no offense was intended. He will only fight when it is right to do so and in the right way.
>
> "But, the other wolf is full of anger. The littlest thing will set him into a fit of temper. He fights with everyone, all the time, for no reason. He cannot think because his anger and hate are so great. It is hard to live with these two wolves inside me for both of them try to dominate my spirit."
>
> The boy looked intently into his grandfather's eyes and asked, "Which one wins?"
>
> The grandfather solemnly replied, "The one I feed."
>
> —*Vickie Smith*

Let's feed buddhi and starve manas whether we are a farmer looking out at the effects of nature's play or an innocent player in a hurtful drama. A social worker who works with battered women once told me that the hardest thing for her clients to get is that nothing is going to change until they stop blaming the perpetrator and start focusing on healing themselves. Entanglement means abuse is happening to me so *I* must be bad.

A shift in perception can begin to transform such a belief into the realization that I must first love myself enough to do what I can to hold the perpetrator accountable and then to work on healing myself in order to attract a different kind of relationship. Like the farmer, I must let go of the belief that, just because something bad has happened to me, *I am bad*. To grow and move forward, I must disentangle and realize that *I am not the field*. I am the Knower of the field.

Slokas 12-18

13.12 I will now teach you what you should know. Once one knows this, one attains immortality. It is Brahman, supreme and without beginning. It is said to be neither being nor non-being.

13.13 Its hands and feet are everywhere, its eyes and heads and faces everywhere. Its ears are everywhere. It stands still, covering everything in the world.

13.14 It appears to have all of the sense-qualities and yet it does not have sense-organs. It is detached and yet it supports all things. It has no qualities [nirguna], and yet it enjoys them all.

13.15 It is at once outside and inside of all creatures. It moves and it does not move. It cannot be explained because it is too subtle. It is both far away and very near.

13.16 It is undivided and indivisible, and yet it appears to be divided among all beings. It is understood to be the support of all beings, and yet it devours them and brings them forth again.

13.17 It is the light of lights, and it is said to be beyond darkness. It is knowledge, and the object of knowledge, and the goal of knowledge. It is set firmly in the heart of all things.

13.18 Thus I have explained briefly the field, and knowledge of the field, and the goal of that knowledge. My devotee understands this and enters into my essence.

It is undivided and indivisible, and yet it appears to be divided among all beings (Sloka 13.16). We see and relate to one another as separate entities. Yet, like the wildflowers of the field, we are nurtured by the same earth, cleansed by the same rain, warmed by the same sun and shaped into blossom by the same master gardener, the cosmic Knower of our field.

In Sloka 13.17, we are told a beautiful thing: *the light of lights, beyond darkness, is set firmly in the heart of all things. All things,* and *all* people. But, not all people have had the benefit of the knowledge and understanding to get untangled. And, even with the knowledge, I'm quite sure I am still unfair and unjust at times due to my incomplete awareness. This is why it's always good to err on the side of compassion and humility. This way, we have a better chance of staying untangled.

And so, we return to our prayer mat again and again and humbly enter into the mystery. We vigilantly watch ourselves throughout the day because we understand that, as we progress, we enable all those around us to progress. We remember it's about the light deep in the hearts of *all* and that, only by loving ourselves better, can we love others better.

Slokas 19-23

13.19   Material nature and the spirit of man [prakriti and purusha] are both without beginning – know this doctrine! And know also that the modifications and the qualities arise within the natural world.

13.20   Nature is said to be the cause of action insofar as actions have effects and instruments and agents. Insofar as there is experience of pleasure and pain, the cause of action is then said to be the spirit in man.

13.21   For the human spirit dwells within nature and experiences the qualities that arise from nature. Its attachment to these qualities is the cause of birth in either good or bad wombs.

13.22   The great lord, also said to be the supreme soul, is also known as the human spirit when it dwells in the body: he is the one who experiences the world, and supports it, and observes it, and consents to it.

13.23   Whoever knows well the human spirit and nature, with its qualities – no matter what his present condition is – he is not reborn again.

Reference the chart (opposite) for a visual of the relationship between Brahman, Purusha, prakriti, the gunas, and the Atman. Purusha, as the essence of Brahman, is the Knower, Observer of the cosmic universe. Prakriti is the field. All of the changes occurring in the field of creation are brought about by the interplay of the gunas, the energetic *qualities that arise from nature* (Sloka 13.21). We, as Atman, are the Knower. We simply observe the field of our experience.

The Knower, the Soul, Rumi said, is simply here *for its own joy*. And, so are we. It's why Mother Teresa told her Sisters to smile.

Slokas 24-30

13.24   By meditating on the self, some men see the self, by means of the self. Others do so by means of the practice [yoga] of Sankhya reasoning, and still others by means of the yoga of action.

13.25   But others, not knowing these doctrines, nevertheless hear them from others and revere them. They take the traditional revelation of the Vedas as their guide and so they too cross beyond death.

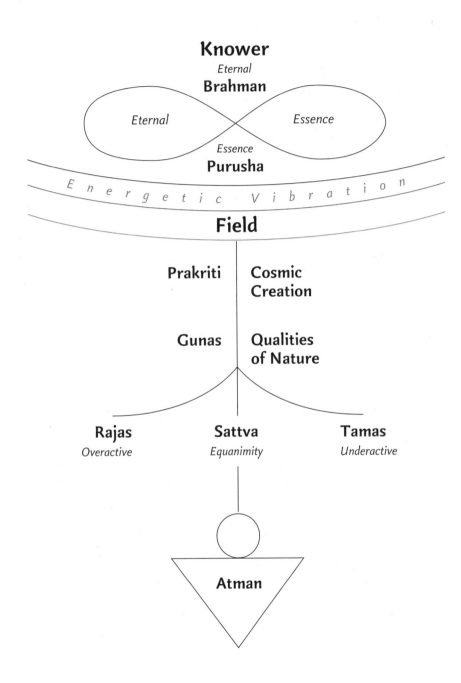

Knower
Eternal
Brahman

Eternal   *Essence*

Essence
Purusha

E n e r g e t i c   V i b r a t i o n

Field

Prakriti | Cosmic
Creation

Gunas | Qualities
of Nature

Rajas
Overactive

Sattva
Equanimity

Tamas
Underactive

Atman

13.26   Any being that is born, whether inanimate or animate, is born from the union of the field and the knower of the field. Arjuna, you should know this doctrine!

13.27   Whoever is able to see in all beings the supreme lord standing there, among those who are dying while he himself does not die – he sees things as they are!

13.28   For when he sees the lord dwelling everywhere, and everywhere the same, he himself does not harm the self in others. Thus he goes to the highest goal.

13.29   Whoever sees that all actions are performed everywhere by nature alone, and thus that the self is not the agent – he sees things as they are!

13.30   When he recognizes the one that dwells within the diversity of all beings, and that from this one they all disperse – then he unites with Brahman.

Any being that is born, whether inanimate or animate, is born from the union of the field and the knower of the field (Sloka 13.26). Now, Arjuna has been given the full explanation of how and why the true self has come into being. Now, he can allow Krishna, Divine personified, the Knower, to drive his chariot. He can rise above personal sentiment to stand firm on the neutral ground of dharma and fulfill his destiny.

And, so can we.

Slokas 31–34

13.31   Because it has no beginning, because it has no real properties, this supreme self is eternal and unchanging. Arjuna, though it dwells in the body, it does not act, nor is it defiled by action.

13.32   Just as all-pervading space – so subtle! – is not defiled by the things that dwell in it, so the self that pervades the body is not defiled by it.

13.33   Arjuna, just as only one sun illuminates this entire world, so the lord of the field alone illuminates this entire field.

13.34   Those who know the difference between the field and the knower of the field, and who know, with the eye of knowledge, this doctrine concerning the liberation of all beings from nature – they go to the highest!

Those who know the difference between the field and the knower of the field—they go to the highest (Sloka 13.34). And, the joy of equanimity arrives because we know how to become untangled. We till the soul of our fields through all seasons and reap a bountiful harvest. Our cup overflows with thanksgiving.

And at day's end, we rest, full and content, in our maker.

And, we are glad.

In the following chapter, we will explore more deeply how we *experience* God through energetic qualities of the field—the gunas.

Key Points

1. We are the Knower of the field, kshetrajna.

2. Understanding the two expressions of our Self, the transient and the eternal, enables us to be *totally present to what is happening in the moment without personally identifying with any of it.*

3. According to Sankhya philosophy, there are twenty-four aspects of the field, or prakriti. All cosmic nature and our self, our bodies, are brought forth by the interplay of these twenty-four aspects.

4. The Knower, observers the entire field of the cosmos, just as we, individual expressions of the Knower, observe the field of our personal experience.

5. Using discernment, all of life becomes our teacher. Understanding, we begin to develop dispassion, vairagya, and our sense of separateness lessens.

6. The cosmic Knower of the field is the same in all, expressed through Purusha, the nature of Brahman behind all the changing forms of nature, and manifested through all creation, or prakriti, through the interplay of the gunas.

7. Recognizing how and why the true self has come into being, we can act with clarity and fulfill our destiny.

8. The Soul is simply here for its own joy. And, so are we.

Terms

Kshetrajna (Kshet-*rah*-jnah) knower of the field

Personal Reflection

1. Define in your own words the Knower of the field.
2. From what, exactly, are you to disentangle?
3. Discuss the difference between having manas or buddhi drive your chariot.
4. Which wolf do you feed most?
5. How does knowing the nature of the true Self help you to fulfill your destiny?

How We Experience the Relationship between Atman and Brahman:
We Experience God through Creation's Energetic Qualities – The Gunas

When we are truly in the present moment
our work on earth begins.

—RESHAD FIELD

CHAPTER 14

May the Pendulum Rest

We know, now, who we are. We are the Knower of the field, kshetrajna. As the Knower, we *experience* our Self in the field of Prakriti through the energetic qualities of nature, the gunas. The gunas are the very essence of prakriti and it is they, not the Knower, who are responsible for all the changes arising in the field from moment to moment. Understanding the gunas helps us to see the origin of all action and to keep from becoming entangled.

Introduced earlier, they are: the rajasic guna, expressed when we are restless or overactive; the tamasic guna, expressed when we are inert or underactive; and the sattvic guna, expressed when we are in balance, present *and* unattached, resting in equanimity.

Slokas 1–4

The Blessed One spoke:

14.1   I will now declare still more concerning this highest knowledge, the supreme among all doctrines. Knowing it, all of the holy men have gone from this world to highest perfection.

14.2   When they rely on this knowledge and have come to have the same
       virtues and duties that I have, when a world-cycle arises they are not
       reborn, and they are not disturbed when one collapses.

14.3   The great Brahman is my womb. I plant my seed in it. The origin of all
       beings originates from this, Arjuna!

14.4   For the forms that originate within all of the wombs of the world,
       Arjuna, the great Brahman is their womb, and I am the father who gives
       the seed.

Within the womb of Brahman, the seed of prakriti creates, sustains and
dissolves all. Change is the nature of consciousness in the field. Brahman,
the unchanging eternal Source of all, observes with neutrality.

Slokas 5–9

14.5   Clarity, passion, dark inertia. These are the qualities that originate from
       nature. Arjuna, they bind the unchanging embodied self within a body.

14.6   Among these, clarity because it is untainted, radiates light and good
       health. It binds one through attachment to pleasure, and through
       attachment to knowledge.

14.7   Passion is essentially desire. Know that it arises from attachment to
       craving. Arjuna, it binds the embodied soul through attachment to
       action.

14.8   And know that dark inertia is born of ignorance. It deludes all embodied
       souls. It binds the soul through carelessness, laziness, and sleep.

14.9   Clarity induces attachment to pleasure, and passion to action, Arjuna.
       But dark inertia obscures knowledge and induces attachment to
       carelessness.

Each guna influences the mind to create attachment to various aspects
of the physical world: rajas to action; sattva to pleasure; and, tamas to
carelessness. As we will see, all three attachments, even pleasure, must be
transcended to enter the inner sanctuary.

Slokas 10–13

14.10 Clarity increases by overcoming passion and dark inertia. Passion
       increases by overcoming clarity and dark inertia, and dark inertia
       increases by overcoming clarity and passion.

14.11   When the light that is knowledge appears in all of the gateways of the
        body, then one will know that clarity has increased.

14.12   Greed, strenuous effort, endless involvement in action, restlessness,
        longing – Arjuna, these arise when passion increases.

14.13   And, Arjuna, when dark inertia increases then these things
        arise – obscurity, lack of effort, carelessness, and finally delusion.

Our attachments, in large degree, determine how we spend our time, and
the quality of our experience. Time spent with the mind influenced by
rajas or tamas just creates more of the same. Time spent in sattva transforms our dense, dark places, leaving us more light.

Slokas 14-15

14.14   If an embodied soul dies at a moment when clarity prevails, then he
        attains to the untainted worlds of those who know this highest truth.

14.15   But if one dies while in a state of passion, one is reborn among those
        who are attached to action. And if one dies while in a state of dark
        inertia, one is reborn in wombs of the deluded.

Recall in Chapter 8, *Going Home*, Krishna tells Arjuna that his state of
mind at the time of physical death will determine his fate.

Slokas 16-17

14.16   It is said that the fruit of an action that is done well consists of clarity
        and purity, and that the fruit of passion is suffering, and that the fruit of
        dark inertia is ignorance.

14.17   Wisdom is born from clarity, just as greed is born from passion, and
        carelessness and delusion are born from dark inertia.

All action creates karma or dharma. Rajasic and tamasic action creates
suffering and ignorance, leaving us in bondage. Sattvic action is pure, setting us free.

Slokas 18-20

14.18   Those who stand firm in clarity rise upward. Those who are passionate
        stand in the middle. Those who incline to dark inertia go downward,
        dwelling in the lowest conditions of nature.

14.19   When one becomes clear in one's vision and recognizes that there is no
        agent other than the conditions of nature, and when one knows what is
        higher than any of these conditions, then one enters into my state.

14.20   When the embodied soul transcends these three conditions of nature
        that are the origins of the body, then he is freed from the sorrows that
        accompany birth and death and old age, and he attains immortality.

Ultimately, in a rajasic state, we spin our wheels, thinking we are going somewhere. In a tamasic state, we actually lose ground. In sattva, we find the key, clarity, to unlock the inner sanctuary.

To transcend these three conditions of nature, (Sloka 14.20), we use discernment, buddhi, to put Krishna, Divine personified, the Knower, in charge of driving our chariot. In this way, we stay in equanimity, sattva, observing our life, the field. From the vantage point of the Observer, we realize that all actions, conditions and circumstances of the field come and go, but we, the Knower, do not. We are the neutral, eternal witness.

Please see the chart (opposite) for a visual summary of Slokas 14.1–20.

The Gunas – Overview

The gunas, energetic forces or qualities of nature, prakriti, could be related to what we commonly call consciousness. And, change is the nature of consciousness in the field. We experience this consciousness as sensation through the senses. The quality of the sensation, from overly excited or withdrawn, to resting in equanimity, is an expression of these forces of nature, the gunas.

Most of us recognize that our consciousness responds immediately to what we are feeling and thinking. We register differences through physical sensation. Consider walking into a situation that elicits fear—whether real or imagined. Once the mind registers *fear*, the feelings and accompanying bodily sensations immediately follow. Conversely, when the mind registers *peace*, different feelings and bodily sensations follow.

This is why training the mind is the first step to shifting consciousness and why the gunas express the qualities of the three basic mind states. Rajas represents an overactive mind state, carried away by passion or excitement and always grasping for the next source of stimulation. Tamas, represents the opposite, an underactive mind, averting action, overcome

The Three Qualities of Nature

PRAKRITI

Womb – the great creator
Creative energy binding true Self to the body

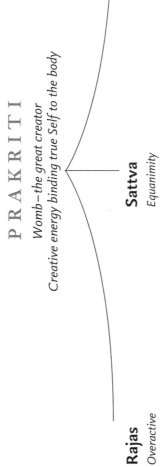

Rajas
Overactive

MIND: becomes attached to craving (7)

BINDS: you to compulsive action (7)

CREATES: greedy, continuous thirsting
after one thing or another (12)

AT DEATH: will be reborn among those
attached to compulsive actions (15)

FRUITS: pain and suffering (16), greed (17)

OUTCOME: we stand in the middle (18)

Sattva
Equanimity

MIND: becomes attached to pleasure (9)

BINDS: to joy and knowledge (6)

CREATES: light that shines through
the gates of the body (11)

AT DEATH: will go to the untainted
worlds of the wise (14)

FRUITS: clarity and purity (16), wisdom (17)

OUTCOME: we rise upward (18)

Tamas
Underactive

MIND: becomes veiled in ignorance (8)

BINDS: to carelessness and laziness (8)

CREATES: sloth and delusion (13)

AT DEATH: will be reborn to parents
ignorant of the truth (15)

FRUITS: ignorance (16), carelessness (17)

OUTCOME: we go downward (18)

by inertia, sloth, carelessness and laziness. Sattvic represents the middle way, clarity, balance and equanimity. If we want to shift our mind state from the polarities of rajas and tamas, we must use buddhi, the discerning aspect of our mind.

Each of us is brought into being by all three gunas. At different times, in response to various life conditions, one guna may dominate over the other two. However, I have noticed that, closely related to innate temperament, one of the three gunas tends to be dominant in most people. Reflect upon the descriptions below and see if one resonates with you.

Rajas

The rajas guna is expressed in those times when our activity is running us around. It is the *do* mode, done for the sake of chasing the next pleasing outcome. The Buddhist would say it is a product of the *desiring* or *wanting* mind. Western psychology might label it manic behavior in its extreme form. It binds us to compulsive action. Always off to the next thing. Yes, this will do it!

It has been said that a wise man is never in a hurry. Notice it did not say not doing anything. Such a wise man could work long hours, yet, without the quality of pushing or forcing. It is the *quality* and the *intention* of the action that is important here. Are we working long hours because focus and passion are bringing forth our life for the greater good or because we're trying desperately to fill some unmet need? Or, if we're at the office, maybe we'd just rather not go home and face the relationship that's not working. The end result is that we stay where we are spinning our wheels.

Tamas

The tamas guna is being expressed in those times when we've checked out—shut down. It is the opposite of the rajas guna. The Buddhist would call it a product of the *averting* or *escaping* mind. Western psychologists might call it depression if extended over a long period of time. It binds us to carelessness and laziness. Too many hours sleeping, watching TV, playing on the computer, overeating, not attending to our responsibilities, are all possible signs the tamasic guna is predominate. Sometimes it shows up as a general *not caring* type of attitude—a kind of just-going-through-the-motions. Because we've chosen not to engage life, we lose ground.

Rajas and Tamas

These gunas often are expressed together. For example, take a person who robs a gas station and doesn't get caught. The action is rajasic because the person is in some way desperately grasping for satisfaction, even to the detriment of others. At the same time, the belief that there is no consequence simply because there is no arrest is the tamasic guna, expressed on the mental level. Or, more commonly, working long hours, and then being surprised when a relationship suffers, also expresses rajasic action and a deluded tamasic mental state.

Both the rajasic and the tamasic guna serve the same function and produce the same outcome: they keep us out of the present moment. We're either moving *to* or *from*, anywhere but *in* to where we're at. Some people may settle into one or the other. Other people might swing back and forth between them in a reactive way. If our moods become severe or we become enslaved by our mood swings, Western psychologists might suspect some mental disturbance. Eastern philosophers would call this *living in duality*. Simply, we swing between *grasping* and *averting*, *happy* and *sad*, because we have not yet found equanimity. We tend to see ourselves, others, and life's circumstances through the lenses of duality because we have not yet embraced all within our self.

We begin to experience the sattvic guna, when we realize, right where we have neglected to look, within, in the present moment, is the treasure we have so desperately been seeking. It's called freedom, *from* the sorrow of being problems to ourselves, *to* the joy of realizing our Self.

Sattvic

Several years ago, I sat with a woman who told me about how she had to admit her teenage daughter for treatment for an eating disorder. For a long time she had tried to "fix" the problem, rajas, or "ignore" the problem, tamas, and, finally, arrived at sattva, where she was able to hold all of these emotions and still do what needed to be done—take her daughter for treatment. The daughter consented to go because she finally felt from her mother the *holding of the truth*—not the manipulation of trying to fix or ignore. Nothing moves without acceptance and no one feels safe until they are truly seen *and* loved. This is devotion. This is sattva.

When experiencing the sattvic guna, the pendulum rests between the polarities. As we discussed in Chapter 6, *The Inner Sanctuary*, I think of it as a kind of door that opens and, when we're not wanting or averting anymore, the Soul quietly, and effortlessly, *becomes us*. We practice creating the conditions to experience and realize this state of bliss when we meditate.

Yet, we are told that even the sattvic quality of mind must be transcended because, like rajas and tamas, it is still simply another mind state. "But, it brings equanimity," you say. "What could be so wrong with that?" The problem is that as we experience increasing peace and equanimity, we can become attached to always being in this blissful state. "So, what's wrong with happiness?" you ask. Nothing. Most would certainly agree it's better than not being happy.

The problem is attachment to one polarity, even a blissful one, leaves us in duality. Needing one, we, inevitably, get the other. So, attached to happy, we, inevitably, get sad. In order to enter into the fullness and spaciousness of the One, we must *transcend both*.

Slokas 21-27

Arjuna spoke:

14.21   Lord, what are the signs that identify the man who has transcended these conditions? How does he go about in the world? And how does he get beyond these three conditions?

The Blessed One spoke:

14.22   Arjuna, as for illumination and activity and even delusion – he does not experience aversion when they arise, nor does he experience longing when they disappear.

14.23   Sitting apart like a witness, he is not disturbed by the conditions of nature. He merely thinks to himself, "these conditions unfold." He stands firm. He is untroubled.

14.24   He stays within himself, indifferent to sorrow and pleasure alike. A clod of earth, a rock, a piece of gold – they are all the same to him! He is wise for whom a friend and a stranger are alike, for whom blame and praise of himself are alike!

14.25   Indifferent to both honor and disgrace, impartial to allies and enemies alike, renouncing all intrigues, such a man is said to have transcended the conditions of nature.

14.26 The man who worships me with the undeviating yoga of devotion, and who has transcended these conditions of nature, is ready to become Brahman.

14.27 For I am the foundation of Brahman, of the immortal and the imperishable, and of the eternal law [dharma], and of absolute bliss!

And, coming empty, we find ourselves full. Needing nothing, all is received.

Welcome Home.

In the following chapter, we'll learn how to enjoy the play here on earth while still remembering to whom we belong. We'll learn our roots are in heaven.

Key Points

1. The gunas are the energetic qualities of prakriti. They are energetic forces of nature expressed as consciousness through the senses.

2. Rajas, tamas and sattva each bind us through attachment to particular qualities: rajas to action; sattva to pleasure; and, tamas to carelessness.

3. The gunas influence our mental and emotional states of mind.

4. The gunas are often expressed in the *intention* behind an action.

5. Rajas and tamas often are interrelated, serving the same function and purpose—keeping us out of the present moment.

6. Sattva, while an advantageous mind state, must also be transcended to rise above duality.

7. Liberation lies beyond happy or sad.

Personal Reflection

1. Considering all three gunas, do you notice one quality of nature expressed most often through you?

2. Provide your own example of an action or activity which has both rajasic and tamasic qualities.

3. In your own words, how is the process of meditation related to

recognizing and understanding how the gunas influence your
experience?

4. A friend expresses to you that s/he has decided to join the "Power
of Positive Thinking" club because s/he wants to discover how to
be happy. Understanding the gunas, and the relationship of the
field to the Knower, what would you say to your friend?

How We Experience the Relationship between Atman and Brahman:
We Discern the Truth Veiled by Maya

That thou mayest have pleasure in everything,
seek pleasure in nothing.
That thou mayest know everything,
seek to know nothing.
That thou mayest possess all things,
seek to possess nothing.
That thou mayest be everything,
seek to be nothing.

—SAINT JOHN OF THE CROSS

CHAPTER 15

Plant Roots in Heaven

To live in and fully enjoy the *field*, we must release our identification with, and attachments to, the world of sense experience, or maya. This is what is meant by cutting down the deep-rooted *Asvattha*, upside-down tree, with the sharp sword of non-attachment.

One of my students, Jan Grossman, who designed the cover for this book, painted a beautiful Asvattha tree mural on a wall at the Fellowship. Picture an image of the roots above in heaven and the limbs reaching down into the world. Metaphorically, it reminds us to whom we belong, the maker and keeper of our days.

Slokas 1–3

The Blessed One spoke:

15.1   There is an eternal fig-tree, with its roots above and its branches below, and they say that the Vedic hymns are its leaves. Whoever knows this tree indeed knows the Vedas.

15.2   First downward and then upward spread its branches. They are nourished by the conditions of nature. Its sprouts are the sense objects and below are its roots, which extend down into the world of men, all bound up with their actions.

15.3   Its form cannot be perceived here as it really is – neither its end nor its beginning nor its foundation. This tree with its fully grown roots – one should cut it down with the strong axe of detachment!

As we do so, we begin to *see* with new eyes, not just all the wondrous creations, but the blessed Creator, *there*, right in front of us. And, wide-eyed, we now realize that, before, we were *blind*, and, now, we *see*. And, suddenly, we start to recognize many other examples of this upside-down tree and the paradox that lies at the heart of the spiritual journey.

It appears that we are separate, different . . . yet,
                    we are One . . . the same.

We strive for perfection . . . yet,
                    we are already perfect.

It sounds egotistical to say we are made of God . . . yet,
                    this realization brings the ultimate humility.

We study . . . yet,
                    knowledge alone will not give us realization.

We think of ourselves on a journey . . . yet
                    there is nowhere to go—we're already Home.

We search . . . yet,
                    we're found.

We plan . . . yet,
                    Providence has other plans.

We think we are born and die . . . yet,
                    we are Eternal.

Slokas 4–6

15.4   And then one should seek out that place where those have gone who do not return again. "I resort to that primordial person [purusha] from whom the ancient process of creation flowed forth."

15.5   To that eternal place go the undeluded, those who have neither pride nor confusion, who have overcome the harmful effects of attachment. They dwell constantly on what relates to the self. They extinguish desire. They free themselves from the dualities that are experienced as pleasure and pain.

15.6   Neither the sun nor the moon nor fire illuminates that place that they go to who do not return again. That place is my highest dwelling.

Yet, not until we begin to *see* and, as a result, *experience* ourselves as *both* the Knower and the field, the eternal *and* the transient, can we begin to surrender into the fullness of being here and yet *not* being here — of being *in* a body but not *of* a body. In such moments, we touch the place from where we *do not return again* (Sloka 15.4) and where *neither the sun nor the moon nor fire illuminates* (Sloka 15.6). In such moments, the stillness of our Soul *informs us*, and we are left in silent wonder.

Sloka 7–8

15.7   In the world of the living, one small portion of me becomes a living being. It remains eternal. It draws to itself the things of nature – the five sense-organs and the mind.

15.8   When the lord takes on a body, or when he leaves one behind, he takes these things with him when he goes, as the wind carries fragrances away from their source.

Sloka 15.8 is a reminder that we, the Knower, carry from lifetime to life-time all we do and experience in the field — *as the wind carries fragrances away from their source*. Through many bodies, over many lifetimes, do we evolve, sow and reap. This is the law of karma.

Slokas 9–10

15.9   Hearing and sight and touch and taste and smell – the lord governs these things and the mind as well. He savors sense-objects.

15.10   But the deluded do not recognize him as he leaves a body, or as he stays in one, or as he experiences it, engaged as it is in the conditions of nature. But those who have the eye of knowledge see him there!

But the deluded do not recognize him as he leaves a body, or as he stays in one, or as he experiences it, engaged as it is in the conditions of nature (Sloka 15.10). As long as we hold onto the belief that we're a body-mind, we stay deluded, clinging feverishly to the sense experience that validates this belief.

Let's look at some of the logical outcomes of *not* cutting down the great Asvattha. Physically, we're likely to do all we can to stay or look young—tucks, lifts, coloring, make-up—anything to disguise the aging of our body. Mentally and emotionally, we're likely to opt only for the good thoughts and feelings, because when we are happy, we mistakenly think *we* are good, and when we are sad, we mistakenly think *we* are bad. Spiritually, we're likely to search *outside* ourselves for that thing that will make us feel connected and whole because we have not yet discovered that what we seek is already within—as close as our very breath. We are caught in the web of illusion. Maya holds us captive.

Few things can pierce this veil of illusion as quickly as a spiritual two-by-four, unceremoniously catapulting us out of our comfort zone: an accident, unexpected diagnosis, a betrayal we don't see coming. It's where we started at the beginning of this book. Notice how it often takes suffering to move us—because it's just too easy to remain comfortable when the ground is soft and the winds are meek. Yet, suddenly jarred, "how to increase earning power" is not an important topic of conversation anymore. All that had once seemed so necessary, looking great, being successful, the admiration of others, begins to fall away. We sense that nothing will satisfy now save our maker, the Potter.

As maya's web is pierced, we are slowly awakened to the truth that death is the only reality—we're not getting out of here alive. As this realization dawns, we are forced to acknowledge the fragility of our attachments. We start to yearn for something more permanent—something that feels real—not fleeting. We start to look for God, and as we do so, the great Asvattha tree begins to weaken and tremble.

However, at this juncture, we hit another paradox as we realize that God is not going to save us from our karma—from walking through the valley of the shadow of death—from walking through the full experience of this world of maya. We are to *walk through* the valleys of our suffering, knowing that the rod and the staff comfort and protect us, knowing we are never alone. To bring down the great Asvattha, we must put our faith and trust in that which is *perceived by* the senses but is not *of* the senses.

One of the places I go before a journey through the valley is to the hymn "Be Still My Soul," inspired by Psalm 46:10 :

Be still my soul, the Lord is on thy side.
Bear patiently the tides of grief and pain.
Trust in thy God to order and provide.
Through every change, his faithful heart remains.
Be still my soul, thy best, thy heavenly friend,
Through thorny ways, leads to a joyful end.

And, being afraid doesn't matter.

Recall in Chapter 5, *Renounce and Be Free*, how Morrie, in the book *Tuesdays with Morrie*, was able to tell Ted Koppel that his disease would get his body but *not* his spirit. But *Tuesdays with Morrie* is not just a story about a courageous struggle or a valiant death. There are many people who suffer greatly every day just to get out of bed. And, still, they do. And, there are many people who face death daily with quiet courage as they pass over into the mystery.

No, the great gift that Morrie gave us was a glimpse of the ability to live and die *without attachment*—without needing conditions to be or not be a certain way. Certainly, he would not have chosen to die a slow and painful death but, seeing the valley before him, he chose to walk through *fully conscious*, because death was not the enemy—*not living fully* was the enemy.

Morrie still dies. Yet, this is the greatest gift. Not even death could kill *Him*. Not the worst scenario. The most painful outcome. The ultimate fear among fears. No. Morrie had cut down the great Asvattha tree, and, his whole experience in dying became a *lesson in living* for millions of people.

And, like Morrie, we too, needing nothing, can dance at our funeral.

This is the realization that Arjuna needs to rise up, defend the dharma, and restore righteousness. By differentiating that which is born and dies, the bodies of the field, from that which is never born nor dies, the Knower, he cuts down the great Asvattha tree, rising in free neutrality to fulfill his destiny.

And, so can we.

Slokas 11–15

15.11 Yogins who exert themselves see that he is present within themselves. But no matter how much they exert themselves, the thoughtless do not see him, because they have not perfected themselves.

15.12   The radiance that belongs to the sun which illuminates the entire world, and that radiance that is in the moon and in fire – know that all radiance is mine!

15.13   I penetrate the earth, and I sustain all beings with my power. And I nourish all the plants of the world. And I have become Soma whose essence is nectar!

15.14   I am the fire that dwells in all men, and I dwell in the body of all that have breath. Joined together with the exhalations and the inhalations of the breath, I cook and digest the four kinds of food.

15.15   I have also entered into the heart of all beings. From me come memory and knowledge and the give-and-take of debate. I am the very thing in the Vedas that is worth knowing. I am the author of the Vedanta [Upanishads] and I am the knower of the Vedas.

But no matter how much they exert themselves, the thoughtless do not see him, because they have not perfected themselves (Sloka 15.11). Again, simple desire is not enough. We must enter the valley of our inner sanctuary, *walk through* our fear to become holy ash, and emerge, born again.

One of the most extraordinary examples of one who, quite consciously and literally, severed the great Asvattha tree at the roots, to walk through the valleys of our world, is the story of the woman known as "Peace Pilgrim." From 1953 until 1981, Peace Pilgrim walked for peace. Her pilgrimage is documented in the book, Peace Pilgrimage, compiled by friends after her death. By 1964, she stopped counting the miles walked at 25,000.

Total abandonment *of* all sense pleasures and securities; total abandonment *to* the Creator. Clearly, the Knower walking through the field. In her words:

> I have no money. I do not accept any money on my pilgrimage. I belong to no organization . . . I own only what I wear and carry . . . I walk until given shelter, fast until given food. I don't ask—it's given without asking. Aren't people good! There is a spark of good in everybody no matter how deeply it may be buried. It is there. It's waiting to govern your life gloriously. I call it the God-centered nature or the divine nature. Jesus called it the Kingdom of God within.
>
> When you have completely surrendered to God's will, the way

seems easy and joyous. It is only before you have completely surrendered that the way seems difficult.

No one walks so safely as one who walks humbly and harmlessly
with great love and great faith.

But, Peace Pilgrim also writes of her time spent *perfecting* (Sloka 15.11)
herself, "However, there's a great deal of difference between being 'willing'
to give your life and actually 'giving' your life, and for me fifteen years of
preparation and inner seeking lay between." She goes on to discuss her
ways of perfecting herself. There were "preparations," such as "bringing
our lives into harmony with the laws that govern the universe"; "purifica-
tions," such as the "purification of desire"; and, "relinquishments," such as
letting go of "feelings of separateness and all attachments."

Sound familiar? And, of course, there were tests along the way. Of these,
she writes:

> Concealed in every new situation we face is a spiritual lesson to
> be learned and a spiritual blessing for us if we learn that lesson. It
> is good to be tested. We grow and learn through passing tests. I
> look upon all my tests as good experiences. Before I was tested, I
> believed I would act in a loving or non-fearing way. After I was
> tested, I knew! Every test turned out to be an uplifting experience.
> And it is not important that the outcome be according to our
> wishes.

And it is not important that the outcome be according to our wishes. Here,
we see perhaps the deepest root in the great Asvattha tree, attachment
to maintaining control over our life. *Complete surrender* is the only blade
sharp enough to sever this root set deep in the soil of fear. The only blade
sharp enough to free us from the illusion of maya. To free us from our
self—to become our Self.

Sloka 16-20

15.16　There are two divine persons [purushas] in the world. One is perishable
　　　and the other is imperishable. The perishable consists of all beings. The
　　　imperishable is called the sublime summit.

15.17　But there is another beside these two, the highest spirit [purusha], called the supreme self [paramatman]. He is the eternal lord who enters and supports the three worlds.

15.18   Since I transcend the perishable, and since I am higher than the imperishable, so in the world and in the Veda I am celebrated as the highest spirit [purushottama].

15.19   Whoever without delusion thus knows me as the highest spirit knows everything! Arjuna, he worships me with his entire being.

15.20   Thus have I taught you this most secret doctrine. Blameless Arjuna, once one has become awakened to this doctrine, then one will have become awakened. And all that one needed to do will have been done.

Recall that Purusha, in Sloka 15.16, is the essence of Brahman behind the changing forms in nature. The *two divine persons* refer to the manifested and the unmanifested aspects of prakriti, pervading the field. Sloka 15.17 and 15.18 refer to the *supreme self* or consciousness, *purushottama*, another word for the Source of all, the Knower.

As we walk in complete surrender as the Knower, through the field of our days, the sharp blade of non-attachment brings down the great Asvattha tree and *all that we needed to do will have been done* (Sloka 15.20). This is the *it's not about us at all* part.

Our only job here is to follow the deepest yearning of our heart—the impulse that makes our face instantly soften, our breath deepen and our burden light.

And, instantly, we are *made* to do our part in the Divine plan.

As we, the Knower, just watch, with joy.

In the following chapter, we will explore how to transcend the ultimate duality—the divine and the demonic.

Key Points

1. To live in, and fully enjoy, the field, we must release our identification with, and attachments to, the world of sense experience, or maya. This is what is meant by cutting down the deep-rooted Asvattha, upside-down tree, with the sharp sword of non-attachment.

2. Often things seem the opposite of what they were before in the new light of wisdom.

3. Nothing pierces the veil of illusion or maya more quickly than the notion of death. We start to look for something permanent. We start to look for God.

4. Simple desire is not enough. We must perfect ourselves in the inner sanctuary.

5. The deepest root in the great Asvattha is *surrender*—releasing control of our life to the Creator.

Terms

Asvattha (*Ahs*-vaht-ha) upside-down tree

Personal Reflection

1. What are you most attached to in the world of maya?

2. If you once were *blind* but now you *see*, what exactly is it that you *see*?

3. What causes you to look for something permanent—to look for God?

4. Do you believe you will *dance at your own funeral?*

5. What would you have trouble leaving behind on a walk with Peace Pilgrim?

How We Experience the Relationship between Atman and Brahman:
We Choose To Develop Divine or Demonic Habits

Turn your face to the sun
and the shadows fall behind you.

—MAORI PROVERB

CHAPTER 16

The Gift of Imperfection

Endowed with the gift of free will, we may plant and manifest anything we want in this field of prakriti, from the darkest of the dark to the lightest of the light. Planting seeds of darkness, we sow more karma, and reap suffering. Planting seeds of light, we sow dharma, and reap joy. Divine behaviors spring from the realization that we are each part of the One. They seek to build connection and lead to liberation, moksha. Demonic behaviors spring from the illusion of maya, that we are separate. They create sorrow and lead to bondage as a result of ignorance.

Slokas 1–3

The Blessed One spoke:

16.1   Fearlessness, purity of character; steadfastness in the yoga of knowledge; gift-giving, self-control, and sacrifice; study of the Vedas and austerity and honesty;

16.2   Non-violence and truth and no anger; renunciation and peacefulness and no slander; compassion for all beings and no greed; gentleness and modesty and no fickleness;

16.3   Radiance, patience, resolve, purity, no deception and no exaggerated

pride – Arjuna, these are the qualities of a man who has been born into
divine circumstance.

In these Slokas, Krishna describes some of the qualities we exhibit in
divine moments.

Virtually all faith traditions agree on what divine behavior looks like. It
is hopeful to me when I remember that at the core of all faith traditions
is a *common* heartbeat or intention. It's called the Golden Rule. Consider
the following ways the Golden Rule is expressed throughout a few of the
most well-known faith traditions:

Hinduism
> This is the sum of duty: do not do to others what would
> cause pain if done to you.
>> —*Mahabharata 5:1517*

Judaism
> What is hateful to you, do not do to your neighbor. This is the
> whole Torah; all the rest is commentary.
>> —*Hillel, Talmud, Shabbath 31A*

Christianity
> In everything, do to others as you would have them do to you;
> for this is the law of the prophets.
>> —*Jesus, Matthew 7:12*

Islam
> Not one of you truly believes until you wish for others what
> you wish for yourself.
>> —*The Prophet Muhammad, Hadith*

Buddhism
> Treat not others in ways that you yourself would find hurtful.
>> —*The Buddha, Udana-Varga 5.18*

Although we are sustained by a common heartbeat and seek to relate to
one another from the common intention of caring for another as we would
care for our self, this does not mean we ignore or gloss over injustice and
harmful behaviors. What it means is that it becomes possible to confront
injustice—indeed, defend the dharma as Arjuna must—without becoming
unjust, because now we *feel deeply* that what we do to others we do to our

self. Only through the realization of our unity does it become possible to respond to wrong action without hating the perpetrator—within our self or the other.

Slokas 4–5

16.4   But, Arjuna, the qualities of a man born into demonic circumstance are: hypocrisy, arrogance, exaggerated pride, anger, harsh speech, and ignorance.

16.5   Divine fortune leads to release. Demonic fortune leads to bondage. But do not worry, Arjuna. You are born into divine circumstance.

Seeing clearly and responding with action born of neutrality and equanimity, we create dharma, a righteous outcome, or heaven on earth. This is why Krishna tells Arjuna in Sloka 16.5, *But do not worry, Arjuna. You are born into divine circumstance.* Because Arjuna has sought refuge and counsel from his Lord, he can align with the divine essence *within himself* to win the war over his inner demons.

Slokas 6–8

16.6   There are two kinds of creation in this world: the divine and the demonic. I have spoken of the divine at length. Arjuna, hear now from me of the demonic.

16.7   Demonic people do not distinguish between activity and the cessation of activity. You will not find purity, or the observance of custom, or truth in them.

16.8   They say that the world has no reality, no religious basis, no god. They deny that the world arises through mutual causation. If not this, then what else? They say that the world is driven by desire.

They deny that the world arises through mutual causation (Sloka 16.8). It is tamasic reasoning to think that our actions do not cause particular effects for which we are held accountable. Just like with little Jacob in Chapter 4, we may think and feel we are bad, but, it is not true. This is the staff of God. Here, we may think and feel we do not reap what we sow, but it's not true. This is the rod. Recall in the last chapter that, *as the wind carries fragrances away from their source,* over many lifetimes do we reap and resolve the karma we have sown.

Slokas 9–11

16.9   Stubbornly maintaining this view, these lost souls with so little insight rise up and seize power through terrible acts of violence, wretched people intent on destroying the world.

16.10   They surrender themselves to insatiable desire. They are intoxicated by their own hypocrisy and pride. They are seized by delusion, and so they seize upon false ideas. They engage in practices that pollute them.

16.11   They devote themselves to anxiety, beyond measure, which ends only when they die. They have convinced themselves that this is all that life amounts to, and so their greatest ambition is to satisfy their desires.

The Dalai Lama said, "The central method for achieving a happier life is to train your mind in a daily practice that weakens negative attitudes and strengthens positive ones." We are reminded of the importance of such a daily practice in Sloka 16.9 where the ultimate outcome of *so little insight* is described.

Similarly, the *Course in Miracles*, a course in esoteric studies from the Foundation for Inner Peace, says that there are only two emotions: love and fear. Simply, Love is connection; fear is separation. When we train our minds in our daily practice using discernment, or buddhi mind, we remember our connection. Untrained, the mind quickly settles in manas mind, and we forget our connection.

Slokas 12–18

16.12   Hope with its hundred snares binds them, and desire and anger preoccupy them. They strive for vast hoards of wealth, by illegal means, in order to fulfill their vain desires.

16.13   "I have gotten this much today, and next I will get this wish fulfilled too. This wealth is mine, and that is too. And I'll have more in the future.

16.14   I have killed this enemy today, and I will kill others as well. I am the lord here. I enjoy myself. I am successful, powerful, and happy!

16.15   I am rich and well-born. Who else can compare with me? I will perform the sacrifices. I will give to the poor. I will enjoy myself!" This is how such ignorant fools talk!

16.16   Distracted by their many worries, they are caught in the web of delusion. Obsessed with satisfying their desires, they fall headlong into a polluted hell.

16.17   Self-absorbed, stubborn, intoxicated with wealth and pride, they perform their sacrifices in name only, dishonestly, ignoring the traditional obligations.

16.18   Egotism, violence, pride, desire and anger – they resort to these, and in their envy they hate me, both in their own and in all other bodies.

I am the lord here. I enjoy myself. I am successful, powerful, and happy! (Sloka 16.14). Thinking such, the ignorant are *caught in the web of delusion,* (Sloka 16.16) and resort to *egotism, violence, pride, desire and anger* (Sloka 16.18). One of my favorite allegories of the spiritual journey that highlights the struggle of light and dark, love and fear, is *Hinds' Feet on High Places,* by Hannah Hurnard. It tells the story of Much-Afraid and her journey following the Good Shepherd to the high places—to the Kingdom of Love.

Initially, Much-Afraid cannot imagine that she might be able to follow the Good Shepherd to the high places because she is a member of the Family of Fearings and her relatives are scattered all over the valley. She fears she could never escape them. She particularly fears her cousin Craven Fear, a great bully, who habitually torments and persecutes her. These Slokas describe Craven Fear perfectly.

Finally, Much-Afraid does muster the courage to leave the valley and begins the journey to the Kingdom of Love. Along the way, she comes upon a great precipice. She can see no way of ascending the terrifying cliff and begins to believe she will have to turn back. Like Arjuna, she sits at the foot of the precipice, in total sorrow, declaring, "I can't do it; I can't." And, just in the moment of doubt, her cousin Craven Fear appears and says,

Ha Ha! My dear little cousin, we meet again at last! How do you find yourself now, Much-Afraid, in this delightfully pleasant situation?

. . . Did you really believe, you poor little fool, that you could escape from me altogether? No, no, Much-Afraid, you are one of the Fearings, and you can't evade the truth, and what is more, you trembling little idiot, you belong to me. I have come to take you back safely and make sure that you do not wonder off again.

Many of us have a similar inner dialogue when we come upon the fears and struggles we believe are insurmountable. But, the Good Shepherd, gives her advice that, of course, sounds very much like Krishna's counsel to Arjuna. He warns her about the use of her mind:

> Much-Afraid, don't ever allow yourself to begin trying to picture what it will be like. Believe me, when you get to the places which you dread you will find that they are as different as possible from what you have imagined. I must warn you that I see your enemies lurking among the trees ahead and if you ever let Craven Fear begin painting a picture on the screen of your imagination, you will walk with fear and trembling and agony where no fear is.

" . . . *where no fear is.*" This is why the demonic forces of darkness or ignorance are often referred to as illusion.

Oh, how we wish we could just go around our fear demons, avert them somehow. Walking *through* the valley of our shadows is not the feel-good part of the journey, and, in the end, it *is* the journey. Fr. Alfred D'Souza writes, "For a long time it had seemed to me that life was about to begin—real life. But there was always some obstacle in the way. Something to be gotten through first, some unfinished business, time still to be served, a debt to be paid. Then life would begin. At last it dawned on me that these obstacles were my life."

Perhaps, the illusion of separateness, and all the dark behaviors created from this illusion, exist to provide us with something to struggle against so that we may discover and develop our strength—*not to defeat others but to defeat the evil within our own hearts.* Only then do peace, harmony and love become the seeds we plant in our own gardens, allowing us to feed others.

Often we pray to be relieved of suffering. Yet, it is the kiln that creates the beauty in the pot. It is the compost that makes the lotus blossom. We become rich and whole *because* of our struggles not *in spite* of them. So when Much-Afraid asks the Good Shepherd to carry her to the High Places, because her feet are disfigured—we all have our good reasons—He answers:

> Much-Afraid, I could do as you wish. I could carry you all the way up to the High Places myself instead of leaving you to climb there.

But, if I did, you would never be able to develop hinds' feet and become my companion and go where I go.

Our job is not to escape the dark, get rid of it or even overcome it. Our job is to shine the light where darkness lives and, like good detectives, see what is there for us. In this way, we journey *through* the valley of our darkness, transforming difficulty into rich compost. In this way, we grow wise — not just old.

Slokas 19-24

16.19 In the endless rounds of rebirth, I cast these vile, hateful, bloodthirsty, lowest of men, over and over again into demonic wombs.

16.20 And deluded they enter, in birth after birth, into a demonic womb. Arjuna, they do not ever reach me. In this way they take the lowest path.

16.21 This is the destruction of the self. This is the three-fold gate of hell. Desire, anger, and greed. One should abandon these three.

16.22 But, Arjuna, a man who is released from these three gates of hell engages in what is good for the self. In this way he takes the highest path.

16.23 If a man neglects the injunctions of tradition, and behaves according to the demands of his own desires, he will not gain success, or happiness, or the highest path.

16.24 Therefore, let traditional law be your authority in deciding what is right to do and what is not. Know what is taught in the law books. You should perform here the actions that you are obliged to perform.

Demonic behaviors that lead us straight through the gates of hell are *desire, anger and greed* (Sloka 16.21). Not realizing our connection to all, we falsely believe we can satisfy any desire without regard for others and not get hurt in the process; hate others without poisoning our self; or, steal from others without suffering loss. Caught in the web of *maya*, we suffer and cause others to suffer.

If I am one with all, then all is available to me. If all is available to me, why would I experience desire, anger, or greed? Each of these emotions expresses a belief in lack or scarcity. I desire or lust *after*; I'm angry *at*; I'm greedy *for* something on the outside I believe will make me feel a certain way on the inside. In these moments, sadly, I have forgotten my connection to all.

I have forgotten that *I am already full, whole and complete.*

Craven Fear may tell us *you belong to me.* But, the Good Shepherd tells us, in Isaiah 49:16, *I have carved you in the palm of my hand.*

You are mine.

In the following chapter, Krishna offers concrete suggestions for creating dharma instead of karma.

Key Points

1. Divine behaviors are described in most faith traditions as a variation on the Golden Rule.

2. The realization of unity is the only thing that enables us to fight hatred without hating.

3. Our experience of the light or dark, love or fear, begins with how we use our minds.

4. We become beautiful pots, the lotus, *because of* not *in spite of* our struggles, challenges and lessons.

5. If we are feeling desire, anger or greed, we are looking *after, at* or *for* something. We have momentarily forgotten that we are *already full.*

6. Remembering our connection to the One, we remember to whom we belong.

Personal Reflection

1. What "darkness" in you feels insurmountable?

2. What does your inner dialogue of fear sound like?

3. *Because of* what experiences have you become wiser?

4. How do you see desire, anger or greed showing up in your life?

How We Experience the Relationship between Atman and Brahman:
We Manifest According to Our Faith

I believe in the sun even when it is not shining.
I believe in love even when feeling it not.
I believe in God even when he is silent.

—JEWISH PRAYER

CHAPTER 17

Make Me an Instrument

Faith has little to do with intellect. Faith is obedience. Faith and abandonment to God's will are inseparable. Faith requires complete humility and fearless courage. Faith is what allows us to step into the dance with our God and become joyful instruments for the greater good.

It is what keeps me dancing the *I am enough and I am nothing* will and surrender dance even when I can no longer see the point, understand the turn of events, remember why or just want to give up. And, faith is why I get up every morning and lay my head on my prayer mat and begin again.

Faith, *shraddha, knows* the sun is still shining on a cloudy day when it can't be seen or felt. It's really the only thing that makes perfect sense to me because it doesn't require the world to be a certain way—it requires *I* be a certain way. It is what *I know* leads me to safety when the rudder is broken and night is falling fast.

Slokas 1–3

Arjuna spoke:

17.1 There are those who neglect the injunctions of tradition, but they faithfully perform sacrifices nevertheless. Krishna, what is their position? Clarity, or passion, or dark inertia?

The Blessed One spoke:

17.2   Among embodied souls there are three kinds of faith. This arises from each one's own nature. There is the quality of clarity, and of passion, and of inertia. Listen now to what I say.

17.3   Each man's faith conforms to his true nature. Arjuna, a man is made up of his faith. What he puts his faith in is what he himself is.

In Sloka 17.1, Arjuna questions the relationship between following *the injunctions of tradition*, or the letter of the law, *shastras*, and simply acting with sincere faith. Krishna answers, in a general way, in Sloka 17.3, telling Arjuna that what a man *puts his faith in is what he himself is*. In the Bible this is expressed in Proverbs 23:7, "*. . . for as a man thinketh in his heart so is he.*"

Slokas 4–6

17.4   Men of clarity offer sacrifices to the gods. Men of passion sacrifice to spirits and demons. And those others, the men of darkness, sacrifice to the dead and to ghosts.

17.5   Some men practice horrible austerities that are not ordained by tradition. They are motivated by hypocrisy and egotism. They are driven by the forces of desire and passion.

17.6   They recklessly starve the cluster of elements that reside in the body. And they starve me as well, the one who dwells within the body. Know that their resolve is demonic.

Our faith is formed and shaped by our core beliefs. These beliefs determine the dominant guna and influence all of our actions. For example, if I understand that full freedom equates to full responsibility, that all life's experiences unfold me to greater awareness, I will commit to the ongoing challenge of embracing the present moment, offer my actions as *sacrifices to the gods* (Sloka 17.4) and, more often, exhibit a sattvic nature.

If I hold a core belief that I must accomplish much to be liked and be successful, I will likely be *driven by the forces of desire and passion* (Sloka 17.5) and settle quite amicably into the "do" mode and exhibit the rajasic guna. Or, if I hold a core belief that I cannot show up for life, that I can do what

I please and escape consequence, then I will likely "check out" and exhibit the tamasic guna.

We return to the ongoing theme that the manifestation of experience begins with how we use our minds. While we may be endowed with a particular temperament based on our karma from previous lifetimes, we are fully able to change and adapt. We can learn to get a lot done, yet not be in a hurry. We can learn to stop and rest, yet not check out. And, with our meditation practice, we can learn to be here, now.

And so we return to our mats again and again to *practice* embracing the present moment. We notice how the mind sometimes wants to run *to* or *from* something, and we *practice* returning again and again to the point of focus, to sattva. Only here is it *all about us—*showing up*—and not about us at all.*

Slokas 17.7–22 offer concrete insight into how the everyday activities of eating (Slokas 17.8-10), sacrifice (Slokas 17.11–13), practicing austerities (Slokas 17.14–19), and gift giving (Slokas 17.20–22) are influenced depending upon which guna is dominant. They speak to the value of self-observation. It is here, when we observe our daily actions with stark honesty, that we learn how the forces of nature are governing us. And awareness is the first step toward change.

Slokas 7-10

17.7   Also the kinds of food that men enjoy are of three kinds. Likewise also are their sacrifices and their austerities and their gifts. Hear how these are classified.

17.8   Food that men of clarity prefer increase one's life-span, strength, courage, good health, contentment and pleasure. Such foods are tasty, mild, firm and easy to digest.

17.9   A man of passion desires foods that are pungent, sour, salty, very hot, sharp, dry, or burning. Such foods cause discomfort and pain and indigestion.

17.10   Food that is preferred by men of dark inertia is spoiled, tasteless, putrid, or stale – such as leftovers or food that is unfit for sacrifice.

Much has been written about the value of particular foods to the body. Culture and climate are additional factors influencing the discussion. Here, we see the thoughts from ancient times.

Slokas 11–13

17.11 A sacrifice has the quality of clarity [sattvika] when it is offered with
attention to the traditional injunctions, and by men who have no desire
for rewards. They concentrate their minds, thinking only "The sacrifice
must be performed."

17.12 Arjuna, know that a sacrifice has the quality of passion [rajasa] when
it is performed in order to gain some reward, or when it is offered
insincerely.

17.13 A sacrifice is considered to have the quality of dark inertia [tamasa]
when it is performed without faith, with no regard for the traditional
injunctions, when the food offerings are neglected, mantras are not
recited, and sacrificial fees are not paid.

The nature of sacrifice speaks to the quality of the heart. With *no desire for
rewards* (Sloka 17.11), a true sacrifice creates its own reward, dharma, the
instant it is offered. All other so-called acts of sacrifice, requiring something in return, create karma.

Slokas 14–19

17.14 Honoring the gods, the twice-born Brahmins, teachers [gurus] and the
wise, and to be pure and honest and chaste and non-violent – this is
called the austerity of the body.

17.15 Words that do not agitate, words that are true and pleasing and
kind – as well as the daily practice of Vedic recitations – these are called
the austerity of speech.

17.16 Serenity of mind, gentleness, meditative silence, self-control, the
purification of one's emotions – these are called the austerity of the
mind.

17.17 This three-fold austerity is considered to have the quality of clarity
[sattvika]. It is performed with the highest faith by men who have no
desire for reward for their actions.

17.18 But austerity that is performed with desire for the respect, honor,
reverence that austerity wins, such austerity is performed insincerely.
It is called the austerity of passion [rajasa]. It is wavering and unstable.

17.19 When austerity is performed because of deluded ideas, or as a form
of self-mortification, or as a means of destroying someone else – it is
considered to be the austerity of dark inertia.

Austerities are the tapas, those practices that burn away the rust, ignorance, enabling our innate beauty to shine. For the body, we strive for *purity* and to practice *non-violence* (Sloka 17.14) to ourselves. For speech, we remember, particularly in challenging moments, it is possible to be both *true and pleasing* (Sloka 17.15). And, for the mind, we cultivate *serenity*, as a result of the *purification of emotions*, in our daily practice (Sloka 17.16). As with sacrifice, the motivation behind austerities, determines what guna is dominant (Slokas 17.17–19).

Slokas 20-22

17.20 As for gift-giving, when it is given with the thought that it ought to be given, when it is given to one who is unable to reciprocate, at the right place and time, and to a worthy person, tradition calls it giving from the state of clarity [sattvika].

17.21 But when a gift is given in order to get a gift in return, or with consideration of reward, or if it is given reluctantly, tradition calls it giving from the state of passion [rajasa].

17.22 When a gift is given at an inappropriate place and time, and to people who are not worthy, when it is given with disrespect and contempt – then it is known as giving from the state of darkness.

Gift giving is not about the gift. It's about the giver. As with the other practices, we really don't need to concern ourselves as much about the appropriateness of the circumstances as with the appropriateness of our heart. When our heart is in the right place, the sacrifice, austerity and gift take care of themselves.

In summary, it's important to remember that, while one guna may sometimes influence our experience more than the other two, our lives are often influenced by combinations of the three. Ultimately, to move away from the polarities exhibited by the rajas and tamas gunas and toward the equanimity of the sattvic guna, we must surrender to the *not about us at all* part of the dance with God.

And, surrender is always an act of faith, shraddha. Yet, it is only from this place that we may truly be used as instruments for the greater good—in just the ordinary unfolding of our day—in the grocery store, talking to our loved ones, doing our work, offering a gift.

Now, it is not about *what we do*. It's about *how we are*.

Slokas 23–28

17.23   OM TAT SAT! This is preserved by tradition as the three-fold explanation of Brahman. By means of it, in the ancient days, the brahman priests, the Vedas, and the sacrifices were established.

17.24   Therefore, those who teach the doctrine of Brahman [Brahmavadins] always recite "OM" before performing sacrifices, giving gifts, and practicing austerities – as required by tradition.

17.25   Those who seek liberation recite "TAT" ["that"] when they perform the various acts of sacrifice, and austerity, and gift-giving – doing so without any concern for rewards.

17.26   The word "SAT" is used in the sense "true" and also in the sense "good." Arjuna, it is also used to refer to actions that are praiseworthy.

17.27   With regard to sacrifice and austerity and gift-giving, steadfastness in these activities is said to be "SAT" – good and true. And all action that is performed for such purposes is called "SAT."

17.28   But whatever is offered or given without faith, or whatever austerity is performed without faith – it is called "ASAT" ["unreal"] Arjuna, because both in this world and in the next it amounts to nothing.

I am fond of telling my students that *we are each made of nothing but ahhhhhhh*. Quite literally, we are made of OM, the internal and eternal hummmmm. And, truly, *we are TAT, That which we seek*. This is the truth, *SAT*, from which all else is known. *OM TAT SAT*.

All else is *ASAT*, untruth.

We *experience* this truth by evoking the sound currents themselves, OM TAT SAT. This is why the Bible says in John 1:1, *In the beginning was the Word, and the Word was with God, and the Word was God*, and why the practice of mantra meditation is our dial-up connection. As we invoke the sound current, we are instantly connected to our Source. During meditation, we tune the dial on the radio of our minds and, in the sweet silence that follows, the signal comes in loud and clear. We *hear* beyond the sounds enabling us to *see* beyond the visible in our daily life.

In addition, we can choose particular mantras, or sound currents, to help strengthen a weak vibration. I witnessed an inspiring example of faith, shraddha, using the sound current to strengthen a weak vibration, with one of my students, Betty Tamposi. At the time, Betty was in a spiritual studies class and had not taken a lot of yoga, so was fairly new to mantra meditation.

Early on a Tuesday morning, I received a phone message from Betty saying that a growth had appeared quite suddenly on her clavicle. Her doctor said it looked suspicious and she was scheduled to have a biopsy that Friday. She asked if I might have some time to meet with her.

During our time together, I introduced Betty to a process I've developed called mantra prayer. It combines intentional prayer with appropriate mantras to strengthen particular vibrations within ourselves. In this case, we used a sound current for healing, *Ra Ma*, to evoke Betty's own inner impulse toward wholeness or health. Thomas Ashley-Farrand writes in *Healing Mantras:*

> Ra is associated with the solar current that runs down the right side of our bodies. Ma is associated with the lunar current that runs down the left side of our bodies. Although these two currents crisscross and meet at the chakras, they are generally associated with the right and left sides of the body. By repeating Rama . . . Rama . . . Rama over and over again, you begin balancing the two currents and their activity so that they can work with the higher stages of energy that will eventually come up the spine. This simple mantra, Rama, qualifies as a healing mantra in its own right.

Betty and I wrote an intentional prayer affirming an outcome to serve the greatest good for all and then we chanted a mantra which included this healing sound current. The particular one we used that day was, *Ra Ma Da Sa Sa Say So Hung*, from Kundalini yoga as taught by Yogi Bhajan, which is well known for its healing properties.

Betty took the mantra prayer practice and gave herself to it wholeheartedly. Two days later, on Thursday, she left a message saying that the growth had visibly shrunk and by Friday morning, the day of her scheduled biopsy, she called to say it was completely gone.

But, what was to be the most important part of this story, for Betty, was her subsequent journey into the full realization that *she had healed herself.* She had not had enough experience with mantra to *believe* that the process would work. In fact, she thought it was a little strange. No, what was required was something she most willingly brought, single-pointed faith, shraddha. And, to where there was darkness, God brought Light.

And, *she was informed.*

In the last chapter, we will see a summary of this Song of God.

Key Points

1. Faith, shraddha, requires complete humility and fearless courage. It's what invites us into the dance with our God and allows us to become instruments for the greater good.

2. Our faith is formed and shaped by our core beliefs. These beliefs determine which guna(s) will most influence our actions.

3. We learn a lot about our true faith by watching how we engage in daily activities such as eating, offering a sacrifice, practicing austerities, or in gift giving.

4. To settle into the equanimity of the sattvic guna, we must surrender to the *not about us at all part* of the dance with God. And, surrender is always an act of faith, shraddha.

5. We are OM TAT SAT. We are the sound current.

Terms

Shastras (Shahs-trahs) recognized scripture or authority
TAT (Taht) that which we seek
SAT (Saht) truth
ASAT (Ah-saht) untruth
Ra Ma (Rah-mah) healing sound current

Personal Reflection

1. Define "faith." What does the word mean to you? Use a concrete example.

2. There are many areas of human experience discussed in this chapter from the standpoint of the three gunas. Were there certain examples which resonated clearly with you and others that did not?

3. Discuss the relationship of *surrender* to faith, shraddha. How does this relationship bring us to be instruments for the greater good?

4. How would you explain the healing that occurred for Betty?

How We Experience the Relationship between Atman and Brahman:
We Choose Right Action Leading to Moksha or Liberation

Let nothing disturb you,
let nothing frighten you;
everything passes away except God;
God alone is sufficient.

—SAINT TERESA OF AVILA

CHAPTER 18

Rise Up!

As in to Chapter 2, many of the key concepts of this Song of God are summarized here. In addition, Krishna expounds on the *trinity* of action and how the gunas impact our understanding, will and happiness. Finally, Krishna shares his counsel for the last time and our hero must decide between joy and sorrow.

And, so must we.

The talk is over. The instruction is complete. It is time for Arjuna to rise up and do his duty. It is a task for which he is eminently qualified. He's a kshatriya, a warrior, and there's a battle to be fought and dharma, righteousness, to be restored. Like us, Arjuna is an ordinary man poised to step into the full glory of his destiny. All that is required is that he allows what he has asked for—Krishna to drive his chariot. In doing so, there is only one possible outcome—victory on the battlefield of life.

In the end, however, Krishna demonstrates the full measure of his love by reminding Arjuna that the choice is his. *"Such is the wisdom which I have taught you, the most secret of secrets! Consider it fully. And then do what you wish."*

Slokas 1-6

Arjuna spoke:

18.1   Krishna, I want to know the truth about renunciation, and about
       abandonment also, and what the difference between them is.

The Blessed One spoke:

18.2   The ancient poets understand that renunciation is the abandonment
       of acts of desire, whereas the learned say that abandonment is the
       abandonment of the fruit of all actions.

18.3   Some men of insight say that action should be abandoned because
       it is harmful. But others say that acts of sacrifice and gift-giving and
       austerity should not be abandoned.

18.4   Hear my judgment on this matter of abandonment, Arjuna, tiger among
       men. Abandonment is known by tradition to be three-fold.

18.5   Works of sacrifice, of gift-giving, of austerity, should not be
       abandoned. In fact, they should be performed. Sacrifice, gift-giving,
       austerity – these things purify men of insight.

18.6   But while such actions should be performed, one should abandon
       attachment to them as well as their fruit. Arjuna, this is my final
       judgment on this!

Arjuna wants to know more about *renunciation* and *abandonment* (Sloka
18.1). The essence of renunciation, sannyasa, introduced in Chapter 5,
requires that our motives and desires for acting be clean. In such moments,
we easily and effortlessly release any identification with the fruits or results
of our actions, tyaga, introduced in Chapter 12. Such unattached action is
born or vairagya, dispassion, introduced in Chapter 2.

When we are not led astray by personal desire or passion, we find equanimity in dispassion, our motives are pure and there is no attachment to
outcome. We simply do our part in the Divine plan realizing, all the while,
it's not about us at all. We're just here to perform a function to serve the
greater good. In this way, we are *in* the world but not *of* the world.

Sometimes, this means offering our skills and gifts to serve a particular
purpose.

Sometimes, it just means offering our place in line.

Slokas 7-11

18.7   To abandon an action that is obligatory is not acceptable. To abandon such action out of confusion is recognized by tradition as an act of darkness.

18.8 Anyone who would abandon an action thinking that it causes pain to others, or out of fear of harm to his own body, does so from a passionate [rajasa] point of view. He will not gain any reward from such renunciation.

18.9 When an action that is required by custom is performed only because it should be performed, Arjuna, while renouncing attachment to it as well as the fruit of it, that kind of renunciation is thought to be rooted in clarity [sattvika].

18.10 The renouncer does not dislike unpleasant action, nor is he attached to pleasant action. He is filled with clarity, and he is wise, and he has severed himself from doubts.

18.11 In fact, it is impossible for one who is still in a body to give up action completely. But a true renouncer is one who is able to give up the fruits of action.

Recall from Chapter 1 that the central theme of the Bhagavad Gita is to overcome fear to rise up and defend the dharma, truth. *Fear* represents all the enemies within, *emotions* that constrict, hold us back, from living our deepest truth. *Fighting for truth is not a sentimental act based on emotion but an act of courage based on clarity.* With such clarity, we do *not dislike unpleasant action* nor are we *attached to pleasant action* (Sloka 18.10).

We simply act to serve the truth, and it sets us free.

Slokas 12–17

18.12 At the moment of death, those who have not abandoned the fruits of their action must confront them. They are of three kinds: the desirable, the undesirable, and the mixed. But this is not the case for true renouncers [sannyasis].

18.13 Arjuna, know that in the teachings of the Sankhya school there are said to be five causes that lead to success in all actions.

18.14 The material basis or the body; the agent; the instruments of various kinds; the different kinds of exertion; divine fate is the fifth.

18.15 Whatever action a man undertakes, with the body or speech or the mind [i.e., physically, verbally, or mentally], whether lawful or not, these five are the causes.

18.16 Since this is the case, anyone who regards himself alone as the agent
has only partial insight. Confused in his thinking, he does not see at all.

18.17 For a man who has no sense of egotism, and whose awareness is not
clouded by attachment, does not really kill, nor is he bound – even if he
must kill all of these people!

In Slokas 18.13 and 18.14, Krishna describes the five causes that make
every action happen. They are the actual *body* doing the action, the *agent*,
ego, the *instruments*, senses, mind and intelligence, *the different kinds of
exertion*, subtle inner activities generated by the *instruments*, and, lastly;
divine fate, the tendencies resulting from the effects of past actions. The
five causes are a part of the field, prakriti, the womb of all creation. In the
field, only the *transient, changing expression of Brahman* is born, lives and
dies—kills and is killed.

We, as Atman, expressions of the eternal, unchanging Brahman, or God,
are never born nor die—nor could we ever kill or be killed.

We simply observe.

Slokas 18

18.18 The impulse to action is three-fold: it involves knowledge, the object of
knowledge, and the knower. And action itself is three-fold: it involves
an instrument, the act itself, and an agent.

This is an important Sloka as it offers a concrete way to understand the difference between the mind in transient prakriti and the Soul of the eternal
Atman. It's helpful here to remember your old school days in English class.
Subject—verb—object. It's how we began to make sense of grammar—and
it's how we begin to make sense of our place in creation.

There are three components to any action: the *knowledge, the object of
the knowledge and the knower*. They are sometimes referred to as the *trinity*.
Re-ordering, we see:

SUBJECT: knower
VERB: knowledge or knowing
OBJECT: knowledge

Another example is:

SUBJECT: seer
VERB: seeing
OBJECT: seen

How does this show us the difference between the mind and the Soul? Most of the time, we experience the world as if *we were our mind*—as if *our mind were the subject watching the world as object*, or:

SUBJECT: we as our mind
VERB: watching
OBJECT: the world

But, when we sit to meditate, *we* start to watch the mind and associated thoughts, feelings and sensations floating by changing from moment to moment. On the day we ask, "Who's watching?" we discover that *we, as Observer or Soul, are the subject watching the field, or mind, as object*, or:

SUBJECT: Observer or Soul
VERB: watching
OBJECT: our mind

Notice that the *mind can function as either subject or object*. But, *we, as the Observer or Soul, can only function as the subject BECAUSE THIS IS WHO WE ARE.* This is a beautiful way to prove to ourselves the difference between the mind and the Soul and is an important starting place to understanding *TAT—That which we really are. That which we seek.*

To understanding *that the very searcher is God.*

In the following Slokas, Krishna summarizes how this subject-verb-object *trinity* is expressed through the gunas. Slokas 18.20–22 summarize the knowledge or object. Slokas 18.23–25 summarize the action or verb and Slokas 18.26–28 summarize the agent or subject.

Slokas 19-28

18.19 The Sankhya doctrine of the three conditions of nature teaches that knowledge, action, and agent are also each three-fold, depending on the three conditions. Concerning these, listen further:

18.20 That knowledge which is rooted in the condition of clarity sees the one unchanging reality that resides in all beings, divided among them and yet not divided. It is important to understand this!

18.21 But that knowledge which is rooted in the condition of passion sees many conditions among all beings, constantly changing, one thing after another.

18.22 But if one's mind is focused completely on only one insignificant task, without considering causes, and without having genuine purpose in it, such knowledge is understood to be conditioned by inertia.

18.23   But an action that is required by tradition and performed by a man who
        has no interest in its result, without passion or hatred, and without
        attachment – such an action is said to be rooted in clarity.

18.24   But when an action is performed by a man who is driven by desire, or
        by one who is driven by egotism, involving too much effort – it is held
        to be action rooted in passion.

18.25   But when an action is initiated out of delusion, without regard for its
        consequences, or for the destruction and violence involved, or for one's
        manly virtue – that action is conditioned by dark inertia.

18.26   The agent who is devoted to liberation, who prefers not to talk about
        himself, who is determined and vigorous, and unchanged by success or
        failure – is rooted in clarity.

18.27   An intensely passionate man who is eager for the fruits of his actions,
        who is greedy and violent and impure, who is consumed by his joys and
        his griefs – he is an agent rooted in passion.

18.28   On the other hand, an agent is said to be rooted in dark inertia when
        he is undisciplined, uncivilized and vulgar, arrogant, dishonest, lazy,
        depressed, procrastinating.

Or:

Sattvic Guna

SUBJECT: is rooted in clarity, determined and vigorous,
            unchanged by success or failure (Sloka 18.26)

VERB: performs action with no interest in its result, without
            passion or hatred, and without attachment (Sloka 18.23)

OBJECT: sees the one unchanging reality that resides in all
            beings (Sloka 18.20)

Rajasic Guna

SUBJECT: is eager for the fruits of his actions, is greedy, violent
            and impure, consumed by joys and griefs (Sloka 18.27)

VERB: driven by desire, egoism, uses too much effort
            (Sloka 18.24)

OBJECT: sees the many conditions, constantly changing
            (Sloka 18.21)

Tamasic Guna

SUBJECT: is undisciplined, uncivilized and vulgar, arrogant, dishonest, lazy, depressed and procrastinating (Sloka 18.28)

VERB: acts without regard to consequences or for the destruction and violence involved (Sloka 18.25)

OBJECT: focuses on only one insignificant task, without considering causes and without having genuine purpose (Sloka 18.22)

Krishna continues, in the following Slokas, focusing on how the dominant guna influences our understanding, or *intelligence* and impacts our will, or *resolve*.

Slokas 29-35

18.29 Arjuna, listen: the classification of intelligence and of resolve according to the conditions of nature is also three-fold. I will explain each of them to you fully and in detail.

18.30 That intelligence which knows what activity is and what its cessation is, what is obligatory and what is not, what is fear and what is fearlessness, as well as what is bondage and what liberation – Arjuna, that insight is rooted in clarity.

18.31 That intelligence which incorrectly perceives what is lawful duty and what is not, what is obligatory and what is not – Arjuna, that insight is rooted in passion.

18.32 And that intelligence which supposes – immersed as it is in darkness – that lawlessness [adharma] is lawful duty [dharma] and which imagines everything to be exactly what it is not – such intelligence is buried in darkness.

18.33 That resolve by means of which one controls the activities of the mind and the breath and the senses as well, that resolve which is practiced with unwavering yoga – that resolve, Arjuna, is based on clarity.

18.34 But when one tries to attend to one's duties, desires, and ambitions with a resolve that is too attached to them, and when one worries too much about the results – Arjuna, that resolve is based on passion.

18.35 And that resolve by means of which the complete fool clings fast to sleep and fear and pain and depression and drunkenness – Arjuna, we call that the resolve of darkness.

Our understanding, *intelligence*, naturally leads us to use our will, *resolve*, in search of differing sense pleasures. *Sattvic* understanding is *rooted in clarity*, discerns clearly the paths to *bondage or liberation* (Sloka 18.30), and *controls the activities of the mind, breath and senses* (Sloka 18.33). *Rajasic* understanding does not easily discern *what is lawful duty and what is not* (Sloka 18.31), is *too attached, and worries too much about the results* (Sloka 18.34). *Tamasic* understanding is *immersed in darkness* (Sloka 18.32), and *clings fast to sleep, fear and pain, depression and drunkenness* (Sloka 18.35).

And, our *intelligence* and *resolve* impacts our state of *happiness* as Krishna describes in the following Slokas.

Slokas 36–40

18.36 But now listen to me, Arjuna. That happiness is also three-fold wherein one comes to rest through long practice, and comes also to the end of suffering.

18.37 That which at first seems like poison but which in the end is like nectar – such happiness is rooted in clarity and arises from the peace that comes from insight into the self.

18.38 And that which arises from contact between the senses and sense-objects and which at first seems like nectar but in the end is like poison – according to tradition that sort of happiness is rooted in passion.

18.39 And that happiness which in its beginning and in its conclusion is mere self delusion arising from sleep, or sluggishness, or negligence – that is held to be rooted in dark inertia.

18.40 There is no one on earth or among the gods in heaven who could be free from these three conditions of nature.

Sattvic happiness is often at first sour but later sweet, while rajasic pleasure is often first sweet and later is sour. For example, it may feel sour to pull ourselves from a warm bed on a cold morning to come to our prayer mat, but, then, the kiln transforms us and the sweet nectar feeds us. Tamasic happiness is marked by self-delusion both at first and later.

And now Krishna reminds our hero once again of the importance of doing the work of his nature.

Slokas 41–46

18.41 Arjuna, Brahmins, and warriors, and villagers, and slaves all have obligatory caste duties which are distinguished by the qualities which arise from the innate nature of each.

18.42 Serenity, self-control, austerity, purity, patience, honesty, as well as knowledge and discrimination, and religious faith – these are the caste duties of a Brahmin which arise from a Brahmin's nature.

18.43 Heroism, energy, resolve, skill, and also the refusal to retreat in battle, generosity, and ruling with authority – these are the caste duties of a warrior which arise from a warrior's nature.

18.44 Farming, cattle-herding, and trade are the caste duties of a villager, which arise from his nature. Service is the caste duty of a slave, which arises from a slave's nature.

18.45 A man achieves success when he is content in doing the work that is his own. Hear how one who is content in doing his own caste duty achieves success!

18.46 That man finds success in his caste duty when he worships the one who pervades this entire world, the one from whom everything here unfolds.

Caste in these Slokas can be likened to our innate nature. By following our inner impulse, we are naturally drawn to certain types of activities and duties. Would a neurosurgeon be asked to build a cabinet? Probably not. Each of us has a part to play *and all duties are necessary to fulfill the Divine plan.*

Slokas 47–49

18.47 It is better to perform one's own caste duty poorly than to perform another's well. By performing action that conforms to one's own nature, one does not accumulate guilt.

18.48 Arjuna, one should not give up the work that one is born to do, even if it is harmful. For harm accompanies all of our involvements, just as smoke accompanies fire.

18.49 One achieves that highest form of perfection beyond action through

renunciation [sannyasa]. Then one's consciousness remains unattached
at all times. One's longings are gone. One has conquered oneself.

Rumi said, "It's as if you were sent to a kingdom to accomplish one thing.
You may accomplish a hundred other things but will feel incomplete until
you accomplish the one thing for which you were sent." As we discussed
in Chapter 2, this one thing is our svadharma, our life's purpose. It's how
we'd spend our time if we only had a year to live.

Sloka 18.47, *It is better to perform one's own caste duty poorly than to perform another's well*, summarizes it beautifully. Whether we are a scholar or
priest, *Brahmin*, warrior, kshatriya, tradesperson or villager, *vaisya*, laborer
or slave, *sudra*. It's not about doing anything perfectly.

It's about being, perfectly, ourselves.

Slokas 50-53

18.50   I will show you how the man who has attained this perfection also
        attains to Brahman. Briefly, this is highest culmination of knowledge.

18.51   Disciplined by a purified awareness [buddhi] he restrains himself with
        firm resolve. He abandons sense-objects, sounds and all the rest. He
        casts off both passion and hatred.

18.52   He cultivates solitude and eats lightly. He is restrained in speech,
        in body and in mind. He devotes himself constantly to yoga and
        meditation. He rests upon dispassion.

18.53   He has freed himself from egotism, force, pride, desire and anger,
        possessiveness. Selfless and serene, he has prepared himself to become
        Brahman.

We become heaven on earth by using discernment, buddhi, to discipline
the mind, control the senses and abandon desire and aversion, *passion and
hatred*, for peaceful equanimity. With our mind in sattva, we realize the
truth of our nature, Brahman.

And, we are freed from being problems to ourselves.

Slokas 54-58

18.54   And having become Brahman and at peace within himself, he does
        not grieve, he does not desire. The same toward all beings, he attains
        supreme devotion to me.

18.55 Through devotion he comes to recognize me, how vast I am, and who I really am. Then, since he knows me as I really am, he immediately enters into me.

18.56 Nevertheless, even as he resorts to me he continues to perform all the actions that he is obliged to do. By my grace he reaches this eternal imperishable place.

18.57 In your mind keep me as your focus and surrender all of your actions to me. Rely on the yoga of insight [buddhi]. Keep your thoughts always fixed on me.

18.58 With your thoughts on me you will be able, by my grace, to overcome all difficulty. But if, in your egotism, you will not listen, then you will perish.

And, freed, we continue to act but now *it's not about us at all*, for *grace has brought us safe thus far, and grace will lead us home.*

Slokas 59–60

18.59 If egotism leads you to think "I will not fight," your resolve will be useless. Nature itself [prakriti] will compel you.

18.60 Arjuna, you are bound by your own action which arises from your very nature. You will do unwillingly the very thing that you wish not to do. This is delusion!

Perhaps, today, we will not rise, perhaps not tomorrow, nor even the next day. But, sooner or later, *we will rise* because the impulse toward wholeness *will not let us go.*

This is how much we are loved.

We can postpone, avoid, even skip out, today, but, ultimately, we cannot *not* face our inner demons and live our truth.

It's why we can't lose the war.

Slokas 61–62

18.61 The lord is present in all beings. Arjuna, he dwells in the territory of the heart. With his magical power [maya] he makes all things revolve like the paddles of a water mill.

18.62 Go to him as your refuge, Arjuna, with your whole being! By his grace you will reach that eternal place, that supreme peace!

When we see with clarity, we see the light in the hearts of all—*beyond* all the anger, pain and suffering. Our devotional gaze cuts like a laser through the ignorance of darkness—and holds our brother and sister close—as we have learned to hold our self.

It's how I held Jacob and how God holds us.

Sloka 63

18.63 Such is the wisdom which I have taught you, the most secret of secrets! Consider it fully. And then do what you wish.

And, the choice is ours. Joy or sorrow?
The choice is now.

Slokas 64–66

18.64 Listen once more to this my final doctrine, the most secret of all secrets! My love for you is firm. Thus I will tell you what is good for you.

18.65 Direct your mind to me. Direct your devotion to me. Make your sacrifices to me. Give me your homage. Thus you will come to me. I promise this to you truly, for you are dear to me!

18.66 Surrender all of your caste duties to me. Come to me as your only refuge. I will set you free from all evil. Do not worry!

And, like a sip of water in the desert, we hear the words of Lord Krishna for the last time:

Keep your mind single pointed.
Keep your heart devoted.
Offer your action up.
Bow your ego down.

Infinitely simple. Completely joyous.

Slokas 67–69

18.67 You must not speak of this to anyone who does not practice austerity or devotion, or to anyone who does not want to hear it, or to anyone who would dispute it.

18.68 But whoever reveals this highest secret doctrine to those who are devoted to me, and who gives me his utmost devotion – without fail, he will come to me.

18.69 No one does more precious service to me than this one, among all men, nor will there ever be any other man on earth more precious to me!

May we concentrate on living our own truth. If someone wants to know about the light that shines through our gaze, or about our quick willingness to confess uncertainty as well as wonder, then let's be happy to share. Perhaps something in our experience can help. After all, we are each given to one other in the most perfect way and time.

Slokas 70-72

18.70 And whoever studies and memorizes our dialogue on sacred duty, Arjuna, I consider him to have worshipped me with a sacrifice that is wisdom.

18.71 And a man who simply listens with faith and without disputing will also be set free, and will attain to the luminous worlds of the meritorious.

18.72 Have you listened to this doctrine with your mind fully focused on it alone? Arjuna, has this delusion born of ignorance departed from you?

And a man who simply listens with faith and without disputing will be set free. It always makes me chuckle at how much misery I can cause myself by disputing, arguing, analyzing and so on. When all I really need to do is *rise up*, everyday, to *sit on my cushion.*

And, *there* is God.

Sloka 73

Arjuna spoke:

18.73 It has departed, Krishna. And by your grace my memory has returned to me. I am firm now. All my doubts are gone. I will do as you say.

Ah, now Arjuna is free of questions and ready to act according to the words of his Lord. When we *hear* this sweet Song of God, we begin to Dance. We *know* we have a part in the Divine plan only we can play. We *respond* to the call of the inner impulse that knows the gift we carry. We start to get that *it's all about us showing up.* And, as we rise, fearless and free, we instantly know *it's not about us at all.*

We *know* to whom we belong now. We *know* the maker and keeper of our days.

We sleep easy and walk free. And Joy becomes us.

Welcome Home.

Sanjaya spoke: **Slokas 74–78**

18.74 Thus I have heard this astonishing dialogue that makes the hair stand
on end, the discourse between Krishna and the great-soul, Arjuna.

18.75 I have heard this supreme secret doctrine by the grace of Vyasa, this
doctrine of yoga, exactly as it was taught by Krishna, the lord of yoga,
himself.

18.76 O king, I remember, I memorize, this astonishing auspicious discourse
between Krishna and Arjuna. And time after time it thrills me!

18.77 And I remember, I memorize, also that wonderfully beautiful form that
Krishna wears. My king, it fills me with wonder. And again and again it
thrills me!

18.78 Wherever Krishna, the lord of yoga, is, and wherever Arjuna his
companion is, there also will be good fortune, and victory, and
prosperity, and steadfast guidance. This I know!

And so we come full circle to remember that we have been listening in on
this ancient and prophetic story told by the pure hearted Sanjaya to the
blind king Dhritarashtra. And, like Arjuna, we, too, have been gifted with
the most sacred knowledge.

Now, what will we do?

Key Points

1. When we are not led astray by personal desire or passion, we find
equanimity in dispassion, our motives are pure and there is no
attachment to outcome.

2. When we simply act to serve the truth, it sets us free.

3. The five causes making every action happen are: the *body;* the *agent*
or ego; the *instruments:* senses, mind and intelligence; *the different
kinds of exertion,* subtle inner activities generated by the *instruments;*
and, *divine fate,* the tendencies resulting from the effects of past
actions.

4. We know our place in creation through the subject-verb-object
trinity.

5. The mind can function as either subject or object. But, we, as the
Observer or Soul, can only function as the subject because *this is
who we are.*

6. Each guna expresses the trinity of subject—verb—object differently.

7. The quality of our understanding, will and happiness are determined by the guna that is dominant.

8. We must perform the duties of our nature to be fulfilled.

9. All duties are necessary to fulfill the Divine plan.

10. We become heaven on earth by using discernment, buddhi, to discipline the mind, control the senses, and abandon desire and aversion for peaceful equanimity. With our mind in sattva, we realize the truth of our nature, Brahman.

11. Sooner or later, *we will rise* because the impulse toward wholeness *will not let us go. It's why we can't lose the war.*

12. When we see with clarity, we see the light in the hearts of all— *beyond* all the anger, pain and suffering.

13. Summary of instruction: keep your mind single-pointed; keep your heart devoted; offer your actions up and bow your ego down.

14. Don't try to convince others about the truth. Instead, live the Truth.

15. Let's *rise up*, everyday, and *sit on our cushion. There* is God.

Terms

Brahmin (*Brah*-min) priest or teacher
Vaisya (*Veye*-shyah) tradesperson
Sudra (*Shoo*-drah) laborer

Personal Reflection

1. There are many ways to get lost but only one way to be found. Describe in your own words the path to moksha or liberation.

2. What does the notion that the mind can be subject or object but the Soul can only be the subject say to you?

3. How would *you* summarize Krishna's instruction to Arjuna?

4. Knowing you can't lose the war, are you ready to *rise up*?

5. What is the most valuable learning you've received from your study of the Bhagavad Gita?

A Glossary of Names and Terms

Abhyasa (Ah-*byah*-sah) steady practice

Adharma (*A*-dar-mah) chaos; untruth

Adideva (*Ah*-dee-*day*-vah) the original One; Primal God

Agni (*Ahg*-nee) god of fire

Ahamkara (Ah-hahm-*kah*-rah) each individual; a singular perceiving entity

Ahimsa (Ah-*him*-sah) non-violence

Ananta (Ah-*nahn*-tah) five-headed king of water snakes

Anantavijaya (Ah-*nahn*-tah-vi-jay-ah) endless victory conch blown by King Yudhisthira

Apara-prakriti (*Ah*-par-rah-*prak*-ri-tee) prakriti expressed in the physical universe

Arjuna (*Are*-joo-nah) Pandava warrior who receives Krishna's instruction

Aryaman (*Are*-yah-mahn) lord of the ancestors

ASAT (Ah-saht) untruth

Ashvatthama (Ash-*vah*-tah-mah) Kaurava warrior

Asvattha (*Ahs*-vaht-ha) upside-down tree

Atman (*Aht*-mahn) individual expression of the One

Bhagavad Gita (*Bah*-gah-vahd *Gee*-tah) the Song of God

Bharata (*Bar*-ah-tah) Lineage of both the Pandavas and Kauravas

Bhima (*Bee*-mah) Arjuna's older brother; leader of the Pandava army; second son of King Pandu, king of the Pandavas

Bhishma (*Bee*-sh-mah) leader of the Kaurava army; blows conch to begin war

Bhrigu (*Bree*-goo) rishi who dwells constantly on the super-consciousness plane

Brahmacharya (*Brah*-mah-*char*-yah) sense control

Brahman (*Brah*-mahn) the eternal, unchanging, omnipresent force; Source of all that is

Brahmin (*Brah*-min) priest or teacher

Brihaspati (Bree-*hahs*-pah-tee) priest of the devas

Buddhi (*Buh*-dee) discerning intellect

Cekitana (Chay-*kit*-tah-nah) Pandava warrior

Chakras (*Chah*-krahs) subtle nerve or energy centers of the body

Chitraratha (*Chit*-rah-rah-tah) chief of celestial musicians

Darshan (*Dar*-shahn) true seeing or blessing

Devadatta (*Day*-vah-*dah*-tah) God-Given conch blown by Arjuna

Dharma (*Dar*-mah) traditional or spiritual law; truth

Dhrishtadyumna (Drish-tah-*dyoom*-nah) son of Drupada; Pandava warrior

Dhrishtaketu (Dir-ish-tah-*kay*-too) Pandava warrior

Drona (*Drow*-nah) archery teacher of warriors on both sides; fights with the Kauravas

Drupada (*Drew*-pah-dah) Pandava warrior

Drupadi (*Drew*-pah-dee) daughter of Drupada; her sons are not named warriors, but represent qualities that arouse a longing for God and the turning away from the material world

Gandiva (Gahn-*dee*-vah) Arjuna's bow

Ganges (*Gahn*-jees) sacred river Ganges

Garuda (*Gar-roo*-dah) half-man, half-bird carrier of Vishnu

Gayatri (*Gah*-yah-tree) mother of all mantras

Gunas (*Goo*-nahs) energetic qualities of nature

Ikshvaku (*Eek-shvah*-koo) great sage

Indra (*In*-drah) king of the gods

Japa (*Jah*-pah) mantra repetition

Jiva (*Jee*-vah) the consciousness of the Soul identified with its incarnate state

Jnana Yoga (*Jnah*-nah Yo-gah) the Path of Wisdom

Kandarpa (Kahn-*dar*-pah) god of romantic love

Kapila (*Kah*-pi-lah) founder of Samkhya philosophy; a great sage

Karma (*Kar*-mah) action and reaction

Karma Yoga (*Kar*-mah) the Path of Action

Karna (*Kar*-nah) Kaurava warrior

Kauravas (*Cow*-rah-vahs) forces of ignorance

King Dhritarashtra (King Drit-ah-*rah*-shtrah) blind king of the Kauravas

King Duryodhana (King Door-*yo*-dah-nah) oldest son of King Dhritarashtra

King of Kashi (King of *Kah*-shee) Pandava warrior

King Pandu (King *Pahn*-doo) king of the Pandavas

King Yudhishthira (King You-*dish*-ti-rah) Arjuna's oldest brother; eldest son of King Pandu, king of the Pandavas

Kripa (*Kree*-pah) Kaurava warrior

Krishna (*Krish*-nah) God within; charioteer and guide of Arjuna

Kshatriya (*Kshut*-tree-yah) someone from the warrior cast

Kshetrajna (Kshet-*rah*-jnah) knower of the field

Kunti (Koon-tee) first wife of King Pandu; mother of King Yudhishthira, Bhima and Arjuna

Kuntibhoja (Koon-tee-*bow*-jah) Pandava warrior

Kurukshetra (Koo-roo-*kshay*-trah) field of action; battlefield where the Bhagavad Gita occurs; the body

Kurus (*Koo*-roos) short for Kauravas

Lokas (*Low*-kahs) luminous spheres

Mahabharata (Mah-ha-*bar*-ah-tah) epic poem of which the Bhagavad Gita is a part

Mahatman (Mah-*haht*-mahn) great exalted one

Manas (*Mah*-nahs) mind

Manipushpaka (Mah-nee-*poosh*-pah-kah) jewel-toned conch blown by Sahadeva

Mantra (*Mahn*-trah) sound current

Manu (*Mah*-noo) father of humanity

Manus (*Mah*-noos) law-givers

Maya (*My*-yah) illusion

Meru (May-roo) sacred Mt. Meru; highest place of divine consciousness in the body

Moksha (*Mok*-sha) liberation

Nakula (*Nah*-koo-lah) Arjuna's younger brother; twin of Sahadeva. Nakula and Sahadeva's mother is Madri (*Mah*-dree), second wife of King Pandu

Narada (*Nah*-rah-dah) a great sage

Nirvana (Near-*vah*-nah) full liberation

OM (*Oh*-m or *Au*-m) cosmic sound vibration

Pancajanya (*Pahn*-cha-*jan*-yah) conch blown by Krishna

Pandavas (*Pahn*-dah-vahs) forces of righteousness

Para-prakriti (*Pah*-rah-*prak*-ri-tee) prakriti expressed in the astral and causal universes

Paundra (*Pound*-rah) Bhima's conch

Prahlada (*Prah*-lah-dah) the pious demon

Prakriti (*Prahk*-ri-ti) nature or creation

Prana (*Prah*-nah) vital energy or breath

Pranayama (*Pran*-nah-*yah*-mah) controlling or restraining vital energy or the breath

Purujit (*Poo*-roo-jit) Pandava warrior

Ra Ma (*Rah*-mah) healing sound current

Rajasic (Rah-*jah*-sik) restless, overactive guna

Rama (*Rah*-mah) an incarnation of Vishnu

Rishi (*Ree*-she) sage

Sadhana (*Sah*-dah-nah) spiritual practice

Sahadeva (Sah-ha-*day*-vah) Arjuna's younger brother; twin of Nakula

Samaveda (*Sah*-mah-*vay*-dah) one of the four Vedas written for liturgical purposes

Sanjaya (Sun-*jah*-yah) visionary; narrator of the Bhagavad Gita

Sankhya (*Sun*-kyah) philosophy concerned with the interplay of nature and spirit.

Sannyasa (Sun-*yah*-sah) state of renunciation; pure of motive behind action

SAT (Saht) truth

Sattvic (*Saht*-vik) balanced guna

Satyaki (*Saht*-yah-kee) Pandava warrior

Satyam (*Saht*-yahm) truth

Shanti (*Shahn*-tee) peace

Shastras (*Shahs*-trahs) recognized scripture or authority

Shibis (*She*-bees) Pandava warrior

Shikandhin (She-*kun*-din) Pandava warrior

Shiva (*Shi*-vah) transformer or destroyer in the Hindu masculine trinity

Shraddha (*Shrah*-dah) sincere belief; faith

Skanda (*Skahn*-dah) god of war

Somadatta (*Sew*-mah-*dah*-tah) son of Somadatta is Somadatti (Sew-mah-*dah*-tee) Kaurava warrior

Subhadra (Soo-*bahd*-rah) wife of Arjuna

Sudra (*Shoo*-drah) laborer

Sughosha (*Soo*-*go*-sha) sweet-toned conch blown by Nakula

Svadharma (*Sva*-dar-mah) predestined duty

Tamasic (Tah-*mah*-sik) inert, underactive guna

Tapas (*Tah*-pas) suffering; burning; spiritual austerities

TAT (Taht) that which we seek

Tyaga (*Tyah*-gah) renunciation of identification with the fruits of our actions

Ushana (*Oo*-shah-nah) poet with great intuitive power

Uttamaujas (Oo-tah-*mau*-jahs) Pandava warrior

Vairagya (Veye-*rah*-gyah) dispassion; non-attachment

Vaisya (*Veye*-shyah) tradesperson

Vajra (*Vah*-jrah) heavenly thunder bolt

Varuna (*Vah*-roo-nah) lord of the gods of the sea

Vasuki (Vah-*soo*-kee) king of snakes

Vayu (*Veye*-yoo) god of wind

Vedas (*Vay*-dahs) ancient scriptures of India

Vikarna (*Vi*-kar-nah) Kaurava warrior

Virata (Vir-*ah*-tah) Pandava warrior

Vishnu (Vish-new) sustainer in the Hindu masculine trinity

Vivasvat (Vee-*vas*-vaht) sun God

Viveka (Vi-*vay*-kah) discrimination

Vrishnis (*Vrish*-nees) clan of Krishna

Vyasa (*Vyah*-sah) illumined sage; author of the *Mahabharata*

Yajna (*Yah*-jnah) sacrifice

Yama (*Yah*-mah) lord of death

Yamas (*Yah*-mahs) restraints in Patanjali's "Eight Limbs of Yoga"

Yantra (*Yahn*-trah) visual

Yoga (*Yo*-gah) the science of practical techniques for realization

Yudhamanyu (Yoo-dah-*mahn*-yoo) Pandava warrior

Yuyudhana (Yoo-*yoo*-dah-nah) Pandava warrior

Works Cited

OPENING QUOTE:
Swami Dayananda Saraswati. *Bhagavadgita Home Study Course*. Arsha Vidya Gurukulam, Saylorsburg, Pennsylvania, 1989.

CHAPTER 1
Swami Satchidananda. *The Living Gita: The Complete Bhagavad Gita and Commentary*. Henry Holt and Company, New York, 1988.

CHAPTER 2
Pressfield, Steven. *The Legend of Bagger Vance*. Harpertorch, New York, 1995.

CHAPTER 3
Winfrey, Oprah. *O, The Oprah Magazine*. September 2002, p.294. New York.

Yogananda, Paramahansa. *God Talks with Arjuna: The Bhagavad Gita, Royal Science of God-Realization*. Self-Realization Fellowship, Los Angeles, 1996.

Dass, Ram and Gorman, Paul. *How Can I Help? Stories and Reflections on Service*. Alfred A. Knopf, Inc., 1985.

CHAPTER 4
Petrie, Jeanette and Ann. *Mother Teresa*, video. Petrie Productions, 1986.

CHAPTER 5
Petrie, Jeanette and Ann. *Mother Teresa*, video. Petrie Productions, 1986.

Albom, Mitch. *Tuesdays with Morrie*. Doubleday, New York, 1997.

Fadiman, James and Frager, Robert. *Essential Sufism*. HarperCollins Publishers, New York, 1999.

CHAPTER 6
Easwaran, Eknath. *Gandhi the Man: The Story of His Transformation*. The Blue Mountain Center of Meditation, Berkeley, California, 1997.

Kornfield, Jack. *The Inner Art of Meditation Video.* Sounds True, Boulder, Colorado, 1996.

CHAPTER 7

Swami Satchidananda. *Meditation: The Path to Happiness Video.* Shakticom, Satchidananda Ashram, Yogaville, Buckingham, Virginia, 1992.

Clark, Glenn. *The Man Who Talks with the Flowers.* Macalester Park Publishing, Austin, Minnesota, 1939.

CHAPTER 8

Yogananda, Paramahansa. *God Talks with Arjuna: The Bhagavad Gita: Royal Science of God-Realization.* Self-Realization Fellowship, Los Angeles, 1996.

Jampolsky, Gerald. *Teach Only Love: The Seven Principles of Attitudinal Healing.* Bantam Books, New York, 1983.

CHAPTER 9

Chawla, Navin. *Mother Teresa: The Authorized Biography.* Element Books, Inc., Rockport, Massachusetts, 1996.

Yogananda, Paramahansa. *Autobiography of a Yogi.* Self-Realization Fellowship, Los Angeles, 1993.

CHAPTER 10

Swami Satchidananda. *The Living Gita: The Complete Bhagavad Gita and Commentary.* Henry Holt and Company, New York, 1988.

Lynch, Ray. *Truth Is the Only Profound: Meditative Reading from the Wisdom-Teaching of Ruchira Avatar Adi Da Samraj.* CD, track 6. The Dawn Horse Press, 1998.

Ashley-Farrand, Thomas. *Mantra: Sacred Words of Power.* Study Guide. Sounds True, Boulder, Colorado, 1999.

CHAPTER 11

Levine, Stephen. *A Gradual Awakening.* Doubleday, New York, 1989.

Lake, Medicine Grizzlybear. *Native Healer: Initiation into an Ancient Art.* Quest Books, Wheaton, Illinois, 1991.

CHAPTER 13

Lynch, Ray. *Truth Is the Only Profound: Meditative Reading from the Wisdom-Teaching of Ruchira Avatar Adi Da Samraj.* CD, track 5. The Dawn Horse Press, 1998.

CHAPTER 15

Pilgrim, Peace. *Peace Pilgrim.* Ocean Tree Books, Santa Fe, New Mexico, 1994.

CHAPTER 16

Hurnard, Hannah. *Hinds' Feet on High Places.* Living Books, Wheaton, Illinois, 1975.

CHAPTER 17

Ashley-Farrand, Thomas. *Healing Mantras.* The Ballantine Publishing Group, New York, 1999.

Acknowledgments

I would like to thank my husband, Doug, for his steadfast love, encouragement and support for both me and my work—day after day . . . my children, Nicole, Alexis, Ross, daughter-in-law Kelly, and Mitch, who each continue to bless and teach me in so many ways . . . and, my two beautiful grandchildren, Greer and Sean, who just bring a sweet joy to my heart.

I would like to honor, with deep gratitude, the Divine Impulse that brought together a most extra-ordinary team to birth this creation. Sid Hall, my publisher, who followed the impulse to come to a gathering when neither he nor I knew why he was there—the Divine One did—and, for his continued patience, help, support, enthusiasm, and overall great ideas, editing and design contributions. Sid's interns, David Jonathan Ross for his special contributions to the book design and Christy Clothier for her expert copy editing and proofreading skills.

A very special thank you goes to George Thompson, my Sanskrit teacher, for creating a most excellent, original translation of the Bhagavad Gita for this commentary and for also reading the draft as it was being created. And, for the beautiful book cover, a special thank you goes to artist Jan Grossman who captured perfectly the extraordinary rising from the ordinary in everyday life. Jan also brought forth the book title which was amended slightly by Sid. And, for her excellent photography skills, I'd like to thank Carol Gaudreau for taking the picture for the back cover.

Finally, I would like to thank Gurucharan Singh Khalsa, Ph.D., for his spiritual and healing guidance; he continues to make the teachings of Yogi Bhajan and the practice of Kundalini Yoga a dominant force in my journey. I'd also like to thank Rabbi Roger Ross and the Rev. Deborah Steen Ross, Directors of the New Seminary for Interfaith Studies for providing the framework for me to call myself simply what I am—an interfaith minister.

Participants' Sharings

The following comments come from participants in Stephanie Rutt's Bhagavad Gita Study Program:

I am an artist. Prior to my study of the Bhagavad Gita I was unable to make that simple statement. Unwittingly, I had lived most of my ordinary life under a veil of self-imposed limitation. Never quite as "perfect" as the masters, the creative aspect of myself was always offered with an assumed apology. Being considered artistic rather than an artist became the comfortable umbrella behind which I could hide. An artist, I imagined, was someone extra-ordinary.

Then came the study, or more correctly the series of studies, as it is still ongoing. I had come to realize that I alone was the keeper of this birth-given gift and that only through me, my eyes and my hands, could it find expression. This is my svadharma, my intimate offering to the world to the best of my ability, the Divine Song through me. Although it was a seemingly subtle internal shift there was a tremendous freedom with this new understanding. I was free to be "perfect in my imperfection."

The battle is not over. The habit of unworthiness runs deep. As I question, "Who am I to be an artist?" the pivotal response follows, "Who am I not to be an artist?" and I am quieted back into action. I continue to take painting classes to refine my technique. Now I am more ready than ever to be a divine tool of expression. Me, Jan Mercuri Grossman, an ordinary person with permission to be an artist. Amen, Satnam, Wahe Guru!

I live my delightfully ordinary life in Amherst, New Hampshire. I practice Kundalini Yoga and pursue spiritual studies at the Tree of Life Fellowship in Milford, New Hampshire. Perhaps the future holds a website for my artwork but as of now I welcome contact via e-mail at jezmercuri@yahoo.com.

—JAN (AHJAN) MERCURI GROSSMAN

I'm doing my dharma imperfectly but it brings out my perfection.

—KAREN HEWS

When I find attachment to what I think ought to be, I find that's the greatest deterrent to seeing God.   —PAMELA EARTHWALKER

When I began my study of the Bhagavad Gita, I put my energy into knowing God. Now I know this is not enough. I need to let God take over until the "me" becomes God.   —JOHN SILVA

Today I cannot think of anyone that I could not pray with. I have had the opportunity to know—either in a clinical setting or when they have been incarcerated—murderers, rapists, and pedophiles. In those settings it is easy to see them as vulnerable and fearful and to have a human face.   —DANA

Sadhana runs the manifestation of the Gunas like a movie on a screen in front of my eyes. It's like the mindfulness meditation technique of naming thoughts—that's planning, that's grasping, that's wishing. When I sit, and settle, sometimes the various states of mind present so clearly. Something will come into my mind that I start to run over and over, and then I'll come back into awareness and may be able to identify where that particular replay is coming from—desire, or fear, resentment or aversion. And when I've seen it in that way it's almost as if it's been, in a small way, diffused of some of its power.

—DEBORAH FARROW

Compassion is empathy without pity.   —KAREN HEWS

My studies [of the Bhagavad Gita] have enriched my life in so many ways and have shown me ways to manage my anxiety symptoms. The Gita has transformed and deepened my relationship with the concept of God. I no longer think of God as the stern and unforgiving disciplinarian I was taught to believe in as a child. I now equate God with all-encompassing and unconditional love for all creation. This in itself alleviates anxiety.

The Gita has taught me patience. In the past whenever I decided I needed something, I wanted it immediately. It was My Will. If that something I needed so urgently did not materialize, I would feel anxious and disappointed. I now realize I do not know what is best for me. I look to Thy Will.

The Gita has brought me self-realization. I am aware of the difference between my Finite Self (my body and mind) and my Infinite Self (soul). Needless to say it is my Finite Self that leads me into a state of "despondency" caused by paralyzing anxiety symptoms. When my mind chatter escalates to foreseeing "bad omens," I try to focus on acting rather than reacting. I imagine Arjuna and Krishna in the chariot on the battlefield. I try to visualize myself as Arjuna turning the reins over to Krishna, relinquishing irrational mind chatter for Krishna's wisdom and guidance. I acknowledge my anxiety, but do not have to *become* anxiety.

—KELCIE

K-A-R-M-A: Know And Renounce My Attachment
—JOHN SILVA

What has been proven to me over and over again is, to be successful, or bear fruit, one must be willing to do the things you don't want to do. Willingness and patience are the virtues that I have needed to bear fruit. In the dark of the morning my alarm goes off and my ego tells me to go back to sleep. My ego continues to provide me with a collection of doubts. I pull myself out of the warm safe bed to show up. My ego is still complaining as I start my spiritual practice, but within a few moments my ego has been pushed away. At times it returns during my meditation, but it only takes a return to the breath to send my ego on its way into the cosmos. It is not hurt and knows that it will be needed later. I am left with a still, expansive quiet that is whole. My back feels a little chilled and my right foot is half asleep, but this bitterness no longer matters. This experience of God I will take into every moment of my day. How sweet it is. Tomorrow when my alarm goes off I have something to tell my ego.   —DANA

In the end we are alone . . . there is no mandate, no must, no guilt-laden should. There is only devotion. And through this devotion, selfless action, and through this action, liberation.

—JAN GROSSMAN

We search and we strive to be that which we are not. We waste our time looking for answers, peace, love, and enlightenment in the world around us. It is usually only in desperation that we look within and realize that we've had it all along. I want to find my answers in quiet humility, not frantic desperation. This is my prayer.   —JOHN SILVA

Until I surrender, it's all just an intellectual playground. And when I do surrender, I am only surrendering to my true self.   —KATHY

Got Gita?   —L.B.

> Deep are the
> roots that draw
> you to the Earth.
> Deep are the branches
> That reach for the heavens.
> Wide is the energy
> That flows through
> Your being.
> You touch Heaven
> With wings of Joy
> You tune your antennae
> You tune your senses
> You tune your pre-sense
> To *love all that is.*
>
>   —S.E.W.

ABOUT THE AUTHOR

REVEREND STEPHANIE RUTT, also known in the Kundalini yoga tradition as SAT DARSHAN KAUR, serves as minister at the Tree of Life Interfaith Fellowship in Milford, New Hampshire, formally the Tree of Life Yoga Studio. In addition, she teaches yoga, sacred dance, and mantra prayer and facilitates spiritual studies groups, from the Hindu and Christian faith traditions, including the annual, eight-month Bhagavad Gita study program. She also maintains a private practice in pastoral mentoring. Currently, she is expanding her experience of the sacred by training to become a dance leader for the Dances of Universal Peace under the mentorship of Halima Sussman.

Rev. Rutt is the founder and Director of the Gifts of Grace Foundation, a New Hampshire charitable organization, which, for the past three years, has made and delivered quilts for local foster care children. She is also the immediate past president of the Souhegan Valley Interfaith Council, where she created and sponsored the "To Hear How Others Pray" series.

Rev. Rutt was ordained an interfaith minister by the New Seminary for Interfaith Studies in New York City in June of 2005. She is a certified teacher in both Kundalini yoga, as taught by Yogi Bhajan, and Kripalu yoga. She holds an MA in Psychology, Guidance, and Counseling, and worked as a mental health counselor and taught for many years in the behavioral sciences at the University of New Hampshire at Manchester in the 1990s. In the summer of 2003, she returned to the University of New Hampshire at Manchester to teach a course called "Bhagavad Gita: Ancient Wisdom."

She lives in Brookline, New Hampshire, with her husband—and her cat, Gabby.

ABOUT THE TRANSLATOR

GEORGE THOMPSON teaches Humanities at Montserrat College of Art. His main research interest is the Rigveda, but his interest extends to Vedic and Avestan Studies in general, Hinduism and Buddhism, as well as to Indo-European and Central Asian Studies. He is preparing an anthology of translations from the Rigveda. Recent articles have appeared in *Nāma-Rūpa: Categories of Indian Thought*, the *International Journal of Hindu Studies*, and the *Electronic Journal of Vedic Studies*. He dwells at length on these old things in the hills of New England.